Real Estate And Stock Market Investing Mastery

How To Generate Tremendous Profits By Taking Advantage Of Proven Stock Market Strategies And Real Estate Investment Opportunities

By

Michael Ezeanaka

www.MichaelEzeanaka.com

Disclaimer

This publication is designed to provide competent and reliable information regarding the subject matter covered. However, it is sold with the understanding that the author is not engaged in rendering investment or other professional advice. Laws and practices often vary from state to state and country to country and if investment or other expert assistance is required, the services of a professional should be sought. The author specifically disclaims any liability that is incurred from the use or application of the contents of this book.

Financial Freedom Mastermind

We run occasional promotions on Amazon where we discount the price of our books. If you want to join an exclusive group of people that get notified when this is about to take place, subscribe to our mailing list by going to:

www.MichaelEzeanaka.com > Financial Freedom Mastermind

Books In The Business and Money Series	
Series #	**Book Title**
1	Affiliate Marketing
2	Passive Income Ideas
3	Affiliate Marketing + Passive Income Ideas (2-in-1 Bundle)
4	Facebook Advertising
5	Dropshipping
6	Dropshipping + Facebook Advertising (2-in-1 Bundle)
7	Real Estate Investing For Beginners
8	Credit Cards and Credit Repair Secrets
9	Real Estate Investing And Credit Repair Strategies (2-in-1 Bundle)
10	Passive Income With Affiliate Marketing (2nd Edition)
11	Passive Income With Dividend Investing
12	Stock Market Investing For Beginners
13	The Simple Stock Market Investing Blueprint (2-in-1 Bundle)
The kindle edition will be available to you for FREE when you purchase the paperback version from Amazon.com (The US Store)	

Download The Audio Versions Along With The Complementary PDF Document For FREE from *www.MichaelEzeanaka.com > My Audiobooks*

Table of Contents

Book 1

Stock Market Investing For Beginners

Your Step-By-Step Guide To Building Wealth And Passive Income Streams Using Proven Stock Market Strategies

By

Michael Ezeanaka

www.MichaelEzeanaka.com

Introduction

Mary is a single mother, she didn't finish high school. She has a hard time getting a job. So, to make ends meet, she decided to become a stay-in housemaid. She worked 6 days a week and almost 16 hours a day. During her fifth year as a house helper, her employer gave her a $2000 bonus. She used that money to invest in the stock market. She met with a financial adviser, opened a stock investment account, and started investing. She continued to put in $120 a month to her investment account. After a few years, her $2000 investment grew to $120,000. She used a little bit of the money to start a small soap business and earned more.

Mary's story is not unique. She's only one of the thousands of people who made a lot of money investing in the stock market.

Stock market investment is a great option for you if you're looking for passive income options and the ability to earn money while you're asleep. But, you must know that not everyone wins big in the stock market. While a lot of people are getting richer through stock investment, a number of investors are losing money, too. While some investors are striking it rich, others lost all the money they invested. The stock market is not only an intimidating subject; it's also a bit of a slippery slope. This is the reason why you should have a deep understanding of how the stock market works before you even start investing.

You've given yourself a great advantage by getting a copy of this book. It contains basic stock market strategies that will help increase your chance of creating a profitable and sustainable portfolio of stocks. This book is written for first time stock market investors, so it's easy to understand. It is basically "stock investing for dummies". It thoroughly explains seemingly intimidating concepts like stock trading, index investing, exchange-traded fund (ETF), index fund investing, penny stocks, and stock trading. It is your ultimate beginner guide to stock investing.

In this book, you'll discover:

- What the stock market is and how can you make money through it
- What a stock is and why they exist
- How the stock market works
- The major players in the stock market
- What an index is
- The difference between a bull market and a bear market
- The role that SEC and other regulators play in the stock market
- How you can invest in the stock market
- What a 401k plan is
- What an IRA is and how it can help you achieve financial independence
- Smart investment strategies that can help you earn bigger returns
- How to pick the right stock to invest in
- Factors to consider when choosing a stock
- How to minimize unnecessary losses
- The right companies to invest in
- The stock research process
- How to build a stock position
- What a stock broker is and how to pick the right one
- How to read your broker trade confirmations
- Types of trades you can place with your broker

- How to manage and diversify your stock investment portfolio
- How to keep your investment to a minimum

And much, much more!

What to Expect From This Book

As I've said before, this book is specifically written for stock market beginners. Its goal is to explain complex financial and investment concepts in a simple way. Most stock market concepts are defined and explained in layman terms. This book also has a glossary or "definition of terms" section towards the end of this book. This will help you understand intimidating stock market terms easily.

In Chapter 1, you'll find basic information that you'll need to understand and eventually master the art of stock market investment. In this chapter, you'll learn what the stock market is and how it works. You'll also learn:

- What stocks are and how they are created
- Why is stock market necessary?
- What's the difference between common and preferred stocks?
- The major stock market players
- What's an index and how to use it
- How you can make money in the stock market
- The role of stock market regulars like the SEC
- What a stock exchange is and why it exists
- What's a bear market
- What's a bull market

You'll learn how to invest in the stock market in Chapter 2. This chapter will help you understand the basic investment plans available to you and how to choose the right one.

In that chapter, you'll learn:

- How to get started in the stock market
- How to invest through a 401(k) plan
- How to invest in an individual retirement plan or IRA
- The difference between a 403 (b) plan and a 401 (k) plan
- How to invest through a taxable brokerage account
- How to invest through a direct stock purchase plan or dividend reinvestment plan

Chapter 3 is about stock investment strategies, such as value investing, growth investing, dividend investing, day trading, and short selling.

Chapter 4 will help you decide how to choose the right stocks to invest in. In this chapter, you'll learn:

- How to set investment objectives
- Factors you need to consider in choosing a stock
- How to tell if a stock is overvalued
- How to build a stock position

Chapter 5 helps you understand your brokerage account statement. This chapter answers questions like:

- What is a brokerage account?
- The types of securities a brokerage account can hold
- Is there a limit to the amount that you can deposit in a brokerage account?
- How many brokerage accounts can one have?
- What's the difference between a full service and a discount broker?

In Chapter 6, you'll learn about the things that you can find in a brokerage trade confirmation, such as the name of the investment you have traded with the ticker symbol, the total shares bought or sold, trade execution date, cost or selling price per share, the commission you paid to the broker, the gross value of the transaction, and more.

Chapter 7 focuses on the types of trades you can place with your broker, such as market orders, limit orders, all-or-none orders, stop orders and stop limit orders, buy to cover orders, trailing stop orders, day and GTC orders, and more.

Chapter 8 talks about the stock research process. You'll learn how to use macro-economic analysis and micro-economic analysis to maximize your investment returns.

Chapter 9 helps you choose stocks for long-term investment. You'll learn the signs that a stock is good for long-term investment, such as competitive advantage, market capitalization, strong balance sheet, high returns of capital etc. You'll also find some high quality stocks you can explore.

Chapter 10 helps you understand the benefit of portfolio management strategies like diversification.

In addition to all of the above, there's also a summary section at the end of each chapter to help you remember important points. The glossary (located at the end of this book) can help you understand complicated stock market concepts.

What Not To Expect From This Book

Gladys had read something about stock market investing online and she got really excited. She opened an investment account and started investing money in stocks.

After *a few months*, Gladys was frustrated not to see significant returns on her investments. And so, she decided to give up.

Stock market investing is not a "get rich quick" scheme. It takes time to grow your investments and achieve great wealth.

This book contains effective *long-term investment strategies* that you can use to become a successful investor. It's definitely not for those who are looking to double their investment in just a few months.

Stock market investing works a bit like gambling. When you're investing in a stock, you're betting on a specific outcome and there are no guarantees. To increase your chance of winning, you have to rely on logic, sound investment strategies, and extensive research. This book will help you do that.

Inspiration #1

"Buy a stock the way you would buy a house. Understand and like it such that you'd be content to own it in the absence of any market."
Warren Buffett

Chapter 1

Understanding The Stock Market

Warren Buffet is one of the most respected and wealthiest people in the world. And he became wealthy by leveraging the stock market. However, to become a wealthy investor like Warren, you must understand the stock market thoroughly – what it is and how it works.

This chapter will help you gain a basic understanding of what a stock is and how you could make money in the stock market.

What is a Stock?

A stock or a share is a piece of a company. The first ever stock was created by the Dutch East India Company (Verenigde Oostindische Compagnie) in 1602 at the Amsterdam Stock Exchange.
Think of a business as a pizza and the slices are its stocks or shares. When you purchase a stock from a company, you own a piece of that company. Let's say that ABC Company has 100,000 shares and you decided to purchase 10,000 shares. This means that you own ten percent of the company – its assets and revenues.

A stock is a form of security or a financial instrument that has monetary value and can be traded. This means that once you buy a stock, you are free to sell or trade it.

But, why do stocks exist and how are they created? Well, companies create and issue shares when they need to raise money for expansion and business growth. Let's look at a story to illustrate this point. Joel started his small candy manufacturing company. Let's call it Candy Corp for the purposes of discussion. He started the company with only three thousand dollars. He bought a second hand machine from another candy company that recently closed shop.

He and his wife, Mara, produced a thousand candies and sold them online. After a year, the business grew so they needed to hire two candy makers, an accountant, a delivery guy, and a customer service representative.

After five years, the three thousand dollar company grew. The demand for Candy Corp's products skyrocketed. Joel also wants to produce more lollipops, jelly beans, and candy sticks. But, the company needs around $1,000,000 to purchase new equipment, hire more people, expand his factory, meet the growing demand and produce new candy types. Joel doesn't have that kind of money. He also doesn't want to borrow money from banks. So, he decided to sell a part of his company and go public. This process is called an Initial Public Offering or IPO, which we'll discuss in a while.

When an entrepreneur starts a business, it's classified as private. This means that his company has a limited number of shareholders (himself and angel investors like investment companies, family members, and friends). But, somewhere along the way, he would need more money to expand his business and cater to more customers. So, to avoid incurring debt and paying for interest charges, he decides to sell a few pieces of his company. He can do this either privately (by raising money from existing shareholders) or publicly (by selling shares to new shareholders).

If he decides to sell his stocks privately, he can sell it to whomever he chooses to sell it to. He can sell it directly to a friend, a business acquaintance, or an angel investor. But, if he decides to sell his company shares faster, he would have to sell it to the public. But, he cannot do this himself. He has to go to an investment bank (let's call it IB). Based on the value of his company, he and IB determine the price of the stock, the amount of shares that they should offer to the public, and the percentage of his business that he would have to give up.

Let's say that the entrepreneur's business is valued at $ 10,000,000 and that he has to sell ten percent of his company to raise an additional capital of $1,000,000 in an initial offering called IPO, which is done in a stock market.

An IPO is the first sale of the stock issued by a company to the public. This is the reason why people call it "going public". It's usually done at a stock market.

What is a Stock Market and How Does It Work?

A stock market is a place where people and company issue, buy, and sell stocks. The stock market has two major purposes. The first is to help companies sell their stocks so they could raise capital for expansion. So, if a company issues 100,000 shares of stock for $10 per share, it could raise up to $1 million dollars capital on its initial public offering.

The second purpose of the stock market is to give investors (the people who purchase stocks) the opportunity to earn from the profits of publicly traded companies. Let's say that an investor purchased a company stock for $10. When the value of the stock goes up to $20, he earns a profit of $10.

There are three types of stock markets, including:

1. Stock Exchanges

A stock exchange is a centralized location where people buy and sell shares. This market is essential to economic development as it gives companies access to capital. It also gives the general public the opportunity to grow their money (through) stocks over time. There are two major stock exchanges in the United States, namely:

New York Stock Exchange

The New York Stock Exchange (NYSE) is the most popular and the biggest stock market (in terms of capitalization) in the world. It is located on Wall Street, Manhattan and it was founded on May 17, 1792. It was previously run by a private company, but it became a public organization in 2005. The parent company of the NYSE is called NYSE Euronext .

Nasdaq

The National Association of Securities Dealers Automated Quotations (Nasdaq) is the second biggest stock exchange in the world (in terms of the capital it generates). It's located on Broadway Street, New York City and it was established in 1941. It's operated by a private company called Nasdaq Inc., which also operates a number of stock exchanges around the United States and in Stockholm, Copenhagen, Tallinn, Helsinki, Vilnius, Reykjavik, and Yerevan.

2. Electronic Communication Network

An ECN or Electronic Communication Network is a computerized network that facilitates the trade of securities and other financial product.

An ECN usually trades currencies and stocks. The first ECN was called Instinet and it was created in 1969. This financial market type is usually used by a number of Forex (foreign exchange) brokers. These brokers trade foreign currencies.

3. Over-The-Counter (OTC) Market

OTC markets are used to buy and sell bonds, currencies, derivatives, and structured products. These markets are also used to trade equities.

Primary vs. Secondary Market

The stock market has two parts – the primary market and the secondary market. The primary market is where the stocks are created. The IPO or initial public offering is an example of a primary market transaction. When you buy a stock in a primary market, you're buying it directly from the company.

The secondary market, on the other hand, is where investors:

- Buy stocks from other investors and/or
- Sell shares they already own.

National exchanges such as NASDAQ and New York Stock Exchange are examples of secondary markets.

Why Do We Need A Stock Market?

The main goal of the stock market is to provide a structured and well-regulated exchange where investors can safely sell and buy stocks of publicly-traded corporations. It also provides companies the opportunity to generate capital by selling shares.

Major Stock Market Players

When you think of a stock market, you'd probably think of testosterone-loaded men in suits. You'd think of figurative wolves and people screaming on the phones. But, these men in suits are only the tip of the iceberg. There are a number of stock market players, namely:

Investors

Investors are people who buy and sell stocks to earn a profit and grow their money. Investors earn money through dividend and capital appreciation. Let's say that an investor bought ten Company M shares for $10 each, so his total investment is $100. After six months, the price of Company M stocks increased to $15. So, if the investor decides to sell his shares, he'll earn a profit (through capital appreciation) of $5.

There are two general types of investors – the "hands on" investors and the "hands off" investors.

Hands-off investors rely heavily on brokers. They don't pick the stocks they invest in. They usually invest in mutual funds, ETFs, and index fund.

Hands-on investors, on the other hand, personally handpick the stocks they invest in. They usually actively work with an experienced broker to build their investment portfolio.

Shareholders

Shareholders are investors who bought stocks from listed companies. They already own a small (sometimes big) part of certain companies.

There are two types of shareholders – common and preferred. Common shareholders, as the name suggests, own common stocks. They have voting rights. They can elect company officials and they have a say in the development of company policies. But, in case of liquidation of assets, they're only paid after the creditors and preferred stockholders get their share.

Preferred shareholders, on the other hand, own preferred stocks. They do not have voting rights. But, they rank higher than the common shareholders. In case of liquidation of assets, preferred shareholders are paid before common stockholders get their share.

Listed companies

Companies listed on stock exchanges are also called "issuers". They sell their shares in the stock market to raise money for expansion. They go through a process called Initial Public Offering or IPO.

Stockbrokers

A stock broker is a third party stock market participant that trades stocks and other securities on behalf of clients or investors. It could be an individual or a brokerage firm.
Representatives of these stockbrokers meet daily at a specific time on the stock exchange trading floor where they buy, sell, and execute orders on behalf of their clients.

There are two main types of stock brokers, namely:

- Traditional – They take orders from their clients in person or via phone.
- Online – They do not interact with their clients. They just take the order from their clients through an online platform.

Venture Capitalists

Venture capitalists are companies (or people) who invest in early stage companies. They often invest between one million to one hundred million dollars or even more. They also usually take a board seat in the company they invest in.

Investment Bank or Underwriter

An investment bank (or underwriter) is an organization that manages the IPO process.
Investment banks draft the necessary documents, find investors, and do the company valuation. They also conduct road shows to encourage people to invest in companies they're representing.

These investment banks usually charge between 2% to 7% of the total amount of money they raised during the IPO. They are many Wall Street investment banks such as JPMorgan, Morgan Stanley, and Goldman Sachs.

Floor Trader

A floor trader is a member of a stock exchange who trades on the floor for his own account.

Floor Broker

A floor broker executes trades on the exchange floor on behalf of clients. He executes orders placed by clients.

Clearing House

A clearing house is a financial institution that facilitates the exchange of securities and payments. Its goal is to make sure that the exchange participants honor their trade settlement obligations.
The clearing house settles member's trade accounts and collects money. It also oversees the delivery of stocks and generates trading data.

Let's say that James sells 50 Company X shares for $2,500 on a stock exchange. Diana buys 50 Company X shares for $2,500.

Diana doesn't have to pay James directly for the stocks she purchased. The stock exchange's clearing house collects $2,500 from Diana's trade account and transfers it to James account.

Analysts

Analysts examine certain stocks to predict future revenues, earnings, and prices.

Online investors

These investors just set up an online account and trades from home.

Financial advisors

These people manage other people's money.

Financial authors

These people do market analysis and publish stock trading theories to help people become intelligent investors.

How Can You Make Money Out of Your Stock Investment

People invest in the stock market to make more money. You can earn money from stock investment in two ways, namely:

Capital appreciation

You may have already heard the motto of every stock broker in Wall Street "Buy low, sell high".
Let's say that you bought a stock for $150 (buying price). Then, two years later, you decided to sell the stock, which is now valued at $300 (selling price). This means that you made a profit of $150. The positive difference between the buying and the selling price is called capital appreciation. This is the easiest way to earn money from the stock market.

Dividends

When a company earns a profit, it can do two things - it can use the money to expand or acquire new properties or it can distribute the profit to its shareholder. But, some companies do both – they distribute a portion of the profit to the shareholders and use the remaining money for expansion. The profit distributed among the stockholders is called "dividend".

A dividend is a portion of the profit distributed to a specific class of stockholders decided by the board of directors.

Dividends are normally distributed on a "per-share" basis. Let's say that you have purchased 200 shares of Company Z which is valued at $100 each. So, your total investment is valued at $20,000 (200 x 100).

Let's say that Company Z is really doing well this year and decides to pay a dividend of $20 per share. This means that you'll get a payout of $4000 (200 shares x 20 dollar per share) and a dividend yield of 20% (the dividend divided by the price of the stock).

You must remember that not all stocks come with regular dividend payments. In fact, not all companies distribute dividends to their shareholders. And when they do, companies can choose which class of stockholders they want to distribute it to (common or preferred shareholders, we will discuss this shortly).

Growing companies are less likely to give out dividends because they'll most likely reinvest their profits to provide "fuel" for further expansion. Large companies, on the other hand, don't need to expand, so they opt to give out dividends to their shareholders on a regular basis.

Common vs Preferred Stocks

Both common and preferred stocks represent ownership of a company. Both are tools that investors can use to earn money in the long run. They have a lot of similarity, but they also have a number of differences.

Common Stocks

Common stocks, as the name suggests, are more common than preferred ones. These stocks are generally cheaper and more risky, too.

A common stock is a type of security that represents ownership of a part of a company. Common stockholders have voting rights (depending on the number of shares they hold). They can vote on corporate policies and possible mergers. They can also elect board directors.

Aside from voting rights, investing in a common stock also comes with a lot of other benefits. For one, it has a higher yield than bonds and other investment products. It also comes with restricted legal liability. This means that the shareholders are not liable when the company is sued. It's also a highly liquid investment. This means that it's easy to purchase and sell.

The downside of being a common stockholder is that they are at the bottom of the company ownership structure. This means that if a company goes bankrupt and decides to liquidate its assets and properties, common shareholders have the rights to the company equity only after creditors, bondholders, and preferred stock holders are paid.

Right To Company Assets Incase of Liquidation	
1st Priority	Creditors/Bond Holders
2nd Priority	Preferred Stockholders
3rd priority	Common Stockholders

If you're a common stock holder, there's no guarantee that you'll get paid when the company goes bankrupt. This is the reason why it's risky.

Preferred Stocks

Preferred stocks are like a hybrid of bonds and stocks. They have features of both a stock and a bond.

Preferred stocks have higher dividend rates. This means that they have higher returns. They're also less risky than common stocks. Why? Well, in case the company decides to liquidate its assets and properties, preferred stockholders get paid before common shareholders.

Like the common stock, a preferred stock also represents ownership of a company. But, it's different from the common share in a sense that preferred stock holders are paid a fixed dividend at regular intervals (could be annually or every quarter).

Let's say that Company X issues new preferred stocks at $50 each. Then, they agreed to pay a dividend yield of $2 a year. This means that this stock has a dividend yield of 4% (annual dividend ($2) divided by the price of the stock ($50). This is a bit similar to how a bond works.

The downside of investing in preferred stocks is that you do not have voting rights. This means that you do not have a say on company policies. You also can't elect board members. Also, when a company faces financial problems, the company can cut dividend payment to preferred stockholders.

Preferred stocks also have low trading volume. This means that you can't easily expand your preferred stock portfolio.

There are also a lot of factors that can decrease the value of a preferred stock such as the interest rate. Let's say that your preferred stock has an annual yield of 4%. When the interest rate rises to 7%, a lot of preferred stockholders may opt to sell their share and reinvest their money on items that pays higher dividends. This could drive the price of the preferred stock lower.

Powerful investors like Warren Buffet have a huge portfolio of preferred stocks. But, before you put your eggs in the preferred stock basket, you must be aware that only a few companies issue preferred stocks. These companies are usually in the financial sector – banks, lending companies, insurance, etc. You should know this because investing in the financial industry is a bit risky as these companies usually have thin profit margins.

Why Do Stock Prices Fluctuate?

The stock market works like an auction house. This means that the price of a stock is basically based on the perceived value of the market players.

The price of a company's stock can change based on a lot of market forces, including the "law of supply and demand". This means that a high-demand stock is more expensive than a low-demand stock.

Let's take Berkshire Hathaway as an example. Its share is currently valued at $115,000 (more or less), the most expensive in the world.

This company is a multinational conglomerate that wholly owns Duracell, Dairy Queen, NetJets, Fruit of the Loom, Helzberg Diamonds, and GEICO. It also owns a part of Apple, Bank of America, Kraft Heinz Company, American Express, Pilot Flying J, and Coca Cola.

But, why is it so expensive? Its supply is too low because current stockholders do not sell their share and yet a lot of people want a share of the pie. It's expensive because the supply is a lot lesser than the demand. Warren Buffet also keeps the prices high to keep short term investors from causing price volatility.

Aside from the "law of supply and demand", there are also other factors that affect a stock's price, including future estimated earnings, a merger, acquisitions, accounting errors, employee layoffs, corporate scandals, and many more.

Let's say that there are two pasta companies - A and B. Company A is using a traditional pasta recipe. It's stable and established, so its stock is sold at $100 each.

Company B, on the other hand, uses avocado sauce. It's interesting, but a bit too inventive, so its stock is sold at a lower price of $50.

Let's say that popular chefs tasted Company B's pasta and thought that it was the best culinary invention next to bread. Because of this, its stock price increased to $100.

Now, let's say that experts discover that Company A's pasta has an ingredient that can cause cancer. Do you think that its stock price would still be $100? Hell, no! This scandal can significantly reduce its stock price. No one would probably want to invest in Company A anymore.

7 Economic forces that affect stock prices:

1. Economic Policy Changes

A new government leader may enforce new policies and this can heavily affect stock prices. Policy changes can either positively or negatively impact prices.

For example, if there's a policy that imposes a sugar tax on soft drinks, the stock prices of soda companies will go down. The stock price of tobacco companies will go up when the government decides to deregulate the cigarette producers.

2. Interest Rates

A country's central bank can increase or decrease interest rates to either stimulate or stabilize its economy. This process is called "monetary policy" and it can affect stock prices.

Let's say that Company K decided to borrow money from the bank for expansion. At that moment, the interest rate was really high, so the company's debt was a bit costly. This decreased Company K's profit and dividend payment. This also decreased the company's stock price.

3. Predictions of Financial Analysts

If economists and financial experts think that the economy is going to expand soon, stock prices can rise. Investors can buy more stocks as they anticipate higher stock prices and future profits.
When the economists predict a possible economic recession, investors panic and end up selling their stocks to invest in safe havens (e.g. Treasury bill, Gold etc.). This drives stock prices down.

4. Inflation

Inflation is the increase of the prices of consumer products. This usually reduces profits as it increases costs and also leads to higher interest rates. The Central Bank may temporarily increase the interest rates in order to make money more expensive to borrow and hence control its supply in the economy. This helps to keep inflation under control as there's less money being spent to acquire products/assets – classic supply and demand. It can also decrease stock prices.

When inflation increases, purchasing power declines, and each dollar can buy fewer goods and services. For investors interested in income-generating stocks, or stocks that pay dividends, the impact of high inflation makes these stocks less attractive than during low inflation, since dividends tend to not keep up with inflation levels.

5. Deflation

Deflation is the complete opposite of inflation. When the prices go down, revenues and profits decrease. This can decrease the stock prices and investors may end up selling their shares.

6. Political Issues and Crime

Political instability often leads to economic instability. For example, a massive act of terrorism such as the 9/11 attacks can decrease economic activities and also reduce stock prices as investors sell their shares to invest in safe havens like gold.

7. Natural Disasters

Natural disasters are scary and difficult to predict. They can destroy lives and economies. They can dampen economic growth and decrease stock prices.

If you want to be a successful investor, you must examine these factors thoroughly.

What a Stock Exchange Is and Why It's Important.

A stock exchange is an organized marketplace where securities such as stocks are traded. Huge amounts of money are moved back and forth in the stock market. More than 50 trillion dollars are traded every year in stock exchanges. This is more than the sum of the value of all the products and services of all world economies.

There are two major stock exchanges in the United States, including:

New York Stock Exchange (NYSE)

The New York Stock Exchange (NYSE) is located on Wall Street, Manhattan. It was founded on May 17, 1792 and it's the biggest stock exchange in the world in terms of the capital it generates.

Stocks are traded in NYSE in two ways – through brokers and electronic systems. Brokers (who represent investors) actively buy and sell stocks in this stock exchange.

National Association of Securities Dealers Automated Quotations (NASDAQ)

National Association of Securities Dealers Automated Quotations (Nasdaq) is the second largest stock exchange in the world in terms of the capital it generates. It is located in Broadway, New York. It is operated by Nasdaq Inc., which also owns stock exchanges in various cities in the world, including Stockholm, Copenhagen, Vilnius, Riga, Tallinn, Helsinki, Reykjavic, and Yerevan.

What is an Index?

Like a store, the stock market has different products with varying values and prices. But, how do you know which one to invest in? How do you make the most out of your investment? Well, you must be familiar with different tools, terms, and concepts that can help you make a wise, informed stock investment decision.

To see how a stock market is performing, many investors look at stock indices. An index is a small sample of stocks that are thought to represent a specific sector or the market in general.

You see, there's no way that one can monitor the performance and the value of all the shares in the stock market. This is the reason why financial analysts just pull a sample of stocks from different industries such as manufacturing, mining, fashion, commodities, real estate, health care, and many more. So, when you see a business reporter announce that the market is up by 3%, he's actually referring to an index or a small sample of stocks.

Indices are used to measure change. They are indicators of the financial health of specific stock markets and industries.

To illustrate this point, let's say that you have invested in a few health care companies. But, the IXHC (or Nasdaq Health Care Index) is continuously decreasing. This information helps you make a wise financial decision. Maybe it's time to reassess your investments and look for other industries to invest in.

There are many types of indices around the globe, but, here's a list of the most popular and widely used indices:

The Standard & Poor's 500 (S&P 500)

This index reflects the average market value (price of share x the number of outstanding or held shares) of five hundred stocks "most held" stocks from different industries. These stocks are held, meaning they are already owned. The companies included in the S&P sample are chosen based on a number of factors, including their market size and how much they represent their industry.

The S&P 500 measures the performance of large-cap and established companies from different industries, such as Abbott Laboratories (health care), Adobe Systems (information technology), Colgate-Palmolive (consumer products), Facebook (communications), Microsoft (information technology), Tiffany & Co (discretionary consumer products), and Wal-Mart (consumer staples).

Dow Jones Industrial Average (DJIA)

The Dow Jones Industrial Average (DJIA) is the oldest and, perhaps, the most popular stock market index. It was created in 1885 as DJA and it was renamed DJIA on May 26, 1896.

This index takes the sum of the thirty largest stocks in the New York Stock Exchange & NASDAQ, and divides it by a divisor. The divisor is used to ensure that a one-point move in a lower-priced component will have the identical effect on DJIA as does a one-point move in a higher-priced component. The current divisor can be found in the Wall Street Journal and is: **0.14748071991788**.

DJIA = Sum (Component stock prices)/Dow Divisor

The stocks included in DJIA are so heavily traded they are great indicators of the overall health of the stock market.

Nasdaq Composite Index

The Nasdaq Composite Index measures over three thousand stocks. It used to exclusively measure tech stocks such as Adobe and Google. But, it has already added stocks from different industries over the last few years.

The Difference between a Bear and a Bull Market

As previously mentioned, the stock market works a lot like an auction house. The prices of the stocks are driven by perception. There are times when the public confidence is really high and optimistic that investors end up buying more stocks. There are also times when the investors become so pessimistic that they ended up selling most of their shares. These occurrences are respectively called "bull" and "bear" markets.

Bear Market

No, we're not talking about the cute, huge, and fluffy mammals. In finance, a bear is a pessimist investor, who believes that the stock market is going downward.

A Bear Market is a condition when a stock's value decline by at least 20 percent for a long period of time (at least two months) because of the investors' pessimism. When this happens, a lot of investors would opt to sell their stocks and this would further fuel the negativity. This phenomenon usually lasts about thirteen months.

There are a lot of factors that push stocks into a bear market, including:

Forecasted Recession

A recession is a condition where there's a decrease in economic activity for a long period of time. This means that there's a decrease in major economic indicators, such as GDP (gross domestic product), manufacturing, disposable income, and employment.

When a country has a sluggish economy for a long period of time, economists may forecast recession. This could push investors to sell their securities and drive the prices low.

Commodity Price Increase

Commodities are investment pieces that include a wide array of industrial and edible products such as wheat, oil, steel, cotton, gold, coffee, sugar, cocoa, corn, live cattle, and gasoline. An increase in commodity prices can lead to inflation. This could negatively impact the stock market and could push it to the bear market territory.

Aggressive Central Bank

Each economy (country) has a central bank. This bank controls the country's money supply and interest rates.

But, sometimes, a central bank can get aggressive in increasing the interest rates to prevent inflation. When this happens, people end up selling their stocks in favor of *high interest* investments, such as certificate of deposit, high interest savings, money market funds, and U.S. savings bonds.

This could decrease the prices of stocks and could encourage investors to sell their shares to prevent losses and maximize their gains.

Extreme Valuations of Stocks

Overvaluation of stocks (vis-à-vis their earnings and intrinsic value) can lead to a bear market condition as exemplified by the economic state of the United States in 2001/2002.

As previously mentioned, a bear market usually lasts for thirteen months. Longer periods of bear market can lead to a stock market crash. This happened in 1973 when the stock market remained depressed for more than ten years.

Is there a way to still make money out of stocks during a bear market period? Yes, you can use a technique that Warren Buffet use called "value investing". This means that you should not look at the price of the stock, but rather, its intrinsic value (its profits, earnings, and assets). We will discuss this investing technique later on in this book.

Furthermore, extremely savvy investors can also benefit from stock market crashes by shorting the right stocks (i.e. stocks that are *most likely* to underperform, especially in bear market conditions).

Bull Market

A Bull Market is a condition in which the stock markets are so high that investors are aggressively buying stocks, acting like bulls. This period could last for months and even years.

A bull market is characterized by very high investor confidence and optimism. It happens when the stock prices increase by 20% for a long period of time (usually two months).

This phenomenon is difficult to predict, so financial analysts usually recognize a bull market after it has happened. The most popular bull market happened in 2003 and ended in 2007.

There are many factors that push the stock market into the "bull" territory, including an increase in GDP (gross domestic product) and a decrease in the unemployment rate.

During a bull market period, the demand for stocks surpasses its supply, causing the stock prices to rise.

Bear Market Vs. Bull Market	
The demand for stocks is lower than its supply – people would rather sell than buy stocks.	The stock demand is higher than its supply – many people are willing to buy stocks, but only a few wants to sell.
Investor confidence is low.	Investors are optimistic and willing to buy more stocks.
The economy is weak and unemployment rates are high.	The economy is strong, creating more jobs and increasing employment rates.

What is SEC and Its Role in The Stock Market

The stock market is a jungle filled with naïve beginners, greedy veterans, and glib stockbrokers. If it's not regulated, the greedy and deceptive predators could easily prey on uninformed investors. This is the reason why stock markets have regulators.

The SEC or the Securities Exchange Commission is a government agency that regulates the buying and selling of securities like bonds and stocks to protect investors from fraud and scams. It was created in 1934, making it the first federal stock market regulator. It regulates the New York Stock Exchange (NYSE) and the NASDAQ Stock Exchange.

The SEC oversees the companies, individuals, and organizations in the stock markets, including brokers, dealers, investors, securities exchanges, financial advisors, and various investment funds.

This government body provides investors access to important documents, such as financial reports and registration statements.

The United States SEC also uses different laws to accomplish its tasks such as the Securities Act of 1933, the Trust Indenture Act of 1939, the Securities Exchange Act of 1934, the Investment Company Act (1940), the Investment Advisers Act (1940), the Sarbanes-Oxley Act (2002), the Jumpstart Our Business Startups (JOBS) Act of 2012, and the Dodd-Frank Wall Street Reform and Consumer Protection Act of 2010.

The SEC has five divisions, including:

- **Division of Trading and Markets** – This division creates and maintains standards to keep the stock markets orderly, efficient, and fair.

- **Division of Economic and Risk Analysis** – This division was created in 2009 and it uses data analytics to proactively identify market risks and violations of the securities law. This department is involved in various activities in the SEC, including policy-making, examination, and enforcement.

- **Division of Enforcement** – This department implements security laws and investigates violations.

- **Division of Investment Management** – As the name suggests, this department regulates several stock market players, such as investment companies and registered investment advisors.

- **Division of Corporate Finance** – This department ensures that investors have access to documents that can help them make sound investment decisions.

But, the SEC is not the only agency that regulates the US stock market. The Financial Industry Regulatory Authority or FINRA is a private company that acts as an SRO or self- regulatory organization.

FINRA was established in 1939 and its goal is to make sure that the stock market operates honestly, openly, and fairly. It oversees all securities licensing requirements and processes. It administers exams needed to become a licensed financial adviser. It also enforces high ethical standards among stock market players to ensure that investors are protected.

Chapter 1 Summary

Below are the some summary points from chapter 1

- Stock market investment is a technique used by investors like Warren Buffet to grow their money and accumulate wealth.
- Some people earn a lot of money from the stock market, while others end up losing huge amounts of money. This is the reason why you must be well-informed before you start investing your money.
- A stock is a part of a company. It is a form of security. If a business is a pizza, a stock is a slice of the pizza.
- Companies create and issue stocks to raise additional capital for expansion.
- When a company decides to sell stocks, it goes through a process called IPO or Initial Public Offering. This process is also called "going public".
- A stock market is a place where stocks are traded.
- The stock market has two parts – the primary market and the secondary market.
- The primary market is where the stocks are created. The secondary market is where investors buy previously-traded stocks and sell stocks they already own.
- There are three types of stock markets, including stock exchanges, ECN or electronic communication network, and OTC (over the counter) market.
- The stock markets have various players including, corporations, investors, brokers, online investors, financial authors, and financial advisors.
- There are two ways that you can make money out of your stock investment – dividends and capital appreciation.
- A dividend is the profit distributed among shareholders.
- Capital appreciation is the positive difference between a stock's buying price and its selling price. It is a form of investor profit.
- A common stock represents ownership of a company. Common stock holders have voting rights. This means that they have a say on how company policies are shaped and they can elect board members. However, they are at the bottom of the payout hierarchy. This means that if the company assets are liquidated, they only get paid after the preferred stock holders get paid.
- A preferred stock acts like a bond. It is more expensive than common stocks and usually comes with dividend. When the company assets are sold, preferred stockholders get their share after creditors and bond-holders are paid.

- Stock prices are affected by many factors, including the law of supply and demand, company news, forecasts, scandals, mergers, and acquisitions.

- An index is a small sample of stocks of companies that are so big that they represent the overall health of the industry they belong to.

- A bear market is a condition when investors are so pessimistic that they end up selling their stocks. This drives down the stock prices.

- A bull market is a condition when investors are optimistic, so they want to invest in stocks.

- The SEC is a stock market regulator that protects investors from fraud and scams.

In the next chapter, we'll discuss how you can invest in stocks.

Inspiration #2

"It's far better to buy a wonderful company at a fair price, than a fair company at a wonderful price."
Warren Buffer

Chapter 2

Getting Started: How to Invest In Stocks

Eden has been working in an advertising agency for fifteen years. She's earning good money, but she's tired and wants to retire early. She always wanted to invest in stocks, but didn't know how.

Much like Eden, many of us want to invest in the stock market, but we just don't know what to do or how to get started.

Investing in the stock market is not as hard as you think. Here are a few steps that you need to follow to get started:

Step 1: Understand the Difference between Stocks and Stock Mutual Funds

Many people think that stock market investing is a complicated animal. Well, not really. You just need to understand the two investment types, namely:

Exchange Traded Funds (ETF) or Stock Mutual Funds

Stock mutual funds allow you to buy small pieces of different stocks in one transaction.
ETFs and Index Funds are stock mutual funds that allow you to track an index and replicate it. For example, the S&P's 500 fund replicates the "Standard & Poor's 500" index.

So, if you decide to invest a little bit of your money in an "S&P's 500" fund, you'll own a little piece of all the companies in it (the size of that piece depends on your investment budget). You can't choose which stock to invest in.

The upside of investing in ETFs is that it is cheaper. It's also *a great way to diversify your stock investments without spending a fortune.* However, the downside of this investment type is that it doesn't allow you to choose specific stocks to invest in. This brings us to the second investment type.

Individual Stocks

You need to invest in individual stocks if you're after a particular company. For example, if you really want a piece of Facebook, you need to buy a few FB stocks on Nasdaq.
You can also build a diversified portfolio out of several individual stocks, but you'd need to have a lot of money to do this.

Step 2: Identify Your Investing Style

You can invest in the stock market in a number of ways. You can invest in employer-sponsored accounts such as the 401(k) plan. You can directly purchase stocks or you can ask a financial advisor to manage your investments.

It's best to invest in a 401k Plan if you're on a budget and you're still working. But, if you're planning to invest a huge amount of money in the stock market, it's best to open a brokerage account or ask a professional money manager to manage your investment.

If you're not really a "hands on" investor, it's best to invest in mutual funds, index funds, or ETFs. But, if you want to choose stocks yourself, then opening a brokerage account is the best option for you.

Step 3: Set a Budget

Before you start investing money in stocks, you must set a budget. How much money are you willing to invest? Remember that the amount of money you need depends on how much the shares cost. Some stocks cost a few dollars, while some shares can cost thousands of dollars.

Step 4: Open a Stock Investment Account

You need an investment account in order to invest in stocks. You can open a 401(k) account through your employer or you could open an IRA (individual retirement account). You can also open a brokerage account if you're more of a "hands on" investor. We will discuss the different types of stock investment accounts in the later part of this chapter.

As mentioned earlier, you can open an investment account with your employer. But, if you decide to open a brokerage account, you should consider the following factors:

Account Minimum

A lot of brokerage firms require a minimum initial investment of $500 or more. If you plan to initially invest just a few hundred dollars on the stock market, you should choose brokers that do not require minimum investments, such as Merril Edge, TD Ameritrade, and Ally Invest.

Commissions

If you decide to invest in individual stocks, you'll have to pay for per trade commissions (usually between 4 to 7 dollars). You should choose a broker with minimal trade commission rate, especially if you're a beginner.

Trading Style

If you're new to stock market investment, you probably don't need advanced trading platforms. But, you may want to choose a brokerage firm that offers educational tools like tutorials, videos, and even seminars.

High volume traders, on the other hand, need state-of-the-art trading platforms and analysis tools.

Account Fees

Most brokerage firms charge account fees such as annual fees, transfer fees, trading platform subscriptions, research fees, market data payments, and inactivity fees. It's best to choose a firm that offers free market data and research services and charges minimal account fees.

Step 5: Start Investing

Once you've opened an account, you can start investing using different strategies, such as value investing, growth investing, income investing, socially responsible investing, diversification, and more. We'll discuss these strategies later on in this book.

401(k) Plan

The 401k plan is a retirement plan that companies offer to their employees as part of the benefits package. It is one of the most common retirement savings accounts. It was created in 1978 through the section 401(k) of the Internal Revenue Code. That's why it's called the 401(k) plan.

The best thing about the 401k plan is that it allows you to save on tax payments. It also allows you to take advantage of your employer's retirement contribution through the "employee matching gift" program. This program is usually offered as an incentive to prevent attrition and encourage employees to stay with the company for a long period of time.

Here's how it works. Let's say that you work in a tech company that sponsors 401k plans and you earn $150,000 a year before taxes. You agree to put 6 percent of your income, which sums up to $9000. This contribution is tax deferred. This means that you don't have to pay taxes for your contribution until you retire (you'll be in a lower tax bracket when that time comes). This means that your taxable income at the moment is $141,000 (your annual income minus your annual contribution).

As a part of the matching gift program, your employer agrees to match $0.50 for every dollar you put into your 401(k) plan. So, the company puts an extra $4500 ($9000 x 0.50 cents). This means that your total contribution is $13,500 a year. See the computation below.

Employee contribution ($9,000.00)
+
Employer contribution ($4,000.00)
____
Total Annual 401(k) contribution ($13,500)

What Happens to Your 401(k) Contribution?

The money invested in your 401(k) account is usually invested in stocks, bonds, and mutual funds. When you sign up for this program, you'll be provided with a list of stocks that you can invest in. Review these stocks carefully.

You must consider your age when choosing the right stocks to invest in. If you're still in 20s, it's okay to take a little risk. You can invest in volatile tech stocks like Netflix, Facebook, and Amazon.

But, if you're already in your late 30s, 40s, or 50s, it's best to go with more stable companies like Hormel Foods Corporation, Costco Wholesale, Cigna, and American Waterworks.

When you decide to quit your job, you can move your 401(k) plan to an IRA (individual retirement account). You can also rollover your existing plan to your new company's 401(k) plan. But, you have to take note that not all companies accept retirement plan rollovers, so it's best to check with your new employer.

You can withdraw your 401k money even before you reach your retirement age, but the IRS (Internal Revenue Service) will have to collect a ten percent early withdrawal penalty. This may not seem much if you saved $3000. But, if you already saved a million dollars, you'll have to pay a bigger penalty.

How to Invest in 401(k) Plan

As previously mentioned, the 401(k) plan is an employee sponsored plan. This means that you have to do it through your employer.

Here's how you can invest in the 401(k) plan:

- When you get hired, choose to be part of your company's 401(k) program.
- Decide how much of your income you want to go to your 401(k) plan.
- Choose the stocks that you want to invest in.
- Review your application and then, submit it to your employer.

At this point, you don't have to do anything else. Your employer will automatically deduct your contribution from your salary. Your company also manages your investment fund, so you don't have to worry about anything.

401(k) Plan vs 403(B) Plan

Like 401(k), 403(b) is also a retirement plan set up by an employer. But, the main difference is that 401(k) is offered by private and for profit employers, while 403(b) is offered by non-profit employers, such as the government or non-profit schools.

If you work as a graphic designer in an advertising agency, you'll have the option to invest in a 401(k) retirement plan. But, if you work for a government agency, your employer will most likely offer a 403(b) retirement plan.

401(k) vs. 403(b)	
401 (K)	403 (B)
Retirement plan offered by private for profit companies	Retirement plan offered by non-profit organizations, such as religious groups, government organizations, and non-profit schools.
Higher administrative costs	Lower administrative costs
Has a maximum contribution limit	Has a maximum contribution limit

Has limited investment options usually selected by your employer or a financial management company	Account holders can invest in a wide variety of annuities and mutual funds
Has an employer matching program	Has an employing matching program

Pros and Cons of the 401(k) Plan

The biggest advantage of the 401(k) plan is that it comes with matching funds. So, you'll get a lot more money than you put in. Let's say, you committed to saving $7,000 a year and your company matches your contribution and also deposits $7,000 to your account each year. This means that you'll have a total annual savings/investment of $14,000. Amazing, right?

The 401(k) plan is also hassle-free. You don't have to manage your investment account. It has high contribution limits and it's protected by the ERISA or the Employee Retirement Income Security Act of 1974.

But, the downside of the 401(k) plan is that it has limited investment options. This means that you can only invest in specific stocks and bonds.

IRA

Joy is a hard worker. Although she didn't finish high school, she found a stable job. She worked as a warehouse manager for thirty long years. The pay is good, but she ended up spending all she got. When she finally retired, she only saved up $10,000, which only covers a few months of her living expenses. Her pension benefits are simply not enough.

Unfortunately, Joy's story is not unique. More and more retirees are broke. To avoid ending up like Joy, it's best to invest in an IRA.

IRA or individual retirement account is a tax-advantaged investment and a savings account that allows you to save for retirement.

There are different types of IRA, namely – traditional IRA, Roth IRA, Simple IRA, Spousal IRA, nondeductible IRA, SEP IRA, and self-directed IRA.

Traditional IRA

A traditional IRA is a tax-deferred retirement savings and investment account. It is the most popular retirement plan. As the traditional IRA is tax-deferred, your contribution is not taxed now, but it's taxed when you withdraw the money in your account. This investment type is great for people who will be placed in a lower income tax bracket when they retire.

So, let's say that you're single and you earn $210,000 per year. Your tax is 35 percent and your yearly retirement savings is $6,500 per year. This means that you have to pay a tax of $2,275.00 per year for your investment. That's too much, right.

Now, if you place your money in a traditional IRA account, you won't have to pay taxes for your retirement plan now. You'll pay when you retire and by that time, your tax is 15%. This means that instead of paying $2,275.00 annual tax for your investment, you'll only have to pay $975. This will save you 57% more money or around $1,300.00 per year!

Here are the key features of traditional IRA:

- It's a tax-deferred account. This means that you only have to pay taxes for your investment plan upon withdrawal.
- It has bankruptcy protection. This means that your creditors can't go after your IRA.
- Your beneficiaries can inherit your IRA funds in case of death.
- You can set up an IRA even if you have another retirement plan.
- You can convert your 401(k) plan into a traditional IRA when you decide to leave your employer.
- You can invest your savings into stocks, mutual funds, and other securities.
- Traditional IRA has a ten percent early withdrawal penalty, except in some cases, such as:
- Death (when this happens, the beneficiaries can withdraw the funds)
- Disability
- Back taxes
- Conversion of Traditional IRA to another retirement plan, such as Roth IRA
- IRS civil suit
- Creditor access
- Medical expenses
- Higher education payments

How you can invest in a traditional IRA

Step 1 – Choose a brokerage company.

Decide what your investing style is. If you're a hands-off investor, you can invest via a Robo-advisor, an online/digital financial advisor that manages your investments with minimal human intervention. Robo-advisors are usually efficient and they're cheaper than regular brokerage firms.

But, if you're more of a hands-on investor, you must choose a broker that has low account and commission fees. Most of all - choose a broker with a good reputation. You don't want to get scammed and lose all your hard-earned money.

Step 2 – Open an account.

Opening a traditional IRA account is not as hard as you think. All you need to do is fill out some forms. You would need to provide personal details, such as your date of birth, social security number or SSN, employment data, and contact information.

Step 3 – Start depositing money into your account.

You can transfer money from your bank account into your traditional IRA. You would need your account number and bank routing number if you're transferring funds for the first time. You can also rollover a 401(k) plan from your former employer into your IRA.

Step 4 – Choose your investments.

When you decide to invest via a robo-advisor, you don't get to choose your investments. But, if you decide to invest through a broker, you'll have to choose which stocks or ETFs that you want to invest in.

Roth IRA

Like the traditional IRA, Roth IRA is a tax-advantaged retirement investment plan. It's named after Senator William Roth of Delaware.

Roth IRA is a lot like the traditional IRA in many ways. But, the major difference is that *it's tax-free (not tax-deferred).* You'll have to pay the tax though annually, but all the taxes paid will be refunded once you withdraw your investment.

Here's how it works. Let's say that you decide to contribute $5,500 per year (for 20 years) and you have a tax rate of 10%. You'll get a tax deduction of $550 per year for 20 years which sums to $11,000. Once you retire, you'll receive a tax refund of $11,000. Amazing, right?

Anyone with taxable income can open a Roth IRA. Here are the top features of this investment plan:

- You can contribute a maximum of $5,500 a year
- It's tax free. But, you'll still get a tax deduction per month. The taxes paid will be refunded when you retire.
- You can open multiple IRAs.
- You can withdraw your Roth IRA funds without paying taxes or penalties five years after you opened the account. But, it's only tax-free and penalty-free in certain cases such as:
    - Disability
    - IRA owner's death
    - Money was used for medical expenses
    - Money was used to pay for insurance premiums
    - The saved money was used to pay back taxes
    - The fund was used for first-time home purchase
    - The IRA fund was used to pay for higher education

Roth IRA is more flexible than the traditional IRA. Plus, you can withdraw it without any penalty in case you're sick, has become disabled, or you need to purchase your first home. Plus, it's something that you can pass on to your heirs.

But, there's one drawback. Single people who have a modified adjusted gross income (MAGI) of more than $137,000 a year or married couple (filing jointly) with an annual MAGI of more than $203,000 cannot open a Roth IRA account (as of January, 2019).

How To Get Started With Roth IRA

Step 1 – Find out if you're eligible to open a Roth IRA.

As previously mentioned, not everyone is qualified to open a Roth IRA. If you're single, head of the family, and you earn more than $135,000, you're not allowed to open a Roth IRA. So, it's best to open either a 401(k) account or a traditional IRA plan.

Step 2 – Choose the right brokerage firm.

Always check the account fees and choose the one with a great reputation and minimal fees. It's also best to choose a brokerage firm with great customer service.

Step 3 – Open your account.

You need to fill out some paperwork when opening your Roth IRA account. You'll need your social security number, driver's license, your bank's routing number, your employer's name and address, and the information of your beneficiaries.

Step 4 – Set up a monthly contribution system.

The next step is to deposit money into your Roth IRA. You can set up a monthly contribution schedule if your bank allows it. That way, you don't have to worry about depositing money into your investment account each month.

Take note that as of 2019, you can contribute only up to $6000 a year if you have an annual income of $189,000 or below.

Step 5 – Design Your Own Portfolio

Choose which stocks or ETFs you want to invest in. You can do this on your own or you can consult a professional financial adviser who can help you make wise investment choices.

Traditional IRA vs ROTH IRA	
Traditional IRA	**ROTH IRA**
Tax-deferred This means that it's not taxed now, but it will be taxed later when you decide to pull out your funds.	Tax-free It's taxed now, but you'll be refunded for all the tax payments you've made when you decide to withdraw the funds.
This investment plan is for people who are in high tax bracket now, but will most likely be in a lower income bracket during retirement.	This investment plan is best for those who may be placed in a higher income bracket during retirement.

You must be under 70.5 years old to contribute	You can contribute at any age
Minors and non-working spouses can contribute	Non-working spouses and minors can also contribute
Annual contribution deadline: April 15	Annual contribution deadline: April 15

Simple IRA

The SIMPLE IRA is the acronym for Savings Incentive Match Plan for Employees Individual Retirement Account. It is a tax-deferred investment account that allows you to save for retirement.

This employee-sponsored retirement savings and investment plan is usually offered by small businesses with one hundred employees or less. Most small businesses favor SIMPLE IRA over 401(k) plan because it is less complicated and a lot cheaper.

As previously mentioned, SIMPLE IRA is a matching investment program just like the 401(k) plan. But, the matching and saving percentage is significantly lower than the 401k plan. Employees can only save up to three percent of their salary and employers can contribute two percent of the employee's salary.

Let's say that you earn $100,000 a year. You can only deposit up to $3,000 a year and your employer has to deposit $2000 into your SIMPLE IRA account.

SIMPLE IRA has a contribution limit of $13,000 as of 2019. If you are over 50, you can add a catch-up contribution of $3,000.

Investing in SIMPLE IRA is quite easy. You just have to check if your employer offers it and then sign up.

SEP IRA

SEP IRA or Simplified Employee Pension Individual Retirement Arrangement is a retirement account used in the United States. This retirement plan is for small business owners and self-employed people. This retirement plan is mainly for entrepreneurs with one or two employees. But, it's also for freelancers and online sellers.

One of the best things about SEP IRA is that it has a higher contribution limit. As of 2019, you can save up to twenty five percent of your income or a total of $56,000, whichever is higher.

Spousal IRA

A spousal IRA is basically a regular traditional or ROTH IRA. But, this investment account allows a working spouse to deposit money on his/her working spouse's account.

To illustrate this point, let's look at Leslie's and Josh's story. They are both nurses and met in the workplace. They fell in love and eventually got married. But, after a year, Leslie got laid off. To make sure that his wife has enough money for retirement, Josh decided to contribute money into Leslie's IRA.

This IRA type is perfect for stay-at-home spouses/parents. But, you should take note that the Spousal IRA is not a joint account. So, even if Josh deposits money into his wife's IRA, the account is not his. This means that only Leslie could withdraw it.

Pros and Cons of IRA

One of the best things about IRA is that it has tax advantages. It's also easy to start and inexpensive. You can set up an IRA on your own without help from a financial planner.

But, the biggest disadvantage of IRA is that it has a contribution limit and low contribution rate. This means that you can only save so much through the IRA. It also has early withdrawal fees.

Taxable Brokerage Account

If you're serious about growing your wealth, you must have a taxable brokerage account on top of your tax-advantaged IRA and 401(k) plan.

A taxable brokerage account (or simply, brokerage account) is an investment account that you have to open through a brokerage firm. You can simply deposit cash into this account through checks or electronic fund transfer.

When you have a brokerage account, your broker will execute the trade orders (to either buy or sell stocks) on your behalf. Brokerage firms usually require a minimum account balance of about $500 to $2000. The money deposited into your brokerage account is called the money market fund. This amount just sits in your account until you decide to use it to buy stocks, bonds, and other securities.

A tax brokerage account can hold different types of investment products, such as common stocks, preferred stocks, bonds, real estate investment trusts or REITs, exchange traded funds or ETFs, mutual funds, or certificate of deposit. We will discuss this in detail later in this book.

There are three types of taxable brokerage account, namely:

A. Cash Account

This is the most basic brokerage account. When you have a cash account, you must pay all your investment transactions in full by the settlement date. This is perfect for beginners.

B. Margin Account

A margin brokerage account allows you to borrow money from the broker. The brokerage firm lends you capital that you can use to purchase stocks and bonds. This account allows you to invest more money in the stock market.

This brokerage account is more risky and it's best for more experienced investors. Margin accounts also have a lot of requirements.

C. Option Account

This is a margin account that's used to buy and sell options or contract to buy. This account can be used for options trading at the Chicago board options exchange. Investing through a taxable brokerage account has a lot of advantages, including:

- You can invest no matter what your income is.
- You can deposit (or contribute) as much as you can.
- You have a wide array of investment choices. This means that you can personally handpick the stocks and ETFs that you want to invest in.
- You can withdraw your money anytime without early withdrawal penalty. You don't have to wait until you're 60.

To open a brokerage account, you just have to follow these steps:

Step 1 – Choose the brokerage firm you want to do business with.

Before you open an account with a brokerage firm, you must do an extensive research. You have to compare the incentives and costs. Check how much the brokerage firms charge per transaction. Choose a broker that charges minimal fees. This will save you a lot of money in the long run.

It's also important to look into the brokerage firm's services. Does the firm give you easy access to research data? Does the company support foreign training? Does it have an advanced trading platform that can be accessed through a mobile app?

Step 2 – File the paperwork.

After you've chosen the brokerage firm, it's time to fill out the new account application. You'd need your driver's license and your social security number. You also need to specify other information, such as your employment status, net worth, investment goals, and more.

Step 3 – Put funds into your account.

You can deposit money into your taxable brokerage account through electronic funds transfer or EFT, check, and wire transfer. You can also roll over your 401k plan into your brokerage account.

Step 4 – Choose the stocks and other securities you want to invest in.

Once you've already set up your brokerage account, it's time to choose the stocks you want to invest in and build your portfolio.'

Pros and Cons of Investing in Taxable Brokerage Account

One of the best things about investing in a taxable brokerage account is that there's no limit to the amount of money that you can put in it. In addition, it does not have early withdrawal fees. But, the downside is that it *does not* have tax advantages. This means that there are no tax discounts and other privileges.

It's best to use a taxable brokerage account when you've maxed out your IRA or 401k plan. It's also perfect for those who want to retire early.

Direct Stock Purchase Plan

A direct stock purchase plan is an investment program that allows you to buy stocks directly from a company without a broker. This means that you don't have to deal with middlemen. Let's say that you want to purchase Company N stocks. Instead of opening a brokerage account, you just have to buy the stocks directly from the issuing company.

This plan is usually inexpensive and perfect for first time investors. You'll only need around $100 to $500 to get started.

But, one of the worst things about the direct stock purchase plan is that it's not liquid. This means that you can't sell your stocks without using a broker, so this investment plan works best for long-term investors.

Here's how you can invest through a direct purchase plan:

Step 1 - Decide what stock you want to invest in.
Step 2 - Check the company's website and go to the FAQ page to see if the company sells their stock directly. If yes, there's usually a link to the company's stock transfer facilitator.
Step 3 – Click on the link. This link usually contains the prices and the minimum amount of money required to open a direct stock purchase plan.
Step 4 – Create an account following the instructions on the company's website. You'll need your SSN, driver's license, name, and bank information.
Step 5 – Specify how many stocks you want to purchase and transfer money into your direct purchase plan.

Dividend Reinvestment Plan

A dividend reinvestment plan or DRIP is an investment program that allows you to reap the benefits of compounding. Investing in DRIP allows you to reinvest the dividends earned from your investments, resulting to more returns and investment profits. When you invest in a DRIP, your investment will grow exponentially.

Let's say that you invest in a few McDonald's stocks. McDonalds usually pays quarterly dividends to its investors. Now, if you sign up for DRIP, your quarterly dividend earnings are automatically used to purchase more McDonalds shares.

One of the best things about DRIP is that it increases your investment exponentially, so it won't sit idle. Plus, it has extremely minimal fees, if there's any. You don't have to worry about those hefty transaction fees that add up.

Chapter 2 Summary

Below are the some summary points from chapter 2

To get started in stock market investment, you need to follow these steps:

- **Step 1** – You have to understand the difference between stocks and stock mutual funds.
- **Step 2** – You must determine what your investing style is.
- **Step 3** – You have to set your investment budget.
- **Step 4** – Choose a brokerage firm and open an investment account.
- **Step 5** - Deposit money into your account and start investing.

There are many types of investment accounts that you can invest in, including the 401(k) plan, IRA or individual retirement account, tax brokerage account, direct purchase plan, and dividend reinvestment plan.

- 401(k) plan is an employer-sponsored investment account. It has tax benefits. It comes with a matching program that allows employers to match their employee's contributions. This investment plan is inexpensive and hassle-free. You can simply sign up through your employer.

- The individual retirement account (or IRA) is a savings and investment account that comes with tax benefits. There are different types of IRA, such as the traditional IRA, the SIMPLE IRA, Roth IRA, Spousal IRA, self-directed IRA, SEP IRA, and non-deductible IRA.

- Traditional IRA is a tax-deferred retirement investment account. This is something that you can open through a brokerage firm. You can use your traditional IRA fund to invest in mutual funds, stocks, and other securities.

- Roth IRA is a tax-advantaged account. It is more flexible than the traditional IRA and with more investment choices. You have to pay upfront taxes for your contributions, but you'll get a tax refund when you retire.

- Simple IRA is an investment account. It's also the acronym for Savings Incentive Match Plan for Employees Individual Retirement. It works a lot like the 401k plan in the sense that it also has a matching program. But, it's cheaper. Most small businesses offer this type of retirement plan.

- You should invest in a 401k plan if you're going to be in a lower tax bracket when you retire.

- SEP IRA (or simplified employee pension) is an investment plan for small business owners, self-employed individuals, and freelancers.

- Spousal IRA is just a regular Traditional or Roth IRA. The difference is that it allows a working spouse to contribute to his/her non-working spouse's account.

- Direct Stock Purchase Plan allows you to purchase stocks directly from issuing companies. This saves you a lot of money because you don't have to go through a broker.

- Dividend reinvestment plan or DRIP allows you to reinvest your dividend earnings. So, if you want your earnings to just keep on growing, you should choose this plan.

- Taxable brokerage plan is best for serious investors and high income earners. But, if you're on a budget, it's best to go with employer-sponsored retirement savings and investment plans.

In the next chapter, we will discuss the basic stock investment strategies and how you can use it to grow your wealth.

Inspiration #3

"There are two types of people who will tell you that you cannot make a difference in this world: those who are afraid to try and those who are afraid you will succeed."
Ray Goforth

Chapter 3

Stock Investment Strategies

Stock market investing is one of the most powerful and effective ways to grow your money. But, to achieve great wealth, you have to invest your money wisely. You must have a sound and foolproof investment strategy. Warren Buffet made a lot of money in the stock market because he is a wise investor. He has mastered the art of growing his money exponentially over time. Below are the top investing strategies that you can use to grow your money.

Value Investing

The best way to earn money from the stock market is to "buy low and sell high". This principle is at the heart of an investment strategy called value investing.

The principle behind "value investing" is quite simple. All you have to do is to find companies that are undervalued in the stock market.

To illustrate this point, let's say that Company V decides to go public. The stock market has estimated its value at $100,000, 000. But, after you studied its earnings and products, you are convinced that it has an intrinsic value (investor's perceived value based on forecasted future earnings) of 1 billion dollars. So, you decided to invest in Company V stocks.

Value investors believe that profit is best made by *investing* for the long haul (in high quality companies), not by *day trading*. They take time to research and determine the value of company assets.

Value investors do not focus on external factors that can affect the company's value, such as daily price fluctuations and market volatility. They believe that focusing on high value companies is the path to building great wealth.

Here are the key principles of value investing:

Value investors do not care about market speculation. They are not looking for the next best thing. They instead look for stocks that are undervalued, so they could earn huge profits in the future.

Stocks are mispriced all the time. Foe example, when some investors are scared they blindly sell everything they own. This creates opportunities for savvy value investors to benefit from. Value investors look at the company's intrinsic value (the value of total assets) over its market value (stock price).

The key to value investing is research. You must know the value of the company's assets. You must also determine how the company is performing in comparison its competitors and find the reason why the stock is sold at a discounted price.

Look for a company with low P/E Ratio as it's *likely* to be undervalued. P/E ratio is calculated as:

P/E Ratio = Market value per share/ Earnings per share

Note: (/) represents the division sign

It's best to invest in stocks with a P/E ratio of less than forty percent. The stock's price should be no more than two thirds (66.67%) of its intrinsic value.

Let's say that Company K has an intrinsic value of $1,000,000 and it has 10,000 shares. This means that its intrinsic value per share is $100. But, its current stock price is currently valued at $50. Should you invest in company K? Yes because its price is only 50 percent of its intrinsic value.

The company you should invest in should have an annual earnings growth rate of 7%. Look at the company's earnings and make sure that its earnings are growing year after year.

It's hard to really determine the intrinsic value of a company. This is the reason why you should give yourself a margin of safety.

The margin of safety is calculated as:

Margin of safety = 1 – (Current stock price/Intrinsic stock price)

Let's say that Company H's current stock price is $40, but you think that its intrinsic stock price is $50. Your margin of safety is 20 percent.

The process of determining a company's stock value is based on detailed and highly accurate analysis of the company's earnings and assets. Still, this process is lined with predictions and a little bit of speculation. So, you may come up with an inaccurate intrinsic value. This is the reason why value investors invest in companies with a high margin of safety. This minimizes the risk.

You should invest in a company with low debt/equity ratio. The debt/equity ratio is a measure of the company's financial health. It is calculated by dividing the company's total debt by its shareholder equity.

Debt to Equity Ratio = Total Liabilities/Total Equity

If a company has a debt to equity ratio of $0.50, it means that it has a debt of $0.50 for every dollar of equity. Companies with low debt to equity ratio are in good financial health because their *profits and earnings are significantly higher than their liabilities*.

Choose a company with a huge growth potential, the ones who haven't tapped certain markets yet.

Be patient. Understand that time is your friend when it comes to value investing. This is why you have to be patient. You'll have to wait for months (if not years) to gain huge profits.

To become a successful value investor, you have to focus on the business, not on its stocks. This means that you should ignore stock trends and news.

You should stop analyzing the overall health of the stock market. You focus on the financial health and profitability of the company you want to invest in.

You must invest in companies that you believe in, love, and understand. And most of all, choose companies that are undervalued. This way, you'll earn huge capital appreciation profits in the future.

Pros and Cons

The major advantage of this investment strategy is that it creates a low risk and high reward scenario. Plus, it's less work in the sense that you don't have to be concerned about the day-to-day stock price fluctuation.

Value investing is a long-term investment strategy, so you get to pay a low tax rate on your investment earnings. You also get to save on transaction fees.

The downside of value investing is that it's sometimes difficult to identify undervalued companies. You have to do extensive research. It's also hard to come up with an accurate company valuation.

Growth Investing

Growth investing is an investment strategy that focuses on capital appreciation (or capital gains). Growth investors usually invest in emerging companies that have the potential to grow exponentially in the future.

Here are the top "growth investing" tips:

Tip 1 - Invest in innovative and fast-growing enterprises.
You should look for companies with revolutionary and ground-breaking technology. And you should invest during their early stages.

In 2012, a Facebook stock was valued at 26.62. At that time, Facebook was already big, but it's still growing. By, January 2019, it's valued at $165.71. So, if you bought 100 FB stocks for $2,662.00, you already have $16,571 in 2019. Not bad, right?

Tip 2 - Cut your losses as fast as you can.
You're going to make investment mistakes. Don't let your losses exceed 20%. If the price of the stock consistently drops day after day, get rid of it so you will not end up losing more and more money.

Tip 3 - Sell a winning stock when its price starts to go down.
When a stock reaches its peak, it will lose its momentum and its price will start to go down. Sell your stock right away when this happens. This will maximize your profit.

To illustrate this point, let's say that you bought 100 Company Y's stocks at $10 each. After one year, the stock price reached its peak at $80. At this point, you already have an investment profit of $7,000. That's not bad at all. So, if the price starts to go down, sell your stocks right before it declined by 20% i.e. $64 (your limit). This way so you could earn an optimal profit. If you wait for a few months, your profit could go down further.

Tip 4 - Long term investments make more money.
Growth investors can make money in just a few months by investing in fast-growing companies. But, you must be patient if you want to maximize your investment earnings.

Tip 5 - Diversify your portfolio.
Don't put all your eggs in one basket. You have to spread your wealth and invest in different companies in various industries. You can buy a few tech stocks, a few health care stocks, and you can invest in real estate properties. Diversifying helps to minimize your exposure to any industry/sector/investment vehicle.

Tip 6 - Buy more shares of your most profitable stocks.
You'll eventually build a huge portfolio over time. To maximum your profit, sell your low performing stocks and buy more stocks of the best performing companies in your portfolio.

Tip 7 - Invest in companies with a good profit margin.

Profit margin is calculated as:
PM = (Revenue – Expenses)/Revenue

You should invest in companies with a high profit margin because these companies likely have a strong brand, are able to charge high prices for their products and are keeping their costs low. You should avoid companies with low profit margin because these companies are not really earning much. They're just getting by.

Value investors invest in stable and established companies, while growth investors place their bets on companies with high growth potential. These companies are usually at their early stages, kind of like what Facebook was in 2012.

To be a successful growth investor, you should actively find unicorns – companies that produce innovative and revolutionary products and technologies.

Pros and Cons

One of the biggest advantages of growth investing strategy is that it's more likely to double your money faster.

Take Facebook as an example. On December 2012, an FB stock is valued at $26.62. A year later, its price rose to $54.00. So, if you invested in an FB stock during its IPO, you've doubled your investment in just one year! Amazing, right?

But, investing in growing neophyte companies is risky. Plus, growth projection estimates are sometimes inaccurate and just based on speculation.

Let's look at Theranos as an example. In 2003, 19 year old Elizabeth Holmes dropped out of Stanford University to start a blood testing company called Theranos. The company claimed to have developed a technology that can improve the efficiency, convenience, and affordability of blood testing and diagnosis.

It was a breakthrough and Elizabeth Holmes became a celebrated Silicon Valley Entrepreneur. She became the youngest female self-made billionaire. Theranos partnered with Walgreens and Safeway and built in-store clinics. Thousands of American people had their blood tested using the groundbreaking Theranos technology.

Theranos was a true "*unicorn*". It was overvalued, but many growth investors believe that it is the future of blood testing and diagnostics and so they invested in Theranos.

Theranos is a private company, but it has initially raised $6 million from investors. It raised a total of more than $600 million from investors. In 2014, the company was valued at $9 billion, making Elizabeth Holmes one of the wealthiest people in the world.

But, there was something off about Theranos. First of all, Elizabeth Holmes is not a doctor or a medical professional. Second, the technology they used was vague. A whistleblower claimed that the capabilities of the company's supposedly groundbreaking technology were extremely exaggerated.

In 2018, SEC charged Elizabeth Holmes with fraud and the company investors lost more than $600 million.

Growth investing is a great strategy. But, you have to be careful in choosing companies to invest in as a lot of startup entrepreneurs exaggerate the capabilities of their technologies to lure investors.

Dividend Investing

Lydia is a Chinese-American living in New Jersey. Her husband, Peter, used to own a huge hardware and home improvement store in the city.

Lydia was living the American dream. She's living in a four bedroom house in a great neighborhood. She's driving a nice car and she can buy all the things she cannot buy when she was in China.

Instead of splurging on designer bags, she decided to invest $500,000 in stable companies that pay annual dividends. After six months, Peter died in an accident. His business started to crumble after his death. Lydia was forced to close it.

It's a good thing that Lydia invested in companies that pay dividends each year. She has about $70,000 dividend earnings per year, enough to cover her mortgage payments and daily needs.

Dividend investing is an investment strategy that involves buying shares of companies that pay dividends. This strategy is best for people who just want to sit back and live off their passive income.

Here are the main principles behind dividend investing:

Invest in quality companies.

Don't invest in cheap low quality stocks, but in high quality ones. To get the most out of your money, you have to invest in companies that are in top financial shape.

You have to invest in a company with low debt/equity ratio. You don't want to place your bet on a company that has no proven history of consistently paying dividends. You would want to invest in a company that raises its dividend payments year after year.

Invest in stable companies.

Remember that slow and steady wins the race. Don't invest in rising superstars. Instead, *invest in companies that have already weathered recessions and various economic setbacks*. Why? So you can sleep at night. Investing in steady companies decreases risk and gives you peace of mind.

Choose a company with rising dividend yield.

As previously mentioned, dividend yield is calculated as:

DY = Annual Dividend/Stock Price

So, if Company Z stock costs $100 and its annual dividend is $10, its dividend yield is ten percent. To get the most out of your money, it's best to invest in a company with high dividend yield.

Also, it's best to choose a company that has a dividend yield of at least 3%. This helps you keep up with inflation.

Better safe than sorry.

You have to pick a stock that has a high margin of safety because this minimizes your risk of being slightly off with your valuation. Buy stocks whose price is below its value. Avoid buying overpriced stocks to lower the risk.

Dividends are not everything.

As a general rule, you should invest in companies that pay a good amount of annual dividends. But, you should not base your investment decisions solely on dividends. Remember that big dividend payout is not always an indication that the company is a good investment. Why? Well, companies who are paying huge amount of dividends are not reinvesting their revenues. This means that there's low opportunity for growth. In addition, the company could be paying an unsustainable amount of dividend to cover up for poor financial performance (because greedy and unsuspecting investors won't care to investigate)

Aside from the dividend payments, you should also consider the company's growth potential and financial health. You should invest in companies with rising revenue and low debt/equity ratio.

You should remember that at the end of the day, dividend stocks are just like other stocks. They are volatile and they are prone to the ups and downs of the stock market.

Pros and Cons

The biggest advantage of dividend investing is that it can provide a steady and a reliable income stream. You'll most likely get a check once or twice a year. Seeing a huge amount of money deposited into your bank account every quarter is exciting and exhilarating.

But, keep in mind that companies can cut dividend payments any time if they're experiencing a setback or decrease in revenue. Dividend payments are not guaranteed, so you must not rely on dividend payments alone. Dividend payments are taxable, so taxes can eat away at your returns.

Also, the prices of dividend stocks, such as Coca-Cola, Colgate-Palmolive, Johnson & Johnson, and AT&T are quite stable. This means that there's not much opportunity for growth or capital appreciation.

Sure, it's great to get a quarterly dividend payment of 3%. But, when you're investing in dividend stocks, you may be giving up the opportunity to earn higher returns from capital appreciation.

Let's look at Lauren and Kelly's story to illustrate this point. In 1997, Kelly bought 100 Coca Cola stocks at $28.94 each. She invested a total of $2,894. She was sure of her investment as Coca Cola is one of the most stable companies in the world and it pays dividends, too.

Kelly's friend, Lauren, decided to invest in a relatively new online bookstore called Amazon. She invested in 1000 Amazon stocks at $2.34 each. Her total investment was $2,340.

In 2019, both Kelly and Lauren decided to sell their shares. Kelly earned dividends along the way and sold her stocks at $48.38. She has a total capital appreciation profit of only $1944 in 22 years.

Lauren, on the other hand, sold her 1000 Amazon stocks at $1,638.88 each. She has a total capital appreciation profit of $1,635,660. Amazing, right?

This story reminds us that dividend payment is good. But, when you invest in dividend-paying companies, you could miss out on opportunities to earn huge capital appreciation profits.

For a more detailed treatment of Dividend Investing, see the book – Passive Income With Dividend Investing: Your Step-by-Step Guide To Make Money In The Stock Market Using Dividend Stock

Day Trading

Day trading is an investment strategy that involves buying and selling stocks and other securities on the same day. There was a time when the only people who can do this were those working for brokerage firms and huge financial institutions. But, with the advent of the internet, anyone can pretty much do day trading via the internet.

As we discussed earlier in this book, the price of a stock is determined by the law of supply and demand. Each time the stock is traded, its price changes.

A stock has a daily opening and closing price. The opening price is the price upon which a stock first trades when the stock market opens on a trading day. The closing price, on the other hand, is the price of a stock when the stock closes on a trading day. The balance between a stock's supply and demand fluctuates several times within a day. This is the reason why a stock's price can either go up or go down in just a few minutes.

Let's say that Company Z's stock price is pegged at $10 on December 10, 2018 at 9:30 when the NYSE opens that day. But, because of rising demand, its stock price rose to $15 at 4 pm just before the stock market closes.

If you bought 100 Company Z stocks at 9 am and decide to sell the stocks at 4 pm, you'll earn a capital appreciation profit of $500. Not bad for a day's work, right?

Benefits of Day Trading

It gives you an opportunity to learn.

Day trading is a great opportunity to test a wide variety of trading techniques and patterns. It helps you learn from your mistakes quickly.

It helps you avoid overnight risk.

The stock price can fluctuate from five to ten percent overnight. And remember, a lot of things can happen in just one night. A scandal can happen. Political issues can arise. Day trading eliminates these risks and helps you sleep like a baby at night.

It's a great home-based business.

As previously mentioned, you can do day trading online, so it can be a great home-based business.

It gives you psychological satisfaction.

You'll feel an adrenaline rush when you start earning a significant amount of money in just a few hours. It gives you a kick and a sense of accomplishment. Day trading is exciting and it's good for your ego.

It's relatively easy.

You don't need to have a PHD in finance to do day trading. Plus, you don't have to be a licensed trader if you're trading penny stocks (stocks that trade under $5). If you're good with stock charts and recognizing patters, then you have a good chance of doing well.

You can see results faster.

You don't have to wait for months or years to see the fruits of your investment. You can earn profits in just one day.

You become your own boss.

Day traders usually work alone and they own their time. They have a flexible working schedule and they work on their own pace. Day trading is great for people who want to become their own boss.

Day trading is also a high-risk investment strategy. You can earn a lot of money in just one day. But, you could lose a lot of money, too.

Day Trading Success tips

Do your homework.

Remember that knowledge is power, especially in day trading. You must do extensive research before you place your bet on a stock. You must also study market volatility and trends.
List down all the stocks you want to trade and track these companies. Check business news often. It's important to keep yourself informed.

Determine how much risk you can tolerate.

You must decide how much you're willing to risk on each transaction or trade. Many seasoned day traders risk only about one percent or less of their account per transaction.

Let's say that you have a $50,000 investment account and you're willing to risk 0.5 percent of your account. This means that your maximum loss per trade should be $250 ($50,000 x 0.005). Do not risk more than $250.00.

You must set aside a lot of time.

You have to watch the prices go up and down by the minute. This is the reason why day trading requires a lot of your time. This is not something that you can do on the side. So, if you have a full time job, this investment strategy is definitely not for you.

You have to start small.

It's best to start small. You have to focus on just one or two stocks during your first few transactions. Don't trade three or more stocks in one trading day.

You can also invest in fractional shares to minimize your losses. For example, if an Apple stock costs $60, you can buy ½ of the stock for $30 instead of purchasing one full stock.

Be realistic.

Don't expect to earn ten thousand dollars per day. You can't win all the time. In fact, a lot of traders only win sixty percent of their trades. You just have to make sure that your wins are bigger than your losses.

Don't let the stock market get on your nerves.

Day trading is sometimes stressful and frustrating. Stay cool. Do not let your fears and greed get the better of you. Also, don't be too optimistic or hopeful. You should use logic in making investment decisions, not emotions.

Pros and Cons

Day trading is exciting. It gives you an adrenaline rush. It also helps you earn money in just a few hours. It's easy to get into and you can do it in the comfort of your home.

But, day trading is a bit tricky because of market volatility. You can earn a lot of money in just a few hours, but you can also lose a lot of money. A lot of day traders incur financial losses in the first few months. This is the reason why you have to do extensive research before you start trading.

Day trading is often costly. To achieve great success in day trading, you have to invest in high quality trading platform and software. You also have to pay a commission fee for every trade.

Day trading sometimes gives you a natural high, but it's also stressful. You'll have to use multiple computer screens so you won't miss trading opportunities.

Short Selling

Short selling (also called going short) is an investing strategy that involves the sale of a stock that the investor has borrowed. It is a strategy that helps investors profit from a stock's decline. It is the complete opposite of the "buy low, sell high" investing principle.

When you invest in a stock, you're placing your bets on the company. When you short sell, you're betting against the company. You short sell because you expect the price of the stock to go down.

To illustrate this point, let's look at Nathan's story. Nathan is doing extensive stock research and heard a rumor that Company X is in deep financial trouble. After some research, he has good reason to believe the company's stock price will go down soon. So, he decided to short sell Company X stock to profit from his stock price prediction.

Nathan called his broker, John, and told him that he wants to short 10 Company X shares. John needs to find 10 Company X stocks to lend to Nathan.

To find stocks for Nathan, John looked at his client's portfolio and his stock inventory. John found 10 stocks in one of his client's investment portfolio. He then sold the share in the market for Nathan at its current market price of $150 each. The $1500 revenue from the sale was credited to Nathan's brokerage account.

As it turns out, Nathan was right. After seven days, Company X's financial struggles were made public and its stock price dropped to $75.

After the stock price dropped, Nathan wants to make a profit from his prediction by buying back the stocks he sold through his broker. Nathan calls John and tells him to cover his position in Company X. John then uses the money in Nathan's brokerage account to buy 10 Company X shares at the current price of $75 each. He then returns the borrowed stocks to his client's portfolio.

Nathan sold ten Company X stocks for $1500 and bought it back for $750. So, he made a profit of $750. But, of course, he has to pay John a small fee for all the trouble. That's awesome, right?

Pros and Cons

Short selling is a great investment strategy for pessimists and sceptics. One of the best things about short selling is that it allows you to earn a huge amount of money without an upfront cost. And most of all, it allows you to make money out of failing companies.

But, you should know that short-selling is a risky investment strategy. You won't know for sure if your prediction is correct. You'd end up losing money if the value of the stock you short sold rises dramatically. Also, short selling (and the pessimism that goes with it) can lead to stock market crash.

You don't have to use just one investment strategy. You can mix up different investing strategies to get the maximum returns. You can also test each strategy to find out which one works for you.

Chapter 3 Summary

To grow your wealth, you have to use an investment strategy that works for you. You can also mix and match different strategies. There are many investment strategies that you can use, including dividend investing, day trading, value investing, short-selling, and growth investing.

Value investing is one of the best investing strategies. It's used by seasoned investors like Warren Buffet. Its main principle is "buy low, sell high". Value investors actively look for undervalued stocks. They also invest in stable and established companies. They do not look at market trends and they do not worry about stock price volatility. They do not care about stock market predictions.

Value investing is a great way to minimize risk. But, it can cause you to lose the opportunity to earn huge capital appreciation profits from rising "superstar" companies.

Growth investing is the opposite of value investing. Growth investors place their bets on companies that are growing pretty fast. They are constantly searching for "unicorns" or the "next best thing" in business. To minimize risk, you have to sell a winning stock once it starts to go down. You must also build a diversified portfolio consisting of companies that are performing well in the stock market.

Growth investing gives you an opportunity to earn a lot of money. But, it's risky, too.

Dividend investing is an investment strategy that involves investing in companies with that pay dividends annually or quarterly. It's also important to choose a company with rising dividend payments.

Day trading is an investment strategy that involves buying and selling stocks the same day. This strategy helps you profit from market volatility. It also gives you the opportunity to learn and sharpen your trading skills. The downside of this strategy is that it's time consuming and you'll have to invest in an advanced trading platform.

Short-selling is an investment strategy where an investor profits from falling stock prices. The investor borrows a stock from his broker and sells it at current market price. Once the stock price goes down, he buys back the stock and returns the stock he borrowed. His profit is the difference between his selling price and buying price.

Short-selling is great because you don't have to pay for anything up front. But, it's too risky. You won't know exactly if the stock goes down anytime soon. If the stock price does not go down, you'll end up with more debt than you can handle.

To lower the risk, you have to invest in companies with low debt/equity ratio and a high margin of safety. These companies are financially healthy.

To maximize your earnings, it's best to diversify your investment portfolio and mix and match different strategies.

In the next chapter, you'll learn how to pick the right stocks.

Inspiration #4

"Compound interest is the eighth wonder of the world. He who understands it, earns it. He who doesn't, pays it."
Albert Einstein

Chapter 4

How to Choose the Right Stocks to Invest In

Mia worked in a software development company for 15 years. She's good at her job, but she was always stressed and tired. So, she decided to give stock market investment a try in order to build a passive income portfolio that'll help her retire early. She met with an old friend named Kate, a financial analyst. Kate helped her invest in high quality and fast-growing stocks.

After two years, Mia earned $650,000 capital appreciation profit. She quit her job and traveled around the world. She soon used part of her earnings to establish her own graphic design company. Her six hundred and fifty thousand dollars grew to over $2 million.

Mia is living her dream life. She owns her time. She has a successful business and she even bought a beach house in Miami.

Chloe was Mia's former colleague. Like Mia, she's been working in the software development industry for about fifteen years. She was also tired. After she heard about Mia's success, she decided to invest in stocks, too.

Chloe didn't know anything about the stock market and didn't know how to choose the right stocks. She invested in companies that are buried in debt and engaged in unethical business practices. So, she ended up losing $10,000.

A lot of people got rich through stock market investment. But, many people lost huge amounts of money, too. This is the reason why you should be careful in choosing the right stocks to invest in. You have to be clear about your investment goals and use the right strategies that work for you and match your risk tolerance level. You must also do extensive research before you place your bet on a stock.

Setting an Investment Objective

Before you start investing, you should be clear about what your investment objectives are. You should also decide what type of investor you want to be. Do you want to be a long term investor? Or, do you want to be a day trader, trading stocks by the minute?

You must be clear about what you want to achieve through stock market investing. How much are you willing to invest? How much do you want to earn each year? What are you willing to risk?

You need to set financial goals like how much you want to earn in one year or in five years. You should also set non-financial goals. Why? Well, your investment earnings are just mere tools that you can use to support your non-financial goals. So, what do you want to achieve? Do you want to have a grand wedding? Do you want to travel to a foreign country at least twice a year?

Factors to Consider In Choosing a Stock

The key to building a profitable investment portfolio is to choose the right stocks. When you're starting, it's costly to buy individual stocks than investing in low cost mutual funds. Below are the factors that you should consider in choosing stocks to invest in.

Growth in Earnings

Before you invest in a company, you should check its earnings and make sure that it's consistently growing over time. The growth doesn't have to be huge. You just have to look for an upward trend in earnings.

For example, let's say that you have an extra $3,000 and you want to invest it in stock. You're looking to invest in 2 companies. Company A is one of the biggest steel manufacturers in the country, while Company B produces the nation's best-selling batteries.

Take time to examine the data below:

Company A: Leading Steel Manufacturer	
Year	Earnings
2005	$2,158,111,202.00
2006	$2,160,369,000.00
2007	$2,080,250,000.00
2008	$1,988,910,000.00
2009	$1,888,630,121.00
2010	$1,780,980,011.00
2011	$1,761,918,870.00
2012	$1,709,919,450.00
2013	$1,670,980,689.00
2014	$1,659,658,905.00
2015	$1,640,050,814.00
2016	$1,590,010,110.00
2017	$1,550,000,289.00
2018	$1,499,110,980.00

Company B: Leading Battery Manufacturer	

Year	Earnings
2005	$750,000,905.00
2006	$805,963,960.00
2007	$815,750,690.00
2008	$909,530,066.00
2009	$915,784,210.00
2010	$918,974,560.00
2011	$990,741,632.00
2012	$1,101,890,390.00
2013	$1,156,120,450.00
2014	$1,190,110,000.00
2015	$1,220,000,980.00
2016	$1,240,780,360.00
2017	$1,310,000.550.00
2018	$1,399,222,080.00

If you look closely, you'll see that Company A has a lot more earnings than Company B. But, its revenue is declining since 2008. This means that the company is facing problems. It could be mismanagement or decreasing market share due to an aggressive competitor entering the space.

Company B, on the other hand, has steady growing earnings since 2006. This company is doing something right and more worthy of your hard earned money.

Stability

Sir Tim Berners-Lee published a paper about a proposed information management program called the "internet" in 1989. He then implemented the first successful communication between a Hypertext Transfer Protocol (HTTP) and a server a few months later.

In 1990, Berners-Lee began writing the World Wide Web (www) – the first ever web browser. The next year, he launched the first ever web page. This forever changed the world. This is what the stock market players call a black swan.

According to risk analyst Nassim Nicholas Taleb, a black swan is an event that's hard to predict that can forever change the world. And if you're wise enough to predict or at least spot a black swan at its early stage, you're going to win big in the stock market and in business. This explains why early internet entrepreneurs like Jack Ma and Jeff Bezos are extremely wealthy.

And soon, promising internet companies decided to go public and the investors went crazy investing their eggs on the "internet business basket".

But, after the tech industry got a little too crowded and the world experienced a stock market crash in 2008, the revenues of internet companies became volatile. So, a lot of investors end up losing huge amounts of money.

But, this is just an example. It doesn't mean that you should not invest in the tech industry. All companies would lose their stock value at some point, especially during periods of recession and economic crisis.

To achieve long term success in the stock market, you have to invest in companies that are strong and stable enough to endure unfavorable economic conditions. Erratic stock price fluctuation is not a good sign.

To illustrate this point, look at the graphs below:

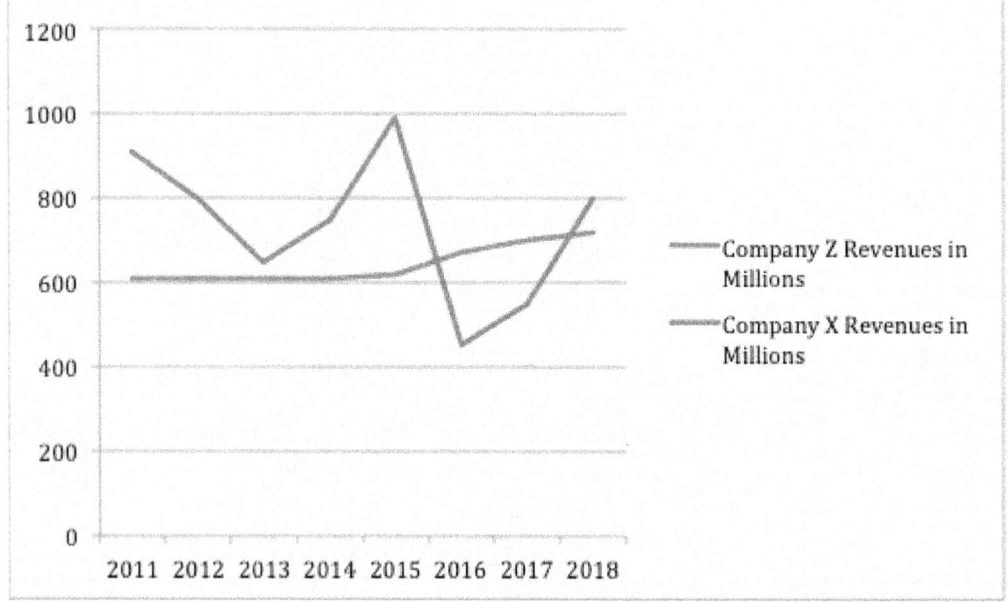

Notice that Company Z's revenues don't fluctuate as much as Company X's. This means that it's more stable and a good choice for long term investment.

The Company's Market Share

Before you invest in a company, look at its market share. Is it one of the strongest in its industry? Is it doing well against its competitors?

If you want a big return on investment, it's best to invest in strong market leaders, such as Microsoft (software), JPMorgan Chase (finance), Facebook (communication), Las Vegas Sands (casino and resorts), Gilead Science (biotech), PepsiCo (beverages), Comcast (cable and broadcasting), and Marriot (hotels).

Profitability

You should not only look at a company's total earnings, you should also look at its profit. Are the earnings higher than the costs? How much profit does the company make per sale? Does the company have a positive cash flow (the amount of money going in is greater than the amount of money going out)?
You should also examine the company's profitability over the years. You would want to invest in a company with an upward profit trend.

Price to Earnings Ratio or P/E Ratio

P/E Ratio is the stock's price divided by its earnings. For example, if a company's stock costs $50 and each investor gets paid a yearly dividend of $5 per stock, its P/E Ratio is 10 (50 divided by 5).

P/E ratio is usually used to measure a company's growth potential. If the P/E ratio is high, it means that investors are willing to pay huge amounts of money for each stock. This could increase the stock price in the future and can result in high return on investment (ROI).

Companies with a low P/E ratio have minimal growth potential. This means that you could possibly lose money when you invest in corporations with low P/E ratio.

But, you should take note that not all companies with a high P/E ratio have promising growth potential. These companies may just be overvalued.

The P/E ratio is a great tool that can help you decide which stock to invest in. But, you should not rely on it entirely.

The Company's Leadership

Like it or not, the company's leadership can greatly affect its future. This is the reason why you should also look into the competency of the company's management team.

Do you feel that the company leaders are competitive and competent? Do you think the company is well managed? Is the company ahead of its competitors because of innovation? Do you see the company leaders as visionaries?

You should also look at the company's culture. Does the company have a toxic environment? Is it involved in many scandals and lawsuits?

Debt to Equity Ratio

As mentioned earlier in this book, equity is the difference between the company's assets and its liability.

Let's say that Company Y's asset amount to $100,000. But, the company's liability amounts to $80,000. This means that the company's equity is valued at $20,000.

Debt to Equity ratio is used to measure a company's leverage and overall financial health. To calculate it, you need to divide the company's total liabilities by its equity.

Assets	Liabilities	Equity
$100,000.00	$80,000.00	$20,000.00

Now, look at Company B's data above. If you divide the company's liabilities by its equity, you'll find that it's debt to equity ratio is $4. This means that Company B has a $4 debt for every $1 of equity. Therefore, Company B is not in good financial health and not fit for long term investment. It's too risky.

To minimize risk, you should invest in a company with a debt equity ratio of 0.30 or below.

Dividend Payments

As previously mentioned, not all companies pay dividends. But, those who do are usually more stable and in good financial health.

It's good to invest in companies that pay dividends. But, you have to be careful. High dividend yields could indicate instability. It can also mean that the company is stagnant as it's not reinvesting its profits on growth and expansion.

Company Reputation

Avoid companies who engage in unethical practices. Companies with a bad reputation are most likely to get involved in scandals.

Company Executives' Investing Habits

Look at the amount of shares that the executives and CEOs are buying or selling to know what's really happening inside the company. If the CEO is selling his shares, it could mean that the company is in deep trouble.

Positive EPS

As previously mentioned, earnings per share or EPS is the portion of profit allotted each common share. A positive EPS is an indicator of a corporation's profitability.

It is usually calculated as:

Earnings per share = Net Income/Number of shares

But, the more accurate calculation is:

Earnings per share = (Net Income - Preferred Dividends)/ Weighted Average Of Outstanding Common Shares

The weighted average of common shares is more accurate because the number of shares changes over time. The company can create new shares in the middle of the year. This data is usually found in the company's income statement, balance sheet, or financial statement.

Look at the data below:

Company D				
Assets	Liabilities	Net Income	Preferred Dividend Payments	Weighted Average Outstanding Shares
$200,000	$35,000	$165,000	$20,000	10,000 stocks

So, if you calculate Company D's EPS should be like this:

EPS = (165,000 – 20,000)/10,000
= $14.5

Company D's EPS is actually a good number, considering that stock market giant Apple has an EPS of $6.45.

You can use the first formula to simplify things. This formula is not as accurate as the second one, but it gives you a pretty good number that you can use to track the profitability of a potential investment opportunity.

Tips in Picking the Right Stocks

Remember that when you buy a company's stock, you become a part owner of that company. So, you have to look at the overall health of the company you want to invest in. Below are a few tips that you can use in picking the right stocks:

Invest in what you know.

You know why you're choosing a particular clothing brand over the other. You also know the ingredients of the dishes you order from your favorite restaurant. To avoid losses, it's important to invest in a stock that you know too well.

Before you invest in a stock, you need to answer the following questions:

- Do you know what products the company offers?
- Have you examined the company's financial statements?
- Is the company profitable?
- Is it buried in debt?
- Do you trust the company executives?
- Is the company innovative?
- Would you buy its products?

Avoid overhyped companies.

You already know what happened to Theranos. Like Theranos, Dropbox is also one of the most celebrated Silicon Valley unicorns. Its stock price is at $30 on May 31, 2018, but it dropped to $19.96 on January 1, 2019. Overhyped companies are great, but the truth is, not all of them can live up to the hype.

Consider the price.

Seasoned investors often look for stocks that are undervalued. As a general rule, stocks with P/E Ratio of 15 and below are considered cheap, while stocks with a P/E of more than 20 is considered a bit overpriced or expensive.

But, you should remember that cheap is not always good and expensive is not always bad. Sometimes, stocks are cheap simply because they're not performing well and some stocks are expensive mainly because they're growing fast. Think Amazon. As of February 2019, an Amazon stock trades at $1,500.00. Yes, it's expensive, but it's worth every penny as it is the world's most valuable public company.

Evaluate the financial health of the company you're investing in.

You must start looking into the company's financial reports. Keep in mind that all public companies release quarterly and annual financial reports. You can easily access these reports through the SEC website. You can click on the link below:

https://www.sec.gov/edgar/searchedgar/companysearch.html

Pick a company with a huge profit margin.

The profit margin is the difference between the company's revenue and expenses. You would want to invest in a company that manages their expenses well.

Do not forget to sell your stocks.

Profit is the ultimate goal of stock market investment. But, you should be clear about how much profit you want to make.

Let's say that you bought Company G's stock at $10.00 and you want to earn a $5 profit. So, when the stock price hits $15, you got to sell right away. Don't be greedy or you'll end up losing a lot of money in the future.

You should believe in the company's management.

Don't invest in a stock if you don't trust the company's CEO. It's really just that simple. Use logic, but also listen to your intuition. Don't invest in anything that doesn't feel right.

How to Tell When a Stock is Over-valued

A lot of financial analysts often overestimate a company's value. You can lose a lot of money if you invest in overpriced stocks.

But, how do you know if a stock is overvalued? Well, you have to review the company's annual financial report, income statement, and balance sheet.

The first thing you want to look at is the stock's P/E Ratio (also called the earnings multiple). Overvalued companies usually have a higher P/E. If a company's stock price is 20 times its earnings, it's definitely overvalued.

To illustrate this point, let's look at two companies – Company N and Company M.

Company M's stock price is $150 while its earnings per share is $200. Therefore, its P/E ratio is 0.75. It's too low, which means that its "earnings per share" is actually bigger than its price.

Company N's stock price, on the other hand, is pegged at $200. But, it's earnings per share is only $10. It has a PE ratio of 20. This means that its price is twenty times its earnings.

If you're a growth investor, you'll most likely go for Company N because it has high growth potential in terms of stock price. It means that investors are optimistic and are willing to pay a high price for its stock.

But, if you're a value investor, you'll most likely invest in Company M because it's undervalued.

A lot of investors just look at the P/E ratio to determine if a company is overvalued. But, there are also other ways to check if a company is priced way above its intrinsic value.

Look at the company's PEG ratio. The Price/Earnings to Growth ratio or PEG ratio is calculated as:

PEG Ratio = PE Ratio/EPS growth rate

This metric is used to evaluate a company's stock price compared to the company's growth and earnings. The lower a company's PEG ratio is the better.

Let's say that Company W has a P/E ratio of 20. That's quite high, right? But, it has an EPS growth rate of 25%, so it's PEG ratio is 0.80. This means that its price is cheap relative to its potential growth.

This metric is best for investors who consider both the company's value and growth rate.

Check the company's Dividend-Adjusted PEG ratio.

If you're investing in a company that pays dividends, you have to look at its dividend-adjusted PEG ratio. It is calculated as:

Dividend-adjusted PEG ratio = PE Ratio/(Earnings per Share Growth Rate + Dividend Yield)

Let's say that Company J has a P/E ratio of 20 and it has an "earnings per share" growth rate of 10 percent. It has a dividend yield of 2%. So, its dividend-adjusted PEG ratio is 1.66. It's pretty low. It means that its price is relatively low relative to its dividend yield and growth rate.

Examine the relative dividend yield.

As previously mentioned, dividend yield is computed as the annual dividend per share divided by its current stock price.

For example, if Company Z's stock price is 10 dollars and it pays 1 dollar per share each year, its dividend yield is 10%.

The dividend yield serves as a signal. You see, highly profitable companies often pay higher dividends. This is the reason why stock market beginners can use dividend yield to examine the company's price relative to its profits.

So, if a company has a high dividend yield, it's most likely undervalued. If a company has a low dividend yield, it's overvalued.

Let's say that you own 100 shares of Company D stocks with a dividend yield of 5%. To maximize your profit, you have to carefully track the company's dividend yield. This helps you determine the profitability of the company. If the dividend yield drops to 2% or below, it means that the business is not earning well, it's overvalued, and it's best to let that stock go.

Check if the company is part of a cyclical industry.

Some industries are extremely sensitive to the ups and downs of the economy. These industries are called cyclical industry because their profits go up when the economy is good and it goes down during an economic crisis.

Companies in cyclical industries usually have unique characteristics. They thrive when the economy is good. Automobile companies, construction contractors, and steel factories are examples of cyclical industries.

When the economy is good, companies in cyclical industries appear to have fast-growing profit and low P/E ratio. So, it would seem that the company is undervalued. But, this situation is actually a "value trap" and can be dangerous and tricky. This can easily deceive stock market beginners. But, more experienced investors know that the P/E ratio of these companies is much higher than they appear.

So, before you judge a company based on its P/E ratio, you must first determine if that company is in a cyclical industry. If so, don't take all the data you see at face value.

Check the company's earnings yield.

Earnings yield is calculated as earnings per share divided by the current stock price.

Earnings yield = Earnings per Share/ Current Stock price

If you look at the formula carefully, you would notice that it's the reverse of the P/E ratio. This metric helps investors determine the return on investment. You can also use this to check if a stock is overvalued.

You can compare a stock's earnings yield with the 10-year Treasury yield. If the earnings yield is less than the Treasury Yield, it's overvalued. But, if a company's earnings yield is high, it's undervalued relative to bonds.

Many investors use earnings yield to make investment decisions. This metric helps you determine if it's best to invest in stocks or you should go with other securities, such as bonds.

Buying an overvalued stock is incredibly risky. You could end up losing a lot of money. So, before you place a bet on a stock, make sure that it's reasonably priced and not overvalued.

How to Build a Stock Position

A stock position is the amount of stocks owned by a dealer, organization, or an individual. When you buy a stock, you are basically taking on a position. There are two types of positions – long positions and short positions.

As we discussed earlier, the term "going short" is a process where you *borrow* a stock and sell it, hoping that the price will go down. When you're "going long", you're basically purchasing the stock (and paying for it up front) because you're hoping that its value will go up.

So, a short position is done when a stock is borrowed and then sold. A long position, on the other hand, is done when a stock is owned and then sold.

There are many strategies that you can use to build a winning or extremely profitable position. One of the ways to do is through "pyramiding". You see, if you gulp an entire cup of hot coffee, you'll burn your mouth. So, you have to take small sips to avoid getting burned. You can use this same strategy to minimize your losses and maximize your return and it's called pyramiding.

If you find a high performing stock, don't invest all your money in it right away. You have to test the water to avoid losing all your money.

Let's say that you found a good stock and you decided to invest $5,000 to buy 100 shares at $50 each. If the stock price falls ten percent, you'll lose $500. But, if you invest just ¼ of your investment money; you'll only lose $125.

Pyramiding involves making multiple stock purchases to build your position. The best way to do this is to divide your purchases into three to five installments.

Let's say that you have a $10,000 investment fund. When you enter a trade, you can use $3,000 to purchase stocks and build your initial position. Make sure to use this money to buy stocks of market leaders and established companies.

Now, don't buy more shares until the price of your current position moves up to at least two percent. Once this happens, invest another $3000. At this point, you have already invested 60 percent of your investment fund.

Once you earn another 2% capital appreciation profit, invest another $2,000. And invest the last $2,000 after the stock price increased by another 2 percent.

This investment strategy is smart. It maximizes your returns, reduces risks, and limits your losses. Pyramiding is an investment strategy to build a winning stock position.

Another way to build your stock position is to write (sell) put options.

A put option is an option to sell stocks at an agreed price on or before a particular date. So, when you're writing a put option, you're essentially obliging yourself to buy shares at a specific price.

To explain this, let's say that you want to buy a few Company V shares. You did extensive research and you found out that the best way to earn maximum profits from your investment is to pay no more than $20. But, there's just one problem – Company V stock is currently valued at $50.

If you're a beginner, you'll most likely wait until the price drops to your desired price. But, if you're an advanced investor, you won't just sit around and wait until the stock price goes down. You can write put options for Company V shares at $20. When you do this, you're essentially promising another party (it could be a bank, a corporation, a mutual fund, or an individual investor) to buy his Company V shares when it reaches $20.

But, why will you do this? Well, in exchange for your commitment, the buyer of your put option contract will pay you a premium per share. One put option contract usually covers 100 stocks. So, if you write 5 put options (total of 500 stocks) and the buyer pays you a premium of $2 per stock, you'll earn $1,000 (500 stocks x $2). You'll also just have to pay a minimum commission fee.

Writing put options is a great way to build your stock position because you'll always be a winner no matter what the outcome is.

If the put option expires and never exercised, you get to keep the $1,000.

If the stock price declines temporarily and the put option contract will be executed, you get to purchase the stock you like at a heavily discounted price. Instead of paying $50 for it. You'll just pay $20 minus $2 premium. So, you'll just pay $18 and get $32 ($50-$18) discount per stock. Not bad, right?

If the company decides to close before the stock price reaches $20, you'll still keep the $1000.

Writing put options is a great way to win in the stock trading game.

Chapter 4 Summary

To win big in the stock market, you have to invest in the right stocks. Otherwise, you'll end up losing a lot of money.

Set an investment objective. What do you want to achieve? You have to set financial goals like how much you want to earn in a year or in five years. You must also set non-financial goals like how often do you want to travel or experiences you want to afford.

When you're choosing stocks, you have to consider different factors such as growth in earnings, stability, the company's market share, profitability, P/E ratio, insider activity, the company's reputation, and the trustworthiness of the company executives.

To pick the right stocks, you have to invest in what you know and avoid over-hyped companies. These companies are usually overvalued and can't live up to the hype. You should also consider the stock price and the profit margin.

You need to sell your stocks once it reaches its peak. This technique maximizes your profit.

Avoid overvalued stocks. Look at the PEG and the P/E ratio to determine if a company is overvalued.

- If a company has a high P/E ratio, it's overvalued.
- A company with a high PEG ratio is also overvalued.

You must also see if the company is in a cyclical industry. Companies in cyclical industry are highly sensitive to economic cycles. Its price is high when the economy is good and it decreases when there's a recession.

When the economy is great, cyclical stocks appear to have fast-growing revenues. This decreases its P/E ratio giving you the impression that the stock is undervalued when in reality, it's overvalued. When you're looking at the P/E ratio of companies in cyclical companies, don't look at it at face value. It can be deceiving.

If a stock's earnings yield is lower than the Treasury Yield (bond), it's overvalued.

Avoid buying overvalued stocks. It's also wise to sell overvalued stocks in your portfolio.

A stock position is the amount of stock an investor owns. There are two types of positions – long and short.

Long position involves buying a stock and paying for it up front. Short position, on the other hand, involves borrowing stocks and selling them in anticipation of a price decline. Once the price drops, you buy stocks to cover what you borrowed. The difference between your selling price and buying price is your profit.

Writing put options is one great way to build your stock position. A put option is the right to sell a stock at a specific price. So, if you want to buy stock A for $20, but its current price is $30, you can write a put option and sell it. The buyer then has the right to sell you his stock when the price goes down to $20 before the expiration date of the contract. The buyer pays you a premium fee for your promise. If the price doesn't go down and the contract wasn't executed, you can still keep your premium earnings. So, there's nothing much to lose.

In the next chapter, we'll talk about brokerage account and statement in detail.

Inspiration #5

"Success is walking from failure to failure with no loss of enthusiasm."
Winston S. Churchill

Chapter 5

Understanding Your Brokerage Account and Statement

You'd be surprised to know that most extremely wealthy people have taxable brokerage accounts. It provides an avenue for them to benefit from the stock market and diversify their income stream. As we've discussed earlier in this book, if you want to invest huge amounts of money and be a successful investor, you have to open a taxable brokerage account.

What is a Brokerage Account?

A brokerage account is a taxable investment account that you can use to buy and sell stocks and other securities. As the name suggests, it's opened through a brokerage firm. It's much like a bank account. You have to deposit money into your account before you can start buying and selling stocks.

You can deposit money into your account through checks or electronic funds transfer. You can also wire money into your account.

Type of Investments A Brokerage Account Can Hold

Brokerage accounts are not just for stocks, there are a number of securities that a brokerage account can hold, including:

Common stock – This represents part ownership of a company. It usually comes with voting rights.

Preferred stock – This stock usually comes with high dividend payments, but it's more expensive than a common stock. Preferred stock shareholders also typically do not have any voting rights.

Bonds – A bond is a debt security. When you purchase a bond, the issuer (usually a government entity) owes you money. You earn money from bonds through interest rates.

Mutual fund – A mutual fund is funded by different shareholders. It's basically a pool of money that's invested in different securities. It's relatively easy to invest in a mutual fund. Plus, it's usually managed by a financial professional. You can buy different mutual funds, too, so you don't have to put all your money in one mutual fund.

ETF – ETF or Exchange Traded Fund is a basket of different securities that's traded as a stock. An ETF is a good investment because it has trading flexibility. It helps you diversify your investment portfolio and manage risk. It's also cheaper than a traditional mutual fund.

REIT – A real estate investment trust or REIT is a company that either finances or operates income-producing real estate properties such as commercial buildings. REITs usually own various income-generating real estate companies, such as hospitals, warehouses, hotels, and malls. You can invest in publicly traded REITs using your brokerage account.

Money market and certificate of deposit – A money market account generally represents pools of liquid mutual funds. It has higher interest rates and has a limited check-writing capacity. A certificate of deposit is basically a time deposit. For example, you agree to deposit $10,000 in your account. You can't withdraw that amount in five years. But, you'll earn an interest rate per year. So, if you earn $1,000 in interest per year, you're going to earn an extra $5,000 for your deposit after five years.

Cash Brokerage Account and Margin Brokerage Account

There are two main brokerage account types – cash account and margin account. A cash brokerage account requires you to deposit cash into your account. You'll have to pay for your transactions in cash and in full when you have a cash brokerage account.

A margin account, on the other hand, allows you to borrow from the broker using some of your assets as collateral to buy securities.

If you're a beginner, it's best to go for a cash brokerage account. Why? Well, margin brokerage accounts are complex and will get you buried in debt if you're not careful.

Limits of Money You Can Deposit in a Brokerage Account

As previously mentioned, other investment plans such as IRA and 401(k) have limits. But, taxable brokerage accounts do not have a limit, so you can deposit and invest as much as you want. But, keep in mind that you have to pay taxes for this type of investment.

How Many Brokerage Accounts Can One Have?

You can have as much brokerage accounts as you want. But, keep in mind that most brokerage firms require a minimum deposit amount of $500 to $2000, so opening multiple accounts can be costly.

But, if you have unlimited resources, you can open multiple accounts with different brokerage firms.

Difference between A Discount Broker and A Full Service Broker

There are two general types of broker:

- A Full service broker and
- A Discount broker.

A full-service brokerage account is great because it comes with a dedicated broker. You can call, text, or email him should you want to make an order. This broker usually knows you personally and sometimes he knows your family. He also knows your finances intimately. He's like a financial advisor. You usually have to meet him regularly to discuss your portfolio.

Full-service brokers usually charge high commission fees. A discount broker, on the other hand, doesn't charge much. But, this type of broker usually operates online. A discount brokerage account is like a Do It Yourself (DIY) investment plan.

So, what should you choose? Well, it depends on what your priority is. If you are on a budget and you really want to save money, it's best to open a discount brokerage account. But, if you really want to have a financial adviser, it's a great idea to open a full-service brokerage account.

Understanding Your Broker's Statement

A broker's statement is a monthly report that contains the activities in your brokerage account. You can choose to receive a paper statement. But, you can usually just check it online.

It pays to examine your statement carefully so you could spot some kind of fraud. When you first receive your income statement, you have to check if it looks professional. An unprofessional-looking statement is a red flag. Legitimate brokerage firms invest time and effort to make sure that their reports look polished and professional.

Here's what you'll find in your broker statement:

- **Statement period date** – A broker's statement reports how your investment is doing at a specific period of time, usually a month. If you don't see a statement period date, that's a red flag.

- **Account number, Account Name, and Address** – This obviously contains your taxable brokerage account number, your name, and your present address. Be worried if this information is incorrect.

- **Contact information** – This contains the contact information of your broker. If you don't see this anywhere in the statement, the brokerage firm you're dealing with may be dubious.

- **Name of the Clearing firm** – This contains the name and the contact number of the clearing firm that holds your investments. FINRA rules require brokerage firms to place this information in their statements. So, be alarmed if you don't see this anywhere in your statement.

- **Account summary** – This gives you an insight with regards to how your account is doing. This can help you review and assess your investment decisions.

- **Fees** – This covers the transaction and commission fees you've paid within the time period.

- **Account activity** – This is where you can see the stocks you've bought or sold within that particular time period.

- **Margin** – If you have a margin account, you'll find this section. This contains the amount you've borrowed to purchase stocks and other securities.

- **Portfolio detail** – This section breaks down your investment by type like stocks, bonds, or mutual funds.

Chapter 5 Summary

A brokerage account, as the name suggests, is an investment account that you open through a brokerage firm. You can use this account to buy and sell stocks in the stock market.

A brokerage account can hold different types of securities, such as common stock, preferred stock, bonds, mutual fund, REIT, ETF, and certificate of deposit.

There are two main types of brokerage account- cash and margin. You need to pay for everything real time if you have a cash account. A margin account, on the other hand, allows you to borrow money from a broker.

There are two general types of brokers – discount and full service. Discount brokers usually just interact with you online. Full-service brokers, on the other hand, conduct face to face meetings on a regular basis.

If you want to save a lot of money, it's best to open a discount brokerage account. But, if you need guidance in choosing the right stocks, it's a good idea to choose a full-service brokerage firm.

You have to examine your broker's statement carefully to spot fraudulent activities or inconsistencies.

In the next chapter, you'll learn how to read your broker trade confirmations.

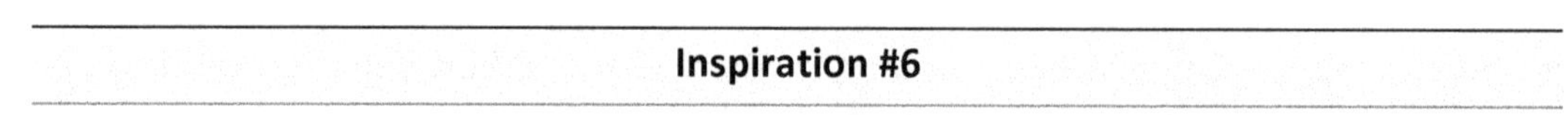

Inspiration #6

"The trick is not to learn to trust your gut feelings, but rather to discipline yourself to ignore them. Stand by your stocks as long as the fundamental story of the company hasn't changed."

Peter Lynch

Chapter 6

How to Read Your Broker Trade Confirmations

SEC requires all brokerage firms to provide their clients broker trade confirmations. But, what is it and why it's important to understand it?

What is A Brokerage Trade Confirmation?

Once you start trading through your broker, you will receive a trade confirmation and it will be mailed to you. But, if you opted for the paperless option, it will be sent to you in a form of a PDF document. This document will be delivered to you each time your broker buys or sells a stock for you.

Here are the things that you can find in your trade confirmation:

- The name of the stock you've traded along with its ticker symbol. A ticker symbol is an abbreviation used to identify a stock. For example, Facebook's ticker symbol is FB while Amazon appears as AMZN in NASDAQ.
- The total stocks you have either bought or sold in that transaction
- The price per share
- Commission paid to your broker
- The date of the transaction
- The total gross value of the transaction. How much did you pay for or earn during this transaction?
- The net value of the transaction. How much did you pay or earn after the commission fees?
- Your account number
- The type of order you used. Did you do a market order or a limit order?

You must look at your trade confirmations carefully. This way, you'll know if your broker executed the orders according to your instructions. Contact your broker right away if you think that there's some kind of mistake.

Your trade confirmations can be useful when you file your taxes. This is the reason why you should keep the original copy of your trade confirmations.

Chapter 6 Summary

Every time you want to buy or sell a stock, you'll receive a trade confirmation in the mail.
Your trade confirmation usually includes information like the name of the stock and its ticker symbol, price per share, total stocks traded, commission payments, account number, the net value of the transaction, and type of order done.

You have to examine that carefully to make sure that your broker executed your order flawlessly.

You must also keep copies of your trade confirmations because you'll need that when you file taxes.

In the next chapter, we will discuss the different types of trades that you can place with your broker.

Inspiration #7

"Go for a business that any idiot can run – because sooner or later any idiot probably is going to be running it."

Peter Lynch

Chapter 7

Types of Trades You Can Place with Your Broker

Once you deposited money from your brokerage account, you're now ready to buy and sell stocks. To do that, you have to make an order with your broker. There are many types of orders, such as market order, limit order, stop order, stop limit order, day order, and trailing stop order.

Market Orders

A market order is a request to purchase to sell or purchase a stock at its current market price. It is the most standard stock order and it has to be executed right away.

For example, when you place a market order to buy 100 Company H stocks at the current price, your broker has to execute the order right away. As long as there is someone willing to sell Company H stocks, your buy order will be executed right away.

Let's say that you own 50 Company M stocks and its price is dropping slowly, so you decide to sell it. You then placed a sell market order. Your order will be executed right away as long as there's someone who's willing to buy Company M stocks.

One thing that you have to remember when you're doing a market order is that you cannot control how much you can pay for a stock. Several factors and stock market players determine the stock market price.

Limit Orders

A limit order is an order to either buy or sell a security at a specific price during a specific time period.

Let's say that you own 100 Company C stocks that are currently valued at $100. At this time, your position is valued at $10,000. To maximize your profit, you decided a limit order to sell 50 stocks when the stock price increases to $185. Then, you placed another limit order to sell the rest of your shares when the stock price increases to $220. If the stocks reached your desired stock price, you'll earn a total profit of $10,250 from your investment.

But, if the stock price reached $185, but didn't reach $220, you'll still earn a profit of $4250 and get to keep 50 Company C stocks.

Now, let's say that you want to buy 100 Company X stocks. Its current price is $100 each. You did extensive research and found out that the only way to maximize your investment profit is to purchase the stocks at $50 each. So, you place a buy limit order at $50. So, your broker buys the stocks for you once it hits fifty dollars or below. If the stock price doesn't drop to $50 at a specific date, your order expires and doesn't get executed.

One of the best things about a limit order is that it maximizes your profit and also controls your loses. It's also a great technique to use if you want to "buy low and sell high".

All-or-None Orders

All-or-None order or AON is an order that has to be carried out entirely or not executed at all.

Let's say that you want to buy 1000 Company W stocks. But, only 500 stocks are available in the market. Your AON order doesn't get executed unless there are 1000 stocks available in the stock exchange. This order is active until it's either executed or cancelled.

Stop Order

Stop Order is also known as stop loss order. It is an order to sell or buy a stock once it reaches a specific price (also called the stop price). It is designed to limit and manage your losses.

Let's say that Katya owns 10 Company V stocks and it's currently valued at $50. Now, let's say that the stock price starts to go down and Katya is in on vacation in an exotic European island. So, she did set a stop loss order of $40. So, once the stock goes down to 40, the broker sells it.

Stop orders are different from the limit order. You see limit orders are done to maximize profits, while stop orders are done to minimize losses.

Stop Limit Orders

A stop limit order combines a limit order and a stop limit order. To do this, you have to enter two prices - a limit price and a stop price. When the market reaches the stop price, your order becomes a limit order.

For example, Company G's stock is currently valued at $50 and it is trending up. You want to take advantage of this trend and, at the same, time try to maximize your profits. So, you place a stop order with your broker and ask him to start buying Company G stocks when it reaches $55, but should stop buying when the price reaches $57.

In this example, the stop price was set at $55 and the limit price was set at $57. When you place a stop limit order, the "stop price" initiates an action (either to buy or sell a stock) and the "limit price" stops the order.

Stop limit order is designed to help limit your losses.

Selling Short and "Buy to Cover Orders"

As previously discussed in this book, selling short is the act of selling a borrowed stock in anticipation of a stock price decrease. Once the stock price decreases, a "buy to cover" is made to cover and return the borrowed stock.

Let's say that an investor called Caleb heard that Company H is engaging in bad business practices and that it's going to get exposed soon. This secret was kept from the public, so the company's stocks are still doing great in the stock market. In fact, one Company H stock costs $200.

So, Caleb called his broker and placed a short trade for 10 Company H stock. His broker took 10 stocks from his stock reserve and sold it for $200 each. He then placed the $2000 revenue in Caleb's brokerage account.

After a week, Company H's evil ways were made public and its stock price decreased to $40. Caleb then placed a 'buy to cover' order for ten stocks. The broker buys 10 stocks for 40 dollars each (using money in Caleb's brokerage account). He then returns those shares to his portfolio. For this transaction, Caleb earns $1600 profit, but would have to pay his broker a small fee for the trouble.

One of the biggest advantage of this strategy is that it doesn't come with upfront costs.

Day Order

A day order, as the name suggests, is an order to either buy or sell stock any time during the trading day. This order automatically expires if it's not executed within the day.

So, let's say that you placed a day order to buy a Company W stock at when the price drops to $10. But, it never reached that price, so the order automatically expires when the stock exchange closed at 4:00 pm.

Extended After-Hours Trading

A stock exchange usually opens at 9 am and closes at 4:30 a.m. But, there's such a thing as "after-hours" trading. It's completed after the stock exchange closes and it's usually done via ECN or Electronic Communication Network. You can still trade via ECN from 4:15 pm to 8 pm. You can also trade a few minutes through ECN a hundred minutes before the stock exchange opens from 8:00 am to 9:15 am.

Extended after-hours trading helps you take advantage of market volatility or some news that happened after stock market hours.

For example, Jared owns 100 Company G stocks valued at $100 each. But, at 4:00 p.m., he saw breaking news that the company CEO was charged with fraud, he immediately logged into his account and placed a market order to sell his 100 stocks at the current market price. Good thing he did because the next day at 9 am, the stock price has already dropped to $50. Jared would have lost half his money.

GTC Order

GTC means **good 'till cancelled**. A GTC order is active until it's manually cancelled by the investor.
Let's say that you want to buy a Company R stock at $20. But, it's current price is $80. So, you placed a GTC limit order to buy a stock once its price drops to $20. This order is going to be active (even after a few years) unless you cancel it.

Trailing Stop Orders

A trailing stop order is a complicated animal. But, don't worry, I'll explain this the easiest way I can.

The trailing stop order is the more advanced form of the "stop order" and has a "trailing amount".

A sell stop order has a stop price below its current market price with a specific trailing amount. Sounds complicated, right? Well, to illustrate this point, let's say that Carly owns one Company S stock valued at $400 when she bought it. Her sell stop price is set at $800.

When the stock finally reaches $800, Carly is already ready to sell her share. But, Company S is really doing well and she doesn't want to miss the opportunity of earning more profits. So, she placed a $40 trailing stop. This follows the stock price upwards. But, if the stock drops by $40, the broker then sells Carly's stock. Let's say that after the stock reached the limit of $800, the stock price kept rising. After a few days, it reached $1,200. But three days after, it dropped to $1,160. So, this is the cue for Carly's agent to sell the stock.

The table below will help you understand this concept:

Carly's Stock S Portfolio

Date	Stock Price	Action
Aug 1	$400	Carly purchased the stock and placed a sell limit order at $800 with a trailing amount of $40
Aug 2	$450	
Aug 17	$800	Reached the stop limit
Aug 18	$950	
Aug 19	$1200	
Aug 20	$1190	
Aug 21	$1180	
Aug 22	$1160	The stock price dropped 40 dollars from its peak price of $1,200 so the broker sells the stock to maximize Carly's profits

Bracketed Orders

Bracket orders are designed to lock in your profit and limit your loss by bracketing the orders. It's basically three orders bundled into one. This order allows you to enter into a position with a target and stop loss.

Remember that bracketed orders are limit orders, so you have to set a limit price, a stop price, and a target price. You can also set a trailing stop loss amount.

The best thing about this order is that it helps reduce your risk and minimize your losses.

How to Place and Cancel an Order

To place an order, you just need to fill up an order form. You have to specify the amount of the order and the order type. You must also set limit or stop prices if you're doing a stop or limit order.

To cancel the order, you just have to log in to your account. Go to your order. There should be an option to cancel the order. Click on that and you're good to go.

Chapter 7 Summary

There are different trades that you can place with your broker, such as limit order, market order, stop order, stop-limit order, and trailing stop order.

A market order is the most basic order. It has to be executed immediately at the current market price.

A limit order is an order to either sell or buy a stock at a certain price during a certain time period.

AON or all-or-none order has to be carried out entirely or not at all. Hence, the name.

A stop order helps you manage your loss. It is an order to either buy or sell a stock once it reaches a certain price called the "stop price'. It is a bit similar to a limit order, but it's different in a sense that stop orders minimize losses while limit orders maximize profits.

Buy to Cover order is an order that's typically used in short selling. It's an order to buy stocks to cover the ones that were borrowed during a short sale.

Day order expires at the end of the trading day.

The stock exchange closes at 4 pm. But, you could still trade via the electronic communication network or ECN during extended trading hours - 4:15 pm to 8 pm and 8 am to 9:15 am.

GTC stands for good 'till cancelled. This order remains active until the investor cancels it.

A trailing stop order helps you specify the amount of profit you're willing to let go.

Bracketed orders bundles three orders.

You need to fill out a form to make an order.

To cancel an order, you need to log in to your account, go to the order, and click on cancel. This process varies depending on what type of brokerage account you're using.

In the next chapter, we'll discuss about the research process and how you can use macroeconomic and microeconomic analysis to make wise investment directions.

Inspiration #8

"Look for small companies that are already profitable and have proven that their concept can be replicated. Be suspicious of companies with growth rates of 50 to 100 percent a year."

Peter Lynch

Chapter 8

How to Research Stocks To Purchase

You can't go to war without a weapon. You can't just buy a stock, you must do extensive research. You must learn to be your own stock analyst. This will help you make a wise and sound investment decision.

To do a comprehensive stock research, you must use two methods used in Economics – micro-economics analysis and macro-economic analysis.

Macro-Economic Analysis

As we've discussed earlier in this book, economic forces such as the law of supply and demand affect stock prices. So, before you invest in a stock, you have to use a top-down global research approach. You must look at the global trends. You must look at the big picture.

As of writing Airbnb is not a public company yet. But, for the purpose of discussion, let's assume that it is. A lot of cities in Europe and in the United States have banned Airbnb. But, it continues to grow in various cities in the world. In fact, you can find a lot of great Airbnb deals in Bali, Malaysia, Singapore, Zurich, Mykonos, and Faro. Plus, it still has a number of untapped markets. If you look at the big picture, you'll see that Airbnb is still a great investment because of its huge growth potential.

Aside from looking at the company's global overview, you must also consider other factors, such as:

Interest Rates

When the interest rate is high, it would be more costly for companies and individual to pay their debts. This decreases their disposable income and their spending. This affects business revenues and can drive down the stock prices.

But, when a country has a low interest rate, people have more disposable income. They'll end up buying more stuff. This could lead to an increase in stock prices.

But, you have to take note that rising interest rates can benefit specific industries, such as the financial sector – banks, mortgage companies, lending companies, and insurance companies.

Cyclical nature of an industry

Before you buy a company's stock, you have to determine if that company belongs to a cyclical industry.

Cyclical sectors such as the automobile industry and the construction industry are sensitive to the ups and downs of the economy. When the economy is good, their prices go up, but it goes down when there's a recession.

Try to avoid investing in companies in cyclical sectors (unless you're very good at timing your investments). You'd want to invest in a stock that can stand economic setbacks.

You must examine the stock market index.

As previously discussed, an index tracks the performance of market leaders. So, it pretty much reflects the overall health of the stock market. If an index is trending up, it means that stock market players are a bit optimistic and a Bull Market may be happening.

Industry-wide research.

Let's say that you want to invest in luxury brands such as Louis Vuitton (LVMH) or YSL. Before you do that, you must look into the overall health of that industry.

If you look closely, you might discover that luxury brands are not doing as well as they used to be because of online shops and China-made products.

Micro- Economic Analysis

When you do macro-economic analysis, you are looking at the economy and the industry. But, micro-economic analysis uses a "bottom-up" approach. This means that you have to do extensive company research.

You have to look into the different aspects of the company, such as:

The company's product – Is the product good? Does it have loyal customers? Is the product going to be relevant ten years from now? Let's say that a music store is selling its stocks. Would you buy it? Well, let's face it, no one buys CDs anymore. We just download music from the internet or check YouTube. Technology is changing by the minute. A widely used product may become irrelevant and unnecessary in the next few years. Just look at what happened to diskettes.

Sales and revenue – Is the company earning money? Are their products doing well in the market?

Debt to Equity ratio – Is the company's debt bigger than its equity? If so, then you should run as fast as you can.

P/E ratio – If the company has a high P/E ratio, it means that it has a high growth potential. But, it also means that the stock is overvalued. A low P/E ratio means that the company has low growth potential, but it also means that it's overvalued. If you're into growth investing, choose a company with high P/E. But, you have to choose a company with low P/E if you're into value investing.

Earnings per share or EPS – A company with high EPS is really doing well. It's profitable. So, assuming other factors check out (e.g. if its not using a lot of unsustainable debt to generate the earnings), it's a good idea to invest in a company with a high EPS.

Company management – Do you trust the people managing the company? Do they engage in unethical business practices? If you don't trust the people running the company, then avoid it at all cost.

Also, make sure that the company's profit is trending upward at least in the last five years.

Chapter 8 Summary

You must do comprehensive research to determine if a stock is a good investment. To do this, you must use two methods macroeconomic analysis and microeconomic analysis.

To do this, you must first look at the worldwide trends. Are the global trends favorable to the stock you're purchasing?

You must also look at the interest rates. Higher interest rates often drive stock prices down.

Don't invest in a company that belongs in a cyclical industry. Cyclical sectors are susceptible to the changes in the economy.

Microeconomic analysis involves extensive company research. You should look at the company's income statement. Is the business earning profits? You must also look at the company's products. Are they doing well in the market?

In the next chapter, we will discuss the signs that a stock is a good investment.

Inspiration #9

The most important quality for an investor is temperament, not intellect. You need a temperament that neither derives great pleasure from being with the crowd or against the crowd.

Warren Buffett

Chapter 9

Signs a Stock is A Good Long-Term Investment

You'd be surprised to know that most extremely wealthy people have taxable brokerage accounts. As we've discussed earlier in this book, if you want to invest huge amounts of money and be a successful investor, you have to open a taxable brokerage account.
A company is profitable when its revenue is higher than its expenses and debts. To illustrate this point, let's look at Miranda's story. She's passionate about fashion and so she decided to build her own bag company.

Miranda started her company with only $70,000. This covered pretty much all her expenses. She operates her business online so she doesn't have a lot of fixed costs. She didn't borrow anything from the bank. In her first year, her company earned $150,000. This means that she has a profit of $80,000 (revenue minus expenses).

Now, let's look at Mark's story. He has a tour bus company operating in Patagonia in Argentina. That year, he spent a total of $10 million, half of which was borrowed from the bank.

But, there are fewer tourists that year and he just earned $8 million. This means that his expenses are higher than his revenue and he's not earning any profit.

Now, if you're an investor, which business would you invest in? If you look at the revenue alone, you'll see that Mark's revenue is way higher than Miranda's. But, Miranda is earning profit. Mark, on the other hand, is operating at a loss. In addition, the tourist industry can be a bit cyclical, as tourism seems to peak during the summer/festive periods whereas bad sales can show consistent sales all through the year. All other things being equal, a wise investor would choose to invest in Miranda's company.

So, how do you know if a stock is a good investment? Well, you have to look for these signs:

High returns on capital with little or no leverage

Leverage is a technical term for borrowed capital. When you're looking for a company to invest in, you have to choose a company that generates high returns on capital with minimal leverage.

This means that you have to choose a profitable company with extremely low debt. You do not want to invest in a company that's buried in debt especially ones that are unsustainable.

Competitive advantage

Let's say that you are looking to invest in the organic food delivery service industry. You believe that it's the next best thing.

Company Z and Company A are both in the organic food delivery service business. But, Company A's ingredients are sourced from a third party farm while Company Z has its own farm.

In this scenario, Company Z has the competitive advantage because its production cost is lower and its ingredients are fresher.

To win big in the stock market, you have to choose a company whose products have a competitive advantage – it could be cheaper, more advanced, or simply more delicious.

You should also invest in companies with high levels of brand loyalty. For example, a lot of customers prefer using an iPhone even if Huawei is also producing high quality products. Let's look at eBay and Amazon. They are almost the same. They are both great. But, Amazon is more successful than eBay because it has created something called "customer obsession". It has created a shopping platform that keeps the customers obsessed and craving for more.

Investing in a company with huge following can lead to great wealth in the future.

The company keeps its shareholders satisfied

Sadly, a lot of companies keep their shareholders in the dark to what's really happening in the company. Just look at what happened to Theranos.

To avoid losing your money, you must invest in a company that puts the interest of their shareholders first before the interest of employees, suppliers, and even customers.

You would want to invest in a company with a management team that has your best interest at heart. You don't want to invest in a company with executives who have no qualms about squandering the organization's assets and resources.

How can you tell if management is on the side of shareholders? One way to go about it is to look at the annual report for previous years. How correct were their estimations, what promises were made, were the promises kept, how honest and transparent were they about ongoing issues? Etc.

The company has a strong balance sheet

The economy experiences a cycle of ups and downs every now and then. Sometimes, the economy is good. Sometimes, it's bad. To minimize risk and maximize your profits, you have to invest in a company that can withstand difficult economic conditions.

But, how do you determine a company's financial health? Well, you have to look at its balance sheet. You should invest in a company with high shareholder's equity. This means that its earnings are way more than its debts.

Choose a company with high revenue, high equity, low expenses, and low debts. Companies with this type of profile tend to have a very strong balance sheet.

Look at the company's market capitalization

Market capitalization or market cap is the total dollar market value of all the company's outstanding shares. It is calculated as:

Market Cap = Company's Outstanding Shares x Current Market Price

A lot of new investors look at the stock price to measure the value of a company. But, this is just a mistake. The stock price is simply not enough. To determine the true value of the company, you have to look at its market cap.

Let's look at IBM and Microsoft as an example. As of February 2019, IBM's stock price is at $136.99, while Microsoft's stock is pegged at $107.01. If you just look at the price, you'll think that IBM is more valuable. However, Microsoft has a market cap of around $800 billion while IBM has a market cap of more or less $130 billion. Market capitalization helps to paint a clearer picture with regards to valuation.

Aside from the market capitalization, you must also look at enterprise value (EV). EV is calculated as:

EV = Market Value + Preferred Stock Equity + Debt + Interest – Cash and Investments

This metric is usually used by investors who want to acquire a certain company. But, it's not enough to look at a company's market capitalization alone. You must also look market cap and enterprise value in relation to its net income (revenue – debts and expenses). You would want the two numbers to be as reasonably close as possible. Why? Well, it's wise to invest in a reasonably valued company. You not only want to invest in a company that's huge in terms of market cap, you also want to make sure that this company is actually earning money and in great financial health.

Best Stocks for Long Term Investment

We've discussed throughout this book that there are a lot of things that you have to consider in choosing the right stock for long-term investment. Not only should you choose a stock with hefty market capitalization, you should also choose a company that produces and sells strong and established brands. Why? Well, these companies usually have a competitive advantage and they're most likely to survive during trying economic times.

A list of potentially great companies for long term investment

Starbucks Corporation (SBUX)

In the United States, you'll probably see a Starbucks shop on every corner. So, one would think that it has reached its growth plateau. But, that's not true at all. In fact, Starbucks has a lot of growth opportunities abroad, especially in Asia. Many hedge fund experts, including Bill Ackman, think that Starbucks is still one of the best stocks to invest in.

Nike (NKE)

We all know that Nike is one of the biggest shoe brands in the world. The brand is worth $29 billion. It is in perfect form. In fact, the company's revenue has increased from $16 billion to $24 billion in just five years.

But, Nike has a market share of 19 percent in the retail footwear market. So, it's definitely great for long term investment.

And, if you invested $2000 on Nike stocks ten years ago, you'll have around $12,310 today.

FedEx (FDX)

FedEx is one of the biggest courier delivery service companies in the world. The massive growth in online shopping has vastly increased the demand for this company's shipping services and, as a result, its stock share price has increased by over 65 percent from 2015 to 2018. This is definitely one to explore further.

Costco (COST)

As we all know, Costco is one of the most popular membership-based warehouse shopping clubs. You could buy just about anything at Costco – fashionable jewelry, fresh flowers, sofa, flat screen TV, watches, vacuum cleaners, and prescription drugs.

Costco has about 760 branches worldwide as of 2018 and it has over 94 million members.
What's more? Costco's earnings have grown over the years with more growth excepted heading into 2020. The company has 20 new warehouse planned for 2019 and is also entering the Chinese market.

In addition, the company also sells low-value *essential* items, which should help reduce the negative impact on its earnings during periods of economic weakness.

Coca Cola (NYSE: KO)

Coca Cola was invented in 1886 by a pharmacist named John Pemberton, who died two years later. His partner, Frank Robinson, worked hard to market this invention. But, it was just not successful.

After Pemberton's death, Asa Griggs Candler rescued the business and, believe it or not, Coca Cola was once marketed as a drug and remedy for headache and fatigue.

But, today, the Coca Cola Company is one of the biggest soda manufacturers in the world. It's not the number one soda in the United States, but it's doing really well overseas.

Procter & Gamble (NYSE: PG)

Procter & Gamble is one of the biggest companies in the world and carries a number of household brands, such as Head & Shoulders, Tide, Olay, Ariel Detergent Powder, Joy, Safeguard, Pampers, Downy, Pantene, and more.

Procter & Gamble has a dividend yield of 3% and it has low P/E. This means that its stocks may be undervalued. This is a great opportunity to multiply your investment over time.

Netflix (NASDAQ: NFLX)

Remember when cable killed VHS? Well, Netflix is about to kill Cable TV. This streaming service company has grown over the past ten years. Its market cap is now bigger than stock market giants like Disney and Comcast, but it still has a lot of room for growth.

General Motors Company (GM)

If you invested $2,000 in General Motors stocks in 2012, you already have $4,400 as November 2018. Many people think that General Motors' glory days are long gone. That's not entirely true.

GM caught a lot of flack late 2018 when management announced a major restructuring of its North American operations. Five factories would be idled as GM shifted production away from lower-margin cars like Cruze and Impala, and toward higher-margin trucks and SUVs.

GM would take between $3 billion and $3.8 billion in up-front charges to make these changes. In exchange, though, the company hoped to grow its annual cash flow by as much as $6 billion by 2020, giving it more resources to invest in high-margin and breakthrough technologies in the future, and also more financial flexibility to weather any recession that may be impending.

This is why I think GM is great for long-term investment. Although the up-front costs may be big, and the political fallout from layoffs unpleasant, GM is making strategic moves that will drive better profitability, as well as improve cyclical resilience.

Lowe's Companies, Inc. (NYSE: LOW)

Lowe's Companies Inc. is the second largest home improvement companies in the world, serving more than seventeen million customers in the United States and in Mexico.
Over the past few years, Lowe's has developed a wide array of products, such as tools, home-building materials, home maintenance products, paint, and décor.

Lowe's has a 2.2% dividend yield and it has about 21 percent five-year dividend growth rate, which makes it an attractive prospect to explore further.

Apple Inc. (NASDAQ: AAPL)

Apple is currently the third biggest smartphone producer in the world, next to Samsung and Huawei. But, it's clearly one of the most powerful tech companies in the United States. Apple has about 33% dividend growth rate in three years and offers a 1.7% dividend yield.

Coupled with the fact Apple is one of the most innovative companies in the world and commands a strong balance sheet as well as brand loyalty, it's a very attractive stock for long-term investment.

Chapter 9 Summary

To choose the right stock to invest in, you must look at the company's profitability.

You must also pick a company that has high returns and low or no debt.

Choose a company whose products have strong competitive advantage. You would want to invest in a company with high customer loyalty rates.

Pick a company that keeps shareholders satisfied.

You must also look at the company's balance sheet.

The next chapter talks about the most powerful portfolio management strategies that you can use to manage your investment portfolio.

Inspiration #10

The secret to being successful from a trading perspective is to have an indefatigable and an undying and unquenchable thirst for information and knowledge.

Paul Tudor Jones

Chapter 10

Portfolio Management Strategies

You can't rely on luck. To win big in the stock market, you've got to have a strategy. You must use logic and do extensive research. Below are the most powerful portfolio management strategies that you can use to grow your money and make the best out of your investment portfolio.

Strategy 1

Don't Use Your Emotions in Making Investment Decisions

Charlie is a seasoned stock market investor and has earned a lot of money in the past from his investments in the manufacturing industry.

After a few decades of winning in the stock market, he decided to invest in sports stocks. He studied different sports stocks including Madison Square Garden Co. (MSG).

MSG owns five professional sports teams, including the New York Knicks. Its stock value is a bit volatile and changes frequently, so it's not great for long term investment.

But, Charlie is a die-hard New York Knicks fan, so he invested in MSG and eventually lost a lot of his hard-earned money.

You're going to lose a lot of investment opportunities if you let your emotions cloud your judgment. You must be extremely objective when you're deciding which stocks to invest in. You must set your personal preferences aside and look at the numbers.

You can support your sports team all you want, but don't buy a team's shaky stock just because you're a die-hard fan.

Strategy 2

Diversification

The wise men of Wall Street always say "do not put all your eggs in one basket". Why? Well, if you lose that basket, you'll end up losing all your eggs.

You should spread your wealth. For example, if you have an investment budget of $20,000 don't spend it all on FB stocks. Buy different stocks and other securities. You can invest in a little bit of stocks and a little bit in bonds and certificates of deposit.

One of the cheapest and easiest ways to diversify your investment is to invest in a mutual fund. You can also invest in exchange traded fund or ETFs and real estate investment trusts or REITs.

It's also wise to invest a little bit of your money in index funds. The best index funds like S&P 500 allows you to own a little bit of the highest performing stocks.

You should also keep building your portfolio. Use your investment profits to expand your portfolio and buy more securities.

Strategy 3

Stop Losses

Lara owns 100 Company Y stocks that she bought at $600/share. After a few months, the stock price rose to $800. This earned Lara a profit of $2,000 ($8000 - $6000).

Lara felt that she could already relax, so she went on a two-week Caribbean cruise. She did not check her account while still on a holiday. When she came back from her vacation, she learned that Company Y's stock price dropped to $400. She ends up losing a total of $2,000.

To keep this from happening to you, you must place a limit or stop order with your broker to keep your losses under control. You can even place a trailing stop order so you could specify the amount of loss you can tolerate.

You can stop your losses manually if you do not want to place a stop order. To do this, you have to monitor the price of your investments on a daily basis. When the price of the stock starts to go down, place a sell market order with your broker.

To win consistently in the stock trading, you have to keep your losses as low as possible.

Strategy 4

Invest in A Company That Pay Dividends

Many "stock trading for beginners" books will tell you to choose a company that pays dividends. And that's good advice. More often than not, dividend payment is an indication that a company is doing great financially. Plus, it's a good source of regular income, too. Who doesn't want to receive checks in the mail every quarter?

But, you must remember that the company can stop dividend payments anytime. Companies that pay dividends usually have a slow growth rate because they are not reinvesting their profits for expansion.

Strategy 5

Non-Correlated Assets

If you want to become a successful investor, you don't only have to diversify your assets. It's also wise to invest in non-correlated assets.

Let's look at Tony's and Noel's story to illustrate this point. They are both new investors and they decided to diversify their portfolio and invest in different stocks.

Tony invested his money in different social networking companies. Noel, on the other hand, decided to take diversification to the next level. He invested in non-correlated companies. He invested a little bit of his money on tech companies. But, he also invested a little bit in mining, food industry, and oil industry.

After a few years, the social networking industry slowed down and Tony ended up losing most of his money. Noel also invested in social networking companies, but he's still doing great because his investments are spread out across different industries.

EXAMPLE OF NON-CORRELATED ASSETS
Gold Company vs Oil Company
Social Media Company vs Gold Company
Oil Company vs Real Estate

Investing in non-correlated stocks reduces risk. It also helps you maximize your profit. For example, if you invest all your money in the luxury bag companies, you'll lose a lot of money if that crashes.

Strategy 6

Tax Considerations

It's great to invest in a taxable brokerage account because it has no limits. But, it's taxable. So, to save money, it's also a good idea to invest in tax-advantaged account.

The 401(k) plan, for example, is a tax-deferred account. This means that you don't have to pay taxes for your contributions up front. You can pay the taxes when you reach your retirement age. At that point, you're already in a lower tax bracket. This will save you a lot of money.

Roth IRA is another tax-advantaged plan. You have to pay taxes for your Roth contributions. But, when you reach your retirement age and you decide to withdraw the money, you will get a tax refund. It's basically tax-free.

So, even if you have a taxable brokerage account, it's still best to invest in a retirement account so you can take advantage of its tax benefits.

Strategy 7

Rebalancing and Asset Allocation

As mentioned earlier, do not put all your eggs in one basket. This means that you should not only invest in stocks, you should also invest in other securities, such as bonds.

So, before you start building your portfolio, you have to decide how to allocate your investment fund. Do you want fifty percent of your investment fund to go to bonds and the rest to stocks?

Let's say that you decided to go with 50-50 asset allocation. But, stocks performed well during the last years, so you decided to sell some of your bonds and buy more stocks. Your asset allocation may shift to 70 (stocks) – 30 (bonds).

When this happens, you must rebalance your asset allocation. You can sell some of your stocks and buy more bonds. This strategy can help reduce your losses if there's a stock market crash.

Strategy 8

Keep your Cost at a Minimum

When you have a tax brokerage account, remember that you have to pay transaction and commission fees per trade. Long-term investment can help you save transaction fees.

Let's say that you bought one Company S stock for $100. Instead of selling your stock and then buying it back when the price goes up or down, just let it sit in your account. Aim for long-term profits instead. This way, you'll earn more capital appreciation profit, plus you'll save on transaction fees.

Don't be afraid to mix and match different investment strategies so you could earn optimal profits and minimize your investment costs and losses.

And lastly, don't hold on to your stocks forever. Long-term investment is good. But, you should sell your stocks if the price is no longer trending up. This can keep you from losing more money.

When a stock's price starts to decline, sell it while its current price is still higher than your purchase price. This way, you'll still going to earn an investment profit.

Chapter 10 Summary

You'll eventually build a huge investment portfolio as you get better in stock trading and stock market investing.

You must use portfolio management strategies that you can use to grow your wealth and your investment portfolio.

Do not make an investment decision based on emotions. Use your brain, not your heart.

Diversify your investments. Invest in different stocks and other securities. If you can afford to buy a real estate property, do that also. Diversifying your investments help reduce risk.

Stop your losses by placing a stop order. This will help limit your losses. You can also do this manually. Sell your stocks when you notice that the price is going down.

Invest in companies that pay dividends. This could be a great source of income. Plus, companies that pay dividends are usually stable.

Don't hold on to your stocks for too long. Long-term stock investment is good. But, sell your stocks when the time is right.

Take advantage of accounts that come with tax benefits. These accounts can save you a lot of money and they're easy to maintain, too.

Glossary

401k Plan

The 401(k) plan is an employer-sponsored retirement fund. The employee agrees to place a percentage of his/her income into the fund and the employer matches every dollar the employee saved.

All-or-None Orders

All-or-none order or AON is an order that must be executed in its entirety or not executed at all. For example, if you place an order to buy 1,000 shares of Company X at $5 per share, the broker cannot execute the order if there are only 500 shares available.

Annuities

An annuity is an investment where payments/deposits are made at equal intervals. Regular monthly deposits to a savings account and monthly insurance payments are examples of annuities.

Bear Market

This is a condition when investors are so pessimistic that they end up selling their stocks. This decreases the demand for stocks.

Bonds

A bond is a financial security that represents a company's debt. Bonds are used by municipalities, states, governments, and companies to raise funds. Investors earn money from bonds through interest.

Black Swan

Years ago, people believed that all swans are white, until they saw a black swan.
In finance and investment, a black swan is an event that has not occurred in the past, so it's difficult to predict.

Black swans have three characteristics:

- It's unpredictable.
- It has a massive impact on the stock market or the economy.
- You can only identify a black swan after it happened.

Investors should watch out for black swans as these events could often lead to either great investment opportunities or losses.

There are a number of black swans that happened in the past, including the invention of the internet, the crash of overvalued internet companies from 2000 to 2002, the 2008 financial crisis, the 9/11 attacks, and Brexit.

Bracketed Orders

Bracketed order is designed to limit loss. It can lock in profits by bracketing an order with a trailing stop, a profit target, or a stop loss.

Bracketed orders have an automated exit strategy. Once your desired condition is met, an order is created to exit the position.

Bracketed orders are efficient because they are automated. It's also flexible. You can add a bracket to all or just a part of your position. You're not required to put a bracket on all of your shares.

Brokerage Account

A brokerage account is an investment account that you can open through a licensed brokerage firm. After you've deposited money into that account, you can start buying securities like stocks, mutual funds, and bonds.

Brokerage Trade Confirmation

The brokerage trade confirmation is a document that you will receive when you start buying and selling stocks through your brokerage account.

Bull Market

This is a condition when the investors are so optimistic that they aggressively purchase stocks. This increases the demand for stocks vis-à-vis its supply.

Buy to Cover Orders

This is a buy order that's used to close out a short position. It is often used in short selling. As the name suggests, this buy order is done to cover a short position or return the stocks borrowed during a short sale.

Capitalization

Capitalization is the sum of a company's stock, long term debt, and earnings.

Cash Brokerage Account

A cash account is a type of brokerage account in which the investor is required to pay all the securities purchased in full. Investors are usually given two days to make a full payment of the stocks they purchased.

Common Stock

A common stock represents an ownership of a company. Common stockholders have voting rights on company policies and other matters. It's a risky investment because common stockholders are usually at the bottom of the payout hierarchy. This means that if a company is liquidated, they'll only get their share after the creditors and preferred stock holders are paid.

Compounding

Compounding is the process in which an asset's earnings, from either capital gains or interest, are reinvested to generate additional earnings over time. This growth, calculated using exponential functions, occurs because the investment will generate earnings from both its initial principal and the accumulated earnings from preceding periods. Compounding, therefore, differs from linear growth, where only the principal earns interest each period.

Cyclical Industry

This is an industry that's sensitive to the economic cycles. The companies belonging to these industries have high revenues when the economy is good and have incredibly low revenues when the economy is bad.

Day Trading

This is a stock investment strategy that involves buying and selling stocks within the same day.

GTC Orders

GTC means "good until canceled". This order will expire if unfulfilled at a certain date. It usually expires within thirty to sixty days.

Debt/Equity Ratio

Debt to Equity Ratio is a metric that's used to measure a company's financial health.
It is calculated by dividing the company's debt by its equity. When a company has a debt equity ratio of 0.5, it means that the company has a debt of 50 cents for every dollar of equity.

Derivatives

Derivatives are financial securities. Their value is derived from a specific asset or a basket of assets, such as interest rates, market indices, currencies, commodities, bonds, and stocks.

Direct Stock Purchase Plan

This investment plan allows you to purchase stocks directly from the issuing company. You don't have to go through a broker.

Dividend Investing

This strategy involves buying stocks with dividend payments.

Dividend Reinvestment Plan

Dividend reinvestment plan or DRIP is an investment plan that allows current shareholders the option of reinvesting their dividend earnings.

The shares purchased through DRIP come from the company's reserve and they're not traded through the stock exchanges. So, trades made through DRIP are commission-free. Plus, most stocks purchased through DRIP are discounted.

Dividend Yield

Dividend yield is the ratio of a corporation's yearly dividend compared to its stock price. It's usually a percentage. To calculate it, you have to divide the company's annual dividend by its share price.

Yearly Dividend ÷ Stock Price = Dividend Yield

Dow Jones Industrial Average (DJIA)

The Dow Jones Industrial Average (or simply the Dow) is a stock market index. It is a sample of thirty companies that are big enough to represent the industry they're in. These companies include IBM, Goldman Sachs, Coca cola, Home Depot, Intel, Verizon, Visa, McDonald's, Nike, and Pfizer.

Earnings per share or EPS

Earnings-per-share is one of the most popular measurements of a company's profitability. It is the company's net income divided by the number of outstanding shares. The company's EPS is positive if it's earning profits.

ECN or Electronic Communication Network

ECN is a computerized system where people could trade stocks and other securities. This system is commonly used by Foreign Exchange (FOREX) traders.

ETF

Exchange-Traded Fund or ETF is a basket of financial assets that trades like a common stock.

Equity

This is the difference between a company's assets and liabilities. Let's say that Company H has total assets of $100,000, but it has debts worth $20,000. So, its owner equity is $80,000 ($100,000 - $20,000).

Euronext

Euronext is the biggest stock exchange in Europe. It is the product of the merger of the Paris, Brussels, and Amsterdam stock exchanges. It also merged with various stock exchanges, including the New York Stock Exchange.

Fractional Share

Fractional share is less than a "full share". It's a result of a stock split. For example, if an Apple stock costs $40, you can buy a ¼ fractional share for $10.

FINRA

FINRA or the Financial Industry Regulatory Authority is a regulatory organization that governs and regulates businesses, dealers, brokers, and other financial professionals. The administer exams and licensing.

Growth Investing

This investment strategy is focused on market capitalization. Growth investors invest in companies that they expect to grow exponentially over time.

Index

An index is a statistical sample that measures the overall health of an industry or a stock market. Investors use indices to make informed and wise decisions.

Index Fund

An index fund is a mutual fund with a stock portfolio that tracks a certain stock market index like the S&P's 500. This investment type has wide market exposure and it's usually inexpensive.

Initial Public Offering or IPO

It's the process companies go through when they offer their shares to the public for the first time. It's also called "going public".

IRA

IRA or Individual Retirement Account is a tax-advantaged investment account that allows you to save for retirement.

Limit Orders

A limit order is an order to buy or sell a stock at a specific price. A sell limit order is often executed when the stock reaches its limit price. For example, you can instruct your broker to sell a stock you own once its price reaches $50.

A buy limit order is executed when the stock reaches the limit price (or lower). For example, you can ask your broker to buy a company's stock once it goes down to $10 or lower.

Macro-Economic Analysis

This analyzes the behavior, performance, and structure of the economy as a whole. It usually covers an economy's gross domestic product (GDP), unemployment, and policies. It also examines inflation, deflation, the "law of supply and demand" and economic forces.

Margin of Safety

The safety margin is the percentage difference between the current stock price and the intrinsic stock price. To calculate it, you need to use the below formula:

Margin of safety = Current stock price/ Intrinsic stock price

A stock with a high margin of safety can give you a higher investment profit because its current stock price is significantly lower than its intrinsic stock price.

Market Cap (Market Capitalization)

Market capitalization or market cap is the total market value (in dollars) of a corporation's outstanding stocks. It measures the company's worth on the market.

Market cap reflects how much investors are willing to pay for a company's stock. So, it's used to speculate a company's future value.

Market Orders

A market order is either a "buy or sell" order that has to be executed immediately at the current market price.

Margin Brokerage Account

A margin account is a type of a brokerage account that allows investors to borrow money from their brokers to pay for their purchased stocks. The purchased stocks serve as the collateral for the loan.

Micro-Economics Analysis

This analyzes the behavior of individuals and companies. This helps investors pick the right stocks and make wise investment decisions.

Mutual Funds

A mutual fund is a pool of money collected from various individual investors. This is invested in different types of securities, such as stocks and bonds. It's best for people who want to diversify their investments. A financial professional manages this fund.

Nasdaq Composite Index

This is an index based on the capitalization of over 3,300 stocks listed on the Nasdaq stock exchange.

National Association of Securities Dealers Automated Quotations (Nasdaq)

Nasdaq is a stock exchange located in Broadway, New York City. It is the second largest stock exchange in the world (in terms of the capital it generates).

New York Stock Exchange (NYSE)

The New York Stock Exchange is the biggest stock market in the world (in terms of capitalization). It is located in the iconic Wall Street.

Option

An option is a contract that gives the recipient the right (but not the obligation) to either buy or sell a known asset at a known price at a pre-defined time frame.

Let's say that Nina and Joey have an agreement. Nina has a car and Joey asks her to give him the right to buy her car for $20,000 in 60 days. Nina agreed not to sell the car to anyone in a month and Bill pays her a 2% or $400 reservation fee.

Joey doesn't have to buy the car, but he has the option to do so. In this example, Bill is the option buyer or the option holder. Nina is the option seller or option writer.

Option Trading

Option trading is the act of selling or buying options.

OTC Market

This is a decentralized market where trades are usually done through dealers. OTC markets are loosely regulated and less transparent than exchanges.

Outstanding Shares

Outstanding shares are the stocks that a company has already issued to investors. It's the sum of a corporation's common stock, preferred stock, and treasury stock.

PEG Ratio

PEG Ratio or "Price/Earnings to Growth" ratio is used to determine a stock's possible true value. It is computed as:

Peg Ratio = Price-To-Earnings/Annual EPS Growth

A low PEG ratio means that the stock is most likely undervalued. Stocks with high PEG ratio are most likely overvalued.

Penny Stocks

Penny stocks are stocks that are traded for less than $5. Most penny stocks do not trade on major stock exchanges. These stocks are highly volatile, so it's best for investors who have a high-risk tolerance.

P/E Ratio

The P/E Ratio is the price per share divided by the earnings per share. If the P/E ratio is high, it means that investors are willing to pay more for every $1 of a company's earnings. Stocks with high P/E have better growth potential. But, this does not mean that high P/E ratio is always better, because these stocks may just be overvalued.

Preferred Stock

A preferred share is a stock that acts like a bond. It usually comes with dividend payouts and it's more expensive that common stocks. Preferred stockholders do not have voting rights. But, in case the company sells its assets, they must be paid in full first before common stockholders get their share.

Profit Margin

A profit margin is the calculated as:

Profit margin = (Revenue – Expenses)/ Revenue

Companies with high profit margins tend to have tremendous brand loyalty that allows them to charge a high price for their products. They're also renowned for keeping their expenses under control, while companies with low profit margins have expense management issues.

Recession

In economics, recession is a condition where there's a significant decrease in economic activity.

Robo-advisor

Robo-advisors are online/digital financial advisors. They manage investors' account with minimal human intervention. They can automatically build a diversified portfolio for you.

S&P 500

The Standard & Poor's 500 is an American stock index based on the capitalizations of 500 companies listed on NASDAQ and the New York Stock Exchange.

Security

Security is a financial or paper asset that can be traded. There are many types of securities, including bonds, banknotes, stocks, futures, swaps, debentures, and futures.

Security Exchange Commission

The Security Exchange Commission (or SEC) is a federal agency that enforces the United States securities laws.

Short Selling

This is the sale of a stock that a seller has borrowed. This is the exact reverse of "buy low, sell high".

Stock

A stock or a share is a security. It represents an ownership of a company. It is also an investment vehicle. Many investors buy and sell stocks to grow their money.

Stock Exchange

A stock exchange is where investors buy and sell shares.

Stock Market

A stock market is a place where people buy and sell stocks and other securities. Its purpose is to help companies raise money for their business and to give investors the opportunity to grow their money through stock investment.

Stock Position

This is the amount of a particular stock or security held by an entity or a person.

Stop Order

A stop order (also known as a stop-loss order) is an order to sell or buy a stock once it reaches a specific price called the stop price. This strategy is used to minimize losses and it's an effective investment risk management technique.

Stop Price

A stop price is a price that generates a market order. Once a stock reaches the stop price a limit order is created.

Structured Product

A structured product is a pre-packaged investment. It can be a single share or a basket of investment products such as stocks, derivatives, currencies, and commodities.

Tax Advantage

Tax-advantage is an economic incentive that's associated with certain investment accounts.

Tax-Advantaged

Tax advantaged accounts are investments that come with tax benefits. These accounts are either tax-deferred or completely tax free. There are a number of tax-advantaged investments, such as retirement plans and municipal bonds.

Tax Brokerage Account

This investment account doesn't have any tax benefits.

Tax-Deferred

Tax-deferred accounts are investment accounts on which taxes are paid at a future date. There are a number of tax-deferred investments, such as traditional IRAs, 401(k) accounts, 403(b) plans, 457 plans, whole life insurance, variable annuities, and Roth IRAs.

Ticker Symbol

This is an abbreviation of the company's name. This is used to represent the company in the stock market.

Trailing Stop Orders

A trailing stop order is an order to either buy or sell a stock if it moves in a damaging and unfavorable direction. This order automatically adjusts to the most current stock price. This helps the investor increase his profits and limits his losses.

Value Investing

Value investing is an investment strategy where you choose a stock that trades below its book value. Value investors invest in stocks that are undervalued.

Book 2

Passive Income With Dividend Investing

Your

Step-By-Step Guide To

Make Money In The Stock Market

Using Dividend Stocks

By

Michael Ezeanaka

www.MichaelEzeanaka.com

Introduction II

Thousands of people in the US have their own business, earning profits regularly, without even showing up at work. For many of us, it is an ideal life - relaxing, watching the business grow, and receiving money from dividend payouts.

This is possible if you own an investment portfolio composed of stocks. Not only mere stocks but company stocks that will allow you to earn passive income.
In our attempt to build wealth, we have invented stocks, which is now considered as one of the best financial instruments in the world.

Savvy investors have a significant percentage of their investment in stocks. In your quest towards financial freedom, you have to understand the nature of stocks, and how you can be successful investing in dividends.

Through the years, more and more people are becoming more interested in the stock market. While in the past, this platform was often reserved for members of the high society, at present, the stock market is now accessible to many and it's indeed a popular instrument for growing private wealth.

This popularity alongside considerable technological advances used in stock trading has liberated the stock market so that anyone can reap its rewards and have the chance to succeed in growing their investments.

But despite the popularity, many are still not fully aware of the benefits and drawbacks of dividend investing. Unfortunately, much information about dividend stocks revolve around conversations over the water cooler with people who are not fully knowledgeable of the financial instrument.

Chances are, you have already heard your friends saying things like "Never trust the stock market. It is only for the rich. You will just lose your money in seconds!" or "My cousin made thousands of dollars with ABC Inc, so I am also investing my savings..."

Much of this misinformation is largely based on the mindset of overnight success, which was specifically popular during the dotcom bubble of the 90s. Unfortunately, people still think that stocks will help them get rich quick without much effort or proper risk assessment.

This sad fact was confirmed when the dotcom bubble popped. It is true that stocks can make you rich, and if you invest in dividend stocks, it will allow you to earn passive income. However, at all times, you should be aware of the risks you are exposed to.

The best way to combat ignorance is through education. The key to making sure that you will be profitable in dividend investing is to **know where you are investing your money.**

This is the reason why I decided to write this book - to educate you on the fundamentals of dividend investing. This book will help you understand:

- The advantages and disadvantages of investing in dividend stocks
- Key technical terms that you will surely encounter while you explore the world of dividend investing
- Different factors that you need to consider when investing in dividend stocks

- Different strategies you can employ when investing in dividends including high dividend yield strategy and high dividend growth rate strategy (The two major schools of thought when it pertains to dividend investing)

And a whole lot more!

The investment principles discussed in this book are not new. I believe there is no need to reinvent the wheel. There are hundreds of investment experts who are already using and advocating the strategies that you will learn here. But I think I have presented these things in a way that an average investor can easily understand.

In the final chapter of this book, a case study will be presented. This case study puts together all the concepts discussed in previous chapters and shows you how a typical dividend investor makes decisions starting from stock purchase to eventual sale – this will help you consolidate your understanding and gain confidence in your ability to invest wisely.

Are you excited yet? lets get right into it!

There are few things that income-seeking investors like more than buying into companies that have paid a dividend for decades or longer. The reason is that a steady history of payouts often establishes to investors the health of a business model.

Only a handful of currently traded companies have paid out dividends for longer than 100 years, and I can find no company that has paid dividends in a concurrent manner for longer than the **Bank of Montreal** (NYSE:BMO), which has been divvying out dividend payments since 1829!

Chapter 11

Why Invest In Dividend Stocks

Investing in dividend stocks can be right for you if you are looking for an investment that provides regular income. Dividend-paying companies regularly distribute a percentage of their profits to investors. Moreover, many dividend stocks in the US are paying investors a fixed amount every quarter, while there are other companies that increase their payouts over time. Hence, it's not unreasonable to expect (after building your portfolio of dividend stocks) a cash stream that resembles an annuity.

Why Some Companies Pay Dividends, While Others Don't

There are several reasons why a company may choose to pass some of its profits as dividends, and another set of reasons why some companies prefer not to issue dividends and instead use all the earnings for growth.

For a stable company with regular earnings that doesn't require reinvestments, dividend payouts can be a good idea because:

- Many investors see dividend payouts as an indicator that the company is strong. It is also a sign that the company has positive projections for earnings in the future that makes the stock more enticing. Remember, higher demand for a company stock will boost its price
- Many investors are looking for steady income that is linked with dividends so they will be more likely to purchase the company's stocks.

US companies that are paying dividends include Verizon (VZ), Wells Fargo (WFC), Exxon Mobil (XOM), Microsoft (MSFT), and Apple (AAPL).

On the other hand, some companies choose not to issue dividends because of the following reasons:

- Startup companies that are rapidly growing will not issue dividends because it needs to invest as much as possible into their growth
- Established companies also choose not to issue dividends if its directors believe it will do a better job of increasing its share price through reinvestment.
- Some companies choose to temporarily suspend dividends to begin a new project, buy out another company, or repurchase some of their shares.
- Companies that choose to reinvest all their profits, rather than issuing dividends may also think about the expensive cost of new stock issuance. To stay away from raising funds through this channel, they decide to keep the profits.
- The decision to begin paying dividends or to increase a current dividend rate is a huge business decision. Firms that will suddenly cancel or even reduce its current dividend payout could be viewed unfavorably and the share price may decrease as a result.

US companies that historically decided not to pay dividends include Tesla, Biogen, Amazon, Alphabet, and Facebook.

Types of Dividends

Basically, a dividend is a cash payout issued by shareholders of a company. But there are different types of dividends, some of which don't involve the payment of cash to stockholders. Below are the different types of dividends:

1. Cash Dividend

Most dividends are considered as cash dividends in form of electronic transfer or check. The value of the cash dividend will be transferred from the company to the stockholders instead of the former using this percentage of the profit for its growth or operations.

If a company decides to issue a cash dividend that is equivalent to the 5 percent of the share price, you can see a resulting loss of 5 percent in the share price. This is caused by the economic value transfer.

Another effect of cash dividends is that the recipients of cash dividends should pay tax on the distribution value, which can lower down its final value.

However, cash dividends can be beneficial for the investors because it will provide you with regular passive income on your investment on top of the possible appreciation of your capital investment.

2. Stock Dividend

Stock dividends are issued by a company to its shareholders without consideration. Most stock dividends are common stocks. When a company issues less than 25% of the total number of outstanding shares, then the transaction is considered as stock dividends. On the other hand, the transaction is considered a stock split if the transaction is in a higher proportion of the outstanding shares.

If a company decides to issue a 5 percent stock dividend, it should increase the number of shares by 5 percent. If you are a stockholder of this company, you will be entitled with 1 share for every 20 shares you own. If you have 1 million shares in the company, you will gain 50,000 additional shares.

However, this doesn't increase the company's value. If the share price of a company is at $10/share, then the value of the company will be at $10 million. After the issuance of the stock dividend, the company's value shall remain the same, but the price will be lower at $9.50 because of the settlement of the stock dividend.

One primary advantage of a stock dividend is you will have a choice. You may either retain your shares and bet that the company will use the cash to increase its share price or you may choose to sell some of your shares so you can convert your stocks into cash.

Cash Dividend Vs. Stock Dividend

Cash dividend seems a better choice if you want an automatic reward for placing your investments in certain companies. But this is not always true.

In various ways, it is better for both the shareholder and the company to choose stock dividends at least once a year. A stock dividend is also good as cash with the extra advantage of not paying taxes upon receipt.

You are a multi-millionaire today if you are one of the early investors who purchased Microsoft's shares in 1986. At least 100 shares of this stock at $21 per share now increased to 28,000 shares. This was the reason why Bill Gates became the richest man in the world.

One of the main reasons for issuing stock dividends instead of cash dividends could be that in doing so, a company and its stockholders can establish stronger links with investors acquiring more of the company with the extra shares.

As long as they are not bundled with a cash option, stock dividends are considered superior to cash dividends. Companies that are paying stock dividends are providing their stockholders the option to convert the shares into cash or keep their profit.

There is no other option if you choose the cash dividend.

However, this doesn't mean that cash dividends are not good. The only downside of this dividend is the limit in your options. You can still choose to reinvest your cash dividends into the company via a reinvestment plan.

Meanwhile, choosing stock dividends is not always a better alternative than taking the cash. Remember, the stock market is very unpredictable. The value of shares could drastically be affected by economic turmoils such as the Great Depression of 1929 and the Global Financial Recession of 2008.

3. Liquidating Dividend

Liquidating dividend are issued when the board of directors of a company decides to return the capital originally paid by stockholders as a dividend. This usually a bad indicator because this dividend is often paid before the business shuts down.

Companies issuing liquidating dividends may choose to pay the bill in one or several installments. US companies are mandated to issue Form 1099-DIV to all its stockholders that contain all the information about the payout.

Even with several tax benefits, liquidating dividends may not be enough to cover initial investment as the fundamental quality of the company may have significantly plummeted.

4. Scrip Dividend

Scrip dividends are issued by companies who don't have enough funds to issue dividends anytime soon.

This type of dividend is basically a promissory note to pay stockholders at a certain date.
The promissory note creates a note payable and may or may not include interest

5. Property Dividend

Companies may choose to issue the non-monetary dividend as an alternative to stock or cash payment. This type of property dividend may either include shares of a subsidiary organization or any physical assets that are owned by the company like real estate, equipment, or inventories.

Property dividends are recorded at the market value of the asset distributed. Investors may choose to hold the asset for possible capital gains, but this is usually for the long-term perspective especially with real estate dividends.

This form of payout scheme is less common compared to cash or stock dividend system. From a corporate perspective, property dividends could be distributed if the main company doesn't have sufficient cash on hand to distribute significant payouts or it doesn't want to dilute its existing share position.

Even though these are considered non-cash dividends, property dividends still have cash value.

How Do Companies Pay Dividends

Companies usually pay dividends in form of a check, but some also issue dividends as stock options.
The normal process for dividend payment is a check that is often sent to shareholders a few days after the former dividend date, the date on which the stock begins trading without the declared dividend.

On the other hand, some companies issue additional shares equivalent to the amount of dividend payout. This alternative is known as dividend reinvestment and often provided as a dividend payment option by mutual funds and individual companies.

Take note that dividends are taxable income regardless of the form you received them.

Dividend Reinvestment Plans or DRIPs provide several benefits to investors. If you want to simply add your present equity holdings with any added funds from dividend payments, a plan can simplify the process as opposed to getting the dividend payment in monetary form and then using the money to buy more shares.

In-house reinvestment plans are often commission-free because you don't need to pay brokerage fees. This attribute makes it enticing for small investors because commission fees are proportionately bigger for smaller stock purchases.

Another advantage of a reinvestment plan is that some companies are offering shareholders the opportunity to buy added shares in cash at a lower price.

The price reduction can go between 1 and 10% on top of the additional benefit of waived broker fees. So you can buy more stock holdings at a discounted price over investors who buy shares in cash through brokerage fees.

When to Expect Dividend Payout

If a company decides to issue dividends, stockholders are notified through a press release, and the news will also be reported via major stock quoting services for easier reference.
Upon announcement, a schedule will be set or a record date, which means all stockholders on this date will be entitled to the payout. The day after the record date is known as ex-date, which refers to the date that the stock starts trading ex-dividend.

Hence, if you acquire shares on an ex-date, you will not be eligible for the payout. Usually, the payable date is 30 days after the record date.

When the payable date arrives, the company will deposit the dividends with the Depository Trust Company (DTC). Payouts are then distributed by the DTC to brokerage companies around the globe where stockholders are holding the shares of the company.

In turn, the brokerage firms will deposit cash payouts to their client accounts or process reinvestment plans upon the instruction of the shareholder.

Preferred Stocks Vs. Common Stocks

Preferred stockholders are usually prioritized when it comes to claiming the company's earnings and assets. This covers the issuance of dividends, wherein preferred shareholders are paid before common stockholders.

Advantages of Dividend Investing

Somehow, receiving dividends is like getting interest on your bank savings. It can be quite nice but doesn't provide the thrill from betting on the rise and fall of share prices. People love the exhilarating experience especially when prices are soaring. However, if you are a conservative investor, dividend stocks provide several benefits over investing on non-dividend stocks.

Below are some of the reasons why it is beneficial for investors to choose dividend stocks:

1. Passive Income

Dividends from stocks can provide you a regular flow of passive income than you may choose to reinvest or spend. This is the main attribute that attracts many retirees who are looking for supplemental income.

2. Lower Risk

Dividend stocks have less volatility in share price and they usually have a lower risk-to-reward ratio. Because of these attributes, dividend stocks can experience a minimal decline in the share price during a market downturn. Lower volatility can also temper the appreciation of the share price during market recovery.

3. More Stable Companies

Dividend stocks are often paid by companies that are more stable. Startup companies usually don't pay dividends as they need to reinvest most of their profits to sustain their growth. The board of directors will only decide to pay dividends only when the company has achieved a sustainable level of success. Meanwhile, the need to distribute dividends will compel the management to be more responsible.

4. Hedge Against Inflation

Inflation is the main enemy of earnings from stock investments. A moderate inflation rate could take a huge bite out of your profits. Even if you earn a 10% return, a 3% inflation can result to only 7% earnings.

Dividends can offset this loss. As companies increase their prices because of inflation, they will earn more money and pay higher dividends.

5. Baby Boomer Boost

The price for dividend stocks could go up as the demand for it will increase because of baby boomers reaching retirement and seeking sources of supplemental income. While this is somewhat of an expert projection, it is still a projection and there's no guarantee that this will really happen. However, the probability of this happening is much higher.

6. Positive Returns in Bear Markets

Companies that are paying dividends will still pay its dues even in bear markets when share prices are dropping or flat. The dividends can help in offsetting any loss from a fall in share prices and there are cases that the results are even positive.

7. Two Ways to Make a Profit

The returns from the dividend stocks could increase when companies pay dividends and when the share prices increase. The only way you can earn positive returns from non-dividend stocks is via appreciation of share price - selling high and buying low.

8. Cash to Purchase More Shares

Once you purchase a certain number of shares of a non-dividend company, you can obtain that certain number of shares. If you like to acquire more shares, you need to use your own money to buy additional units. If you invest in dividend stocks, you can buy additional shares through reinvestment of all or some of your dividends. There is no need to use your money in your pocket to buy more shares. Most investors are also enrolled in special programs, which allow them to automatically reinvest their dividends.

9. Ownership Retention and Profit Collection

Among the most disappointing attributes of owning shares of non-dividend stock is that all your profits are locked in the investment. You can only access your profits by selling some of your shares. Through dividend stocks, you can retain ownership of the company while still collecting your returns.

While dividend stocks pose less risk compared to non-dividend stocks they also carry some risk and may not be suitable for all types of investors. Aside from the benefits, you should also understand the drawbacks of dividend investing. This will help you decide if this type of stock market investment is really right for you.

Each time you sign an investment agreement with an intermediary such as a mutual fund manager or a broker, you will usually read a lengthy disclaimer about the results not guaranteed. To put this simply, you may earn money from your investments today, but there is no certainty that it will be the same case tomorrow. Just like any other kind of investment, dividend investing also carries some risk.

Disadvantages of Dividend Investing

1. High Dividend Payout Risk

Investing in stocks with a high dividend payout ratio comes with risk. Take note that the company's dividend payout ratio reflects how much of its profits are used to reinvest in growth, pay its debts, serve as cash reserve versus how much is being paid to shareholders.

It can be a delicate balancing act for most companies to figure out the percentage of its profits to allocate for dividends. They surely like to entice and retain investors with high payouts, but also need to keep enough of their earnings to support further growth, and, at the same time, maintain their capacity to raise dividend in the future.

In reality, once the dividend payout ratio of a company becomes too high for sustainability, this can force the business to reduce or cancel payouts altogether.

2. Dividend Policy Changes

Dividend policy refers to the company's plan for figuring out its amount for dividends and any possible increases based on projected earnings. Once a company makes changes to the policy, specifically those that result in reducing or canceling payouts, it will have adverse effect on its share price.

Based on the clientele effect theory the price of a stock is strongly connected to the reaction of investors to policy changes of the company. So when these changes happen, many investors will purchase or sell their company shares.

When a company is forced to cancel its dividends for any reason, you may lose your passive income.

3. Double Taxation

Another disadvantage of investing in dividend stocks is that the payouts are subject to double taxation. First, you need to pay tax when you receive your payouts because the company issuing the dividends from its net profit has to pay tax on its yearly earnings. These earnings generate the dividend payments of the company.

Second, you need to pay tax again as you receive the payouts as personal income that you have earned over the course of a certain tax year.

Therefore, you are paying tax twice as an individual and as a part owner or a company.

In general, dividend investing is less risky compared to non-dividend stock investing. However, before you can maximize the returns from this type of investment, you need to be very familiar with both the benefits and drawbacks before you buy your first shares.

Managing Risks in Dividend Investing

There is always risk in stock market investing due in part to it unpredictable and variable nature. That being said, there are several factors that can increase risk, some are within your control and some are not.

Even though we cannot eliminate the risk, it is still possible to minimize our exposure by becoming more aware of the factors the influence the market behavior. As a saavy investor, you can manage the risks in dividend investing by dealing with factors that you can control.

1. Diversifying Your Investments

You must never invest all your money in one company stock regardless of how promising the business is. Its competitors may dominate the market. The management may be corrupt or incompetent. Or the firm or its whole industry may lose the favor of investors for any reason. These are beyond your control.

The good thing is that you have absolute control over where you want to pour your money. You can greatly minimize the risk by spreading your stock investments in different stocks.

2. Minimize Human Error

Human error is the largest risk factor with dividend investing, and it may result from the following:

- Lack of knowledge
- Misaligned investment strategy and investment goals
- Insufficient research and analysis
- Using emotions over logic in choosing stocks
- Failure to keep track of market conditions
- Allowing panic and fear influence investment decisions

Doing your due diligence is the best way to eliminate human error. You certainly know the risk involved in not being prepared if you have taken an exam you have not studied for. Aside from the unsettling feeling of having not knowing the right answers, you will experience panic that will not help your situation.

3. Use Reason Over Emotion

The Efficient Market Hypothesis is one of the prevailing theories about the mechanics behind the stock market. This hypothesis describes investors as logical people who are capable of understanding all available information in the market to make reasonable decisions for maximum profits. However, most people are not logical or rational.

Many investors are buying stocks based on advice from their family or friends and sometimes from people they don't know. Some investors buy or sell their stocks because of what they heard over the news, or because a new company is making a product they adore and they are sure that it will be a big hit in the market. They know nothing about the history of the stock, its management, or the company as a whole.

To effectively manage the risks in dividend investing, it is best to avoid these three major emotions: Love, Fear, and Greed

Love:

You must never fall in love with your investments. Remember, these are lifeless things that are not capable of loving you back. But it is interesting that they can betray you and hurt you.
Some investors are so in love with the company they hold stocks in that they refuse to sell even when indicators show that the company's inherent value has deteriorated and the share price is falling. You need to bail out when a stock declines sharply.

Review your stocks regularly and scrutinize each investment on its recent performance. If it is not contributing to your portfolio's growth, you can sell your shares, which you can easily do because stocks are very liquid.

Fear:

Investors who experienced losing money in the stock market are susceptible to fear that it paralyzes them from taking any action. Rather than taking on some risk with high potential investments, they are putting their money in safe investments with low rates of return.

Greed

Greed is the opposite of fear. Most investors who have made a lot of money in the stock market would usually want more.

Some investors are vulnerable to the bandwagon effect, pouring their money into the "hottest" companies and industries. This inflates a bubble that will eventually burst.

Greedy investors usually tend to invest in instruments they don't fully understand or they can't afford and then fall into the trap of increasing their investments to recover their losses.

Interesting Fact #2

Dividend investors also love a company that has a history of boosting its dividend. Only a handful of companies are elite enough to join what's referred to as the Dividend Aristocrats club -- those companies that have raised their dividend for 25 or more consecutive years. No company, though, is more elite than ATM and security systems manufacturer **Diebold** (NYSE:DBD), which earlier this year increased its dividend for a record 60th consecutive year.

Chapter 12

Key Technical Terms

Remember, one success ingredient for generating profits in dividend investing is due diligence. And before you even scrutinize each stock that you want to buy and include in your stock market portfolio, you should first learn the key technical terms that you will surely encounter in this field.

In this Chapter, we will briefly discuss some of the technical terms you will encounter while assessing each stock for your dividend investment.

Payout Ratio

Payout Ratio, also known as the Dividend Payout Ratio, refers to the **proportion of profits issued as dividends** to shareholders. This is usually expressed as a percentage, but can also be expressed as a cash flow proportion.

To determine the Payout Ratio, you can use the following formula:

(Total Paid Dividends / Net Income) x 100 = Payout Ratio

or

(Dividends Per Share (DPS) / Earnings Per Share (EPS)) x 100 = Payout Ratio

By the end of a certain period, usually at the end of a fiscal year, some companies issue payout dividends. The source of the dividend is the ***net earnings*** of the company and represent a return to shareholders.

The payout ratio is an important financial metric that is used to figure out the sustainability of the dividend payments of a company. This is the number of dividends issued to shareholders that is relevant to the total net income of the firm.

For instance, ABC Company with profits per share of $2 and dividends per share of $0.70 has a payout ratio of 35 percent. XYZ Company with profits per share of $2 and dividends per share of $1 has a ratio of 50 percent. So which of these two companies has a more sustainable payout ratio.

It really depends on the sector because there is no single number that can define a suitable payout ratio.

Companies in cyclical industries like energy and resources **usually have lower dividends** because their profits are not constant and dependent on the economic cycle. Hence, the name.

On the other hand, companies in defensive industries like telecommunications, pipelines, and utilities have predictable and stable profits and cash flows and **could support much higher payouts compared to cyclical sectors**.

In our earlier example, if ABC Company is a commodity producer and Company XYZ is a regulated firm, XYZ's payout sustainability may be better compared to ABC, even though ABC has a lower absolute payout ratio compared to XYZ.

Some companies only pay out a percentage of their profits, while some pay out all of their profits to shareholders. If the company is paying out some of the profits as dividends, it will keep the rest of the portion.

Retention ratio (which you will learn a bit later) will allow you to measure the level of earnings retained by the company.

A reduced payout ratio signifies that the company is using more of its profits to operate or to grow the company. In this case, the retention ratio will be higher.

A high payout ratio could mean that the company is sharing more of its profits with its shareholders. The retention ratio will be lower in this case.

A payout ratio higher than 100 percent signifies that the company is paying out more dividends compared to its earning. While this may seem good for investors, this move is not sustainable.

Companies who are regularly issuing dividend payouts have a target range for their payout ratios and define them as cash flow or sustainable earnings.

A stable payout ratio over the years signifies that the company has a viable record of dividend payouts.

Many blue-chip companies have stable payout ratios over the years despite their dividend increases.

Retention Ratio

Retention Ratio, also known as Plowback Ratio, refers to the percentage of profits retained by the company. This percentage is called retained profits.

Instead of distributing as dividends, the company may choose to retain the earnings to further expand business operations, start a new project, or acquire new assets.

Retention Ratio is the opposite of the Payout Ratio, which measures the proportion of profits distributed to stockholders as dividends.

Use the following formula to determine the company's Retention Ratio:

(Net Income - Dividends) / Net Income = Retention Ratio

For a per-share basis, this ratio can be also expressed as:

1 - (Dividends Per Share / Earnings Per Share)

Dividend Yield

Dividend Yield refers to the ratio of the company's yearly dividend in comparison to its share price. This figure is expressed in percentage and can be determined using the following formula:

Yearly Dividend / Share Price = Dividend Yield

The yearly dividend used in the formula can be the most recent dividend x 4, the total dividend paid over the past four quarters, or the total dividends issued by the company during the most recent fiscal year.

The dividend yield can also signify the dividend-only return of investment. The yield will fall if the price of the stock rises, and it will rise if the price of the stock falls assuming the dividend is not lowered or raised.

This usually looks high for stocks that are quickly falling because the dividend yield has an inverse relationship with the share price.

Let's say that the stock of Company M is trading at $20 and yield a yearly dividend of $1 for every share. Meanwhile, let's say that the stock of Company H is trading at $40 and yields a yearly dividend of $1 for every share.

Using the formula above, we can say that the dividend yield of Company M is at 5 percent (1/20=0.05), while the dividend yield of Company H is only 2.5 percent (1/40=0.025).

All other factors being equal, the better choice is Company M because it has twice the dividend yield compared to Company H.

Although high dividend yields are enticing, they can affect the potential growth cost. The money that the company is issuing as dividends to stockholders is the money that the company cannot use for generating capital gains or for expansion. Stockholders can earn more returns if the value of their stock grows while they are holding their units.

Historical data reveals that a concentration on dividends can boost returns instead of slowing them down.

Based on a study conducted by Hartford Funds, more than 82% of the total returns since 1960 from S&P 500 are from dividends. This has traction because it operates under the assumption that investors are willing to reinvest their dividends to the company. This significantly compounds their capacity to earn more money in the long-term.

Basically, established companies that are no longer expanding fast enough tend to have the most dividend yields. Companies that are in utilities or staple industries are good examples of industries that are paying the best average dividend yield.

In tech stocks, the average dividend yield is lower. But the rule about established companies also applies to the same sector.

It is also important to take note that the **dividend yield cannot tell you much about what type of dividend that a company is paying**. For instance, the dividend yield in the market is highest with REITs (Real Estate Investment Trusts). But these are from ordinary dividends that are a bit different compared to the traditional qualified dividends.

BDCs (Business Development Companies) and MLPs (Master Limited Partnerships) also have very high average dividend yields. These business organizations are all required by the government to pass through most of their profits to shareholders.

Concerns with Dividend Yields

It is not safe to assess a stock based solely on the dividend yield simply because dividend data might be obsolete or based on erroneous data.

Most companies have a very high yield as their stock plummets. This usually occurs before cutting the dividend payout.

You can use the most recent financial report of a company to compute its dividend yield. This is fine during the first quarter after the company has released its yearly financial report.

This information will no longer be reliable if you need data for 2nd to the 4th quarter. As an alternative, you can get the total of the last four quarters of dividends that can cover the trailing year of dividend data. Using this data can be good, but may not be enough if the dividend has been raised or cut.

Most companies are paying dividends every quarter. So, investors are taking the last quarterly dividend, multiply it by 4 and use the result as the yearly dividend. This method can reflect any recent change in the dividend. However, not all companies pay a uniform dividend every quarter.

Some companies - especially non-US organizations - choose to pay a minimal quarterly dividend than a large dividend at the end of a fiscal year. Therefore, you may get an inflated dividend yield if you perform the computation after the distribution of the yearly dividend.

Some companies are also issuing payouts more regularly than every quarter. Therefore, using the figure for a monthly dividend will result in too low a dividend yield.

In choosing how to compute the dividend yield, you should look at the record of dividend payouts to choose the most suitable approach that will provide you the most reliable results.

You should also be cautious in assessing a company that seems distressed with a higher dividend yield. Remember, the share price is the denominator of the formula for dividend yield. So, a strong fall in the price may significantly bloat the quotient.

Ex-Dividend

Ex-dividend refers to the stock that is trading devoid of the value for the next dividend payout. The day that the stock begins trading without the value of the next dividend payout is known as the ex-dividend date or ex-date.

If you buy a stock on or after the ex-dividend date, you are not entitled to the announced dividend. **If you buy a stock *before* the ex-dividend date, you are entitled to the payout.**

The stock normally drops in price by the amount of the expected payout because buyers are not entitled to the next payout on the ex-date.

Once a company decides to issue a dividend payout, the board of directors will determine a record date. You should take note of the record date because this is when you should be on the company's list as a stockholder so you can receive the dividend payout.

After establishing the record date, the ex-dividend date is also set based on the rules of the stock exchange on which the stock will be traded. Hence, the ex-dividend date is usually one business day prior to the record date.

For instance, when a company announced a dividend on 3 June with a record date on Monday, July 11, the ex-dividend date will be 8 July Friday because this is one business day prior to the ex-dividend date.

The ex-dividend date happens before the record date because of the manner stock trades are paid. Once a trade happens, the record of this transaction is not paid for two more business days. This is called the T+2 payment. Hence, if you own the stocks on 7 July but sold the stocks on 8 July, you are still a shareholder of the company based on the record because the trade is not yet complete. But if you sold your shares on 7 July, then the trade would be settled by 11 July, and the new owner will be entitled to the dividend payout.

There are some slight changes when the company decides to issue a dividend in stock rather than cash. With stock dividends, the ex-dividend date will be recorded on the first business day after the settlement of the dividend.

Let's say, ABC company declared in a press release dated 8 April 2017, that it will start trading ex-dividend on 8 April. The record date was determined as 9 April. Prior to this, the company already announced the dividend payout of $0.62 per share scheduled for 2 May, so stockholders who bought the stocks from the company before the ex-date of 8 April will be entitled to the cash payment.

Importance of Knowing Ex-Dividend Date

Understanding the mechanics behind and around ex-dividend payment is crucial. You need to purchase a dividend-paying stock at least two days prior to the record date because it will take two days to settle the trade.

Knowing when the ex-date happens can help you plan your trade entries, especially if your investing strategy is focused on income. But because the price of the stock drops by about the equal value of the payout, purchasing shares before the ex-dividend payment is unlikely to yield any profits. Likewise, investors purchasing stocks on the ex-dividend date or after *can take advantage of a lower share price.*

The Movement of Stock Price on the Ex-Dividend Date

By average, a stock could drop by a bit less than the dividend payout. The fluctuation triggered by small dividend is quite difficult to detect because the stock prices are moving daily. It is easier to observe the movements of the stock prices during large dividend payouts.

The ex-dividend date is surrounded by other crucial dates in the process for dividend distribution.

Record Date

This date refers to the exact date that the company is reviewing its list of shareholders. This is usually one day after the ex-dividend date. However, this is not a primary deciding factor for dividend investing.

Declaration Date

Also called announcement date, the declaration date refers to the date when the company announces dividend payout. This is an important date because any changes in the payout may cause the share price to fluctuate as traders are still adjusting their investments based on the news.

Payment Date

This is the date when dividend payouts are credited or checks are sent to investor accounts. Because the payment date is known prior to this, the event must not have any effect on the price of the stocks.

Price-Earnings Ratio (P/E Ratio)

P/E Ratio refers to the ratio for valuing a business organization that measures its present stock price relative to the per-share profits. This is also known as the earnings multiple or the price multiple.

Below is the formula used for calculating the P/E ratio:

Market Value per Share / Earnings per Share

In general, the P/E ratio indicates the dollar amount that an investor is expecting to invest in a company so it can receive a dollar off from the company's profits. This is the reason why this ratio is also called the price multiple because ***it will show you how much investors are willing to pay for every dollar of profits.*** If a company is presently trading at a multiple (P/E) of 15, this indicates that an investor is willing to pay $15 for a dollar of the present profits.

The EPS (Earnings Per Share) should be known to calculate the P/E ratio. The EPS is usually derived from the last four quarters. This type of P/E ratio is known as the trailing P/E that can be calculated by finding the difference between the share value of the company at the start of the 12-month period from its value at the end.

There are also instances that the price-earnings can also be taken from the estimates of the profits projected during the next four quarters. This type of price-earnings is known as a forward or projected P/E. Another form of P/E uses the sum of the estimates for the next two quarters and the figures from the last two actual quarters.

Basically, a high P/E indicates that investors are projecting higher profits growth in the future in comparison with companies with lower P/E. On the other hand, a lower P/E can signify that a company might be undervalued at present or that the company is doing great well relative to its historical trends. If a company is posting losses or has no profits, in both cases, P/E is written as N/A. While it is possible to get a negative P/E, this is very rare.

P/E Ratio is also considered as a way for standardizing the value of one dollar of profits in the stock market. Theoretically, you can get the median of P/E ratios over a certain period so you can establish a standard P/E ratio. You can use this as a benchmark to guide you with regards to whether a certain stock is ideal to buy.

Limitations of the P/E Ratio

Similar to any other fundamentals designed to guide investors in buying stocks, the P/E Ratio has its limits that you should consider. Be that as it may, please be aware that there is no *single metric* that can provide you with an absolute insight into your investment decision.

One major limitation of using P/E ratio rises in comparing P/E ratios of various companies. Growth rates and valuations of companies may usually vary wildly between sectors because of the different ways that companies are earning money to the different timelines during which organizations are earning their profits.

Therefore, you should only use Price-Earnings Ratio as a tool for comparison when you are ***considering companies in the same industry***. This type of comparison is the only type that can provide you with reliable insight. Your assumptions will not be highly reliable if you compare the P/E ratios of an energy company and a media company.

Comparing the P/E ratios of several companies in the same sector is much more meaningful. For instance, a telecommunications company may have high P/E ratio, but this might be an indication of a trend in the sector instead of one emerging from that specific company. If the entire industry has high P/E ratios, the high P/E ratio of a single company in that industry may be less of a concern.

Furthermore, because the debt of a company could affect both its profits and prices of shares, leverage can also affect the P/E ratios. Let's say that there are two companies in the same sector. They have a different take on their payables. Company A has lower debt and has a lower P/E ratio than Company B that has higher debt. But if the industry is doing well, Company B has the higher potential to earn more mainly due to the risks it has taken.

Another major limitation of P/E ratio is one that dwells inside the equation used to figure out P/E itself. Objective and accurate presentations of P/E ratio could depend on accurate inputs of the market value of shares as well as accurate earnings for share estimates.

Even though the market establishes the value of shares and so this information is available from different reliable references this is less likely to happen for profits that are usually reported by companies and so they are not completely reliable. Because profits are an essential input for computing P/E, changing them can also change the P/E ratio.

Here are the things you need to remember when you are looking into the P/E ratios of company stocks you want to buy:

- The average market P/E ratio is 20 to 25x profits
- A high P/E ratio signifies that investors are projecting higher growth for the company
- Companies that are losing money don't have P/E ratio
- Estimated profits can be used to obtain the forward-looking price-earnings ratio

Dividend Growth Rate

Dividend growth rate refers to the yearly growth of the percentage rate that a specific stock's dividend experiences over a specific period of time.

This metric is crucial for using the dividend discount model, which is a form of security pricing model. This operates under the assumption that the estimated future dividends will determine the price of a given stock discounting the excess of internal growth over the estimated dividend growth of a company.

Using this model, a certain stock could be considered as undervalued if the outcome is higher compared to the current price of the share of the company. You can figure out the intrinsic value of a certain stock if you estimate the expected value of cash flow using the dividend discount model.

A record of stable dividend growth may signify future dividend growth that also indicates profitability for a specific company. If you calculate the dividend growth rate, you can use any interval time you want. You can also compute the dividend growth rate using the least squares approach or just by looking at the yearly figure over a specific period.

How to Compute the Dividend Growth Rate

You can determine the dividend growth rate by taking an average using the linear method. For example, let's say that a company issued the following dividend payments to its stockholders over the last 5 years:

2014 = $1.00
2015 = $1.05
2016 = $1.07
2017 = $1.11
2018 = $1.15

To determine the growth from 2014 to 2018, you can use the formula below:

Year X Dividend / (Year X - 1 Dividend) - 1 = Dividend Growth

The following are the growth rates for our example above:

2014 Growth Rate = N/A
2015 Growth Rate = $1.05 / $1.00 - 1 = 5%
2016 Growth Rate = $1.07 / $1.05 - 1 = 1.9%
2017 Growth Rate = $1.11 / $1.07 - 1 = 3.74%
2018 Growth Rate = $1.15 / $1.11 - 1 = 3.6%

The average yearly growth for the company is 3.56%.

Meanwhile, you can use the dividend discount model to value the stock of a company. This model is based on the concept that a stock will be worth the sum of the future payments to stockholders that is discounted back to the current date.

The formula uses three variables to obtain the current price (P). These are:

r = equity capital cost
D1 = dividend value for next year
g = the growth rate of the dividend

The formula for the dividend discount model is:

P = D1 / (r-g)

Using the example above, if the dividend for 2019 will be $1.18 and the equity capital cost is 8%, the price of the stock for every share will be $26.58 as shown in the equation below:

P = $1.18 / (8%-3.56%) = $26.58

Return On Equity (ROE)

Return on Equity (ROE) is a metric of financial performance that can be determined by getting the ratio of the net income and equity of the shareholders. This metric is considered as the return on net assets because the equity of the shareholders is equal to the assets of the company less its debt.

ROE is written as a percentage and can be computed for any company if equity and net income are both positive numbers. Net income is computed prior to the payout of common stocks and after the payout of preferred stocks on top of lender interests.

Low or high ROE will dramatically vary from one sector to another. ***The comparison will be more meaningful if you use this metric to assess one company to another company in the same sector***. But take note that even with the same sector, comparing the ROE of a company that is paying a huge dividend with a firm that doesn't pay dividend could be misleading.

Trailing 12 months or the net income over the last fiscal year can be found in the income statement, which will provide you an overview of the company's financial activity over this period.

On the other hand, the balance sheet will show the equity of the shareholders. This balance sheet refers to the running balance of the organization's whole history of changes in liabilities and assets. It is ideal to compute ROE based on the average equity over this period because of the mismatch between the income statement and the balance sheet.

ROE = Net Income / Average Shareholder Equity

The average equity of a shareholder is computed by adding equity at the start of the period to equity at the end and dividing by 2. You can use the balance sheets (quarterly) to come up with a more reliable equity average.

Let's say that Company XYZ has a yearly income of $1,900,000. The average equity of shareholders stands at $15,000,000. The ROE of this company would be 12.6%.

It is not ideal to compare the ROE of two companies if they are not the same. But some investors consider this metric near the long-term average of 10 to 15% as an ideal ratio. Meanwhile, anything that is lower than 10% will be considered poor ROE.

The Role of ROE in Determining the Growth Rate

Even though there could be some concerns, ROE can be a good starting point for projecting the future estimates of the growth rate of stock as well as the dividend's growth rate. These two metrics could be employed to make comparison easier between companies that are within the same industry.

To get the estimate of the future growth rate of a company, you can multiply ROE by the retention ratio of the company. The retention ratio refers to the percentage of net income that is reinvested or retained by the company to fuel its growth.

Let's say that two companies, YumTime and TacoMadness both have the same net income and ROE, but different retention ratios. The ROE of YumTime is 15% while its returns are at 30% of its net income to shareholders in a dividend. This means that the company is reinvesting 70% of its net profit.

On the other hand, TacoMadness also has an ROE of 15% but only issues 10% of its profits to its shareholders, which means that the company is reinvesting 90% of its profits for growth.

YumTime Growth Rate is 10.5% because:

15% (ROE) x 70% (Retention Ratio) = 10.5%

TacoMadness Growth Rate is 13.5% because:

15% (ROE) X 90% (Retention Ratio) = 13.5 %

This assessment is known as the ***sustainable growth model***, which you can use to estimate the future of a specific company and determine stocks that can be risky because they are going over the sustainable growth ability.

A company that has a slow growth rate compared to its sustainable rate might be undervalued, or the stock market is just ignoring the red flags. In both cases, the growth rate that is below or above the sustainable rate requires deeper due diligence.

By earlier assessment, TacoMadness may seem more enticing compared to YumTime. However, this ignores the benefits of a higher dividend rate that can attract investors. You can change the calculation to make the estimate of the dividend growth rate of the stock that could be more essential for investors who are looking for regular passive income.

By multiplying ROE by the payout ratio, you can get an estimate of the dividend growth rate. The payout ratio refers to the portion of net income that is issued to common stockholders via dividends. This approach can provide us the sustainable dividend growth rate that makes YumTime more attractive:

YumTime Growth Rate is 4.5% because:

15% (ROE) x 30% (Payout Ratio) = 4.5%

TacoMadness Growth Rate is 1.5% because:

15% (ROE) x 10% (Payout Ratio) = 1.5%

A stock that is showing growth beyond its sustainable rate may indicate some red flags that should be thoroughly investigated.

Using ROE for Stock Comparison

A bad or good ROE will largely depend on what is common for the peers of the stock. For instance, companies in the utility sector usually have big asset and debt accounts on the balance sheet in comparison to a small amount of net profit. The common ROE for a utility company could be 10% or even lower.

On the other hand, companies in the retail industry usually have smaller balance sheet accounts that are relative to net income but may have ROE of 18% or even higher.

As a reference, you can target companies with ROE that is equal or just a bit above the average for the sector. For instance, let's say a company TechX has sustained the 18% ROE over five years in comparison to other companies in the industry that only sustained 15%. You may say that the company's management is a lot more efficient at using its assets to generate income.

Using ROE to Spot Red Flags

Many investors often wonder why a stock with an above average ROE is good instead of a company that has double the average of other companies in the same sector. In the first place, companies with very high ROE seems to have higher value.
There are cases when very high ROE can be a good thing if the net income is extremely large in comparison with the equity because the performance of a company can be strong. But more often than not, high ROE is caused by a small equity account in comparison to net income that signifies risk.

Negative ROE

ROE is often not calculated if a company has a negative income. However, ROE can be negative if the company has negative equity because of a prior period of losses, long-term pattern of share buybacks or excessive borrowings. The denominator in the computation, in this case, will result in a negative number.

The most common concern with negative ROE is *inconsistent profitability or excessive debt*. But there are exceptions to this rule for companies that are profitable and have been using their profits to purchase their own shares.

For some companies, this is an alternative way of issuing dividends and it could reduce the equity enough to make the ROE negative.

As an investor, you should investigate further if you encounter stocks with high or negative ROE. In rare circumstances, a negative ROE ratio might be caused by efficient management and cash flow supported share buyback scheme.

Also, take note that companies with negative ROE should not be assessed against other companies with positive ROE.

Inconsistent Profits

Let's say you are evaluating a company that is not making money for three years now. The losses are recorded on the balance sheet in the equity portion and tagged as a retained loss.

The losses have reduced shareholder equity and resulted in a negative value. But this year, the company landed a huge project that boosted its profitability. After this windfall, the denominator in the ROE formula will be very small considering the company has been losing money. This makes the ROE of the company high and unreliable.

For trained investors, the high ROE of the company will signify that it has no profitable track record in the past four years. Investing in this stock would be riskier compared to those with lower ROE and consistent profit trends.

High Debt

Companies that are aggressively borrowing can increase ROE because equity is equal to assets less debt. Higher debt may result in lower equity.

A usual scenario that may cause this concern happens when a company is borrowing huge amounts of debt to purchase its own stock. This could boost the company's earnings per share but it will not affect its performance or actual growth rates.

Looking at ROE in comparing stocks can be helpful, but *you should be careful in comparing stocks with different dividend strategies or stocks of companies that operate in different industries.*

Debt Equity (D/E) Ratio

You can determine D/E Ratio by dividing the total liabilities of a company by its shareholder equity. You can find these figures on the balance sheet of a company you are evaluating.

The D/E Ratio is used to assess the financial leverage of the company. This is also known as the gearing ratio. Below is the formula for computing the D/E Ratio:

Debt/Equity Ration = Total Liabilities/Total Shareholder Equity

In the balance sheet, the assets should be equal the total shareholder equity less the liabilities. This is an alternative form of the balance sheet formula (Shareholder Equity + Liabilities = Assets).

These balance sheet categories may contain individual accounts that are usually considered "equity" or "debt" in the conventional form. Take note that the ratio can be affected by pension plan adjustments, intangible assets, retained earnings/losses.

Better due diligence is required so you can fully understand the true leverage of the company. Some of the accounts in the main balance sheet categories tend to be ambiguous, so you may need to modify the D/E ratio to be more viable and easier to compare between different assets.

You can also improve your assessment of the D/E Ratio by including growth expectations, profit performance, and short-term leverage ratios.

How to Use D/E Ratio for Corporate Fundamental Analysis

Because the D/E Ratio is used to measure the debt of the company relative to the net value of its assets, this is often used to measure the extent to which the company is taking on debt as a way of leveraging its assets.

High D/E Ratio is usually associated with high risk. This signifies that the company is aggressive in funding its growth using debt.

At the end of 2018, ArrowStrike had total liabilities of $43.54 billion, total shareholder equity of $31.9 billion, and a D/E Ratio Of 1.36. On the other hand, Orinoco Inc had total liabilities of $13.2 billion, total shareholder equity of $8.80 billion and a D/E ratio of 1.50 at the end of the year.

ArrowStrike: $43.54 / $31.9 = 1.36
Orinoco Inc: $13.2 / $8.80 = 1.50

In fast assessment, it may appear that the higher leverage ratio of Orinoco Inc signifies higher risk. But this conclusion can be too generalized and more due diligence is in order.
If the company is using debt to finance its growth, it would possibly earn more profits than it would have without the debt. If the leverage can boost the profits by a higher amount compared to the interest (cost of debt), then stockholder will benefit.

However, if the interest outweighs the income generated the share values may fall. The interest may vary with market conditions, so unprofitable debt may not be significant at first.

Adjustments in assets and long-term debt tend to have the biggest effect on the D/E ratio because they are often bigger accounts compared to short-term assets and debt.

If you want to assess the short-term leverage of the company and its capacity to pay its debt for a fiscal year, you can use other ratios and metrics.

For instance, if you need to compare the solvency or the short-term liquidity, you can use the current ratio (short-term liabilities + short-term assets) or the cash ratio (short term liabilities + cash and marketable securities) rather than the long-term measure of leverage such as D/E ratio.

Limits of D/E Ratio

It is crucial to look into the sector of the company you are evaluating if you are using D/E ratio. Because various sectors have various growth rates and capital needs, a high ratio might be common in one sector, while a low ratio may be common in another.

For instance, tech companies usually have D/E ratio under 0.5, while capital-intensive sectors such as auto manufacturing tend to have a ratio above 2.

Utility companies usually have a very high ratio in comparison to market averages. A utility has a lower growth rate but is often able to sustain a constant income stream that allows these companies to borrow at a lower interest rate.

High leverage ratios in slow growth sectors with steady profits signify efficient capital use. The non-cyclical consumer sector tends to also have high D/E ratio because these companies have a stable income and can borrow money at a lower interest rate.

You should take note that not all stock analysts are consistent about debt. For instance, preferred stock is often considered as equity, while the liquidation rights, par value, and preferred dividend make this form of equity look a lot more like debt.

Adding preferred stock in total debt may increase the D/E ratio and make a company less attractive. Adding preferred stock in the equity portion of the ratio can lower the ratio and increase the denominator. This can be a huge issue for companies such as real estate investment trusts (REITs) when preferred stock is added in the D/E ratio.

Let's say that Avante Inc has $1.2 million in total shareholder equity (excluding preferred stock), $1 million in total debt (excluding preferred stock), and has $500k in preferred stock.

D/E ratio with preferred stock as part of total liabilities:

Debt/Equity Ratio 1.25 = ($1m + $500k)/$1.25m

D/E ratio with preferred stock as part of shareholder equity:

Debt/Equity Ratio 0.57 = $1m/($1.25m + $500k)

Other financial accounts like unearned profits will be categorized as debt and may distort the D/E ratio. Let's look at a company with a prepaid contract to build a new warehouse for $2 million. Because the work is not complete, so the $2 million is still categorized as a liability. On record, the company has purchased $1 million of materials and inventory to complete the project that has increased shareholder equity and total assets.

If you include these figures in the D/E computation, the numerator will be increased by $2 million while the denominator by $1 million that will increase the ratio.

Changes to D/E Ratio

The total value of assets less liabilities is equal to the equity portion of shareholders. However, this is not the same thing as assets less the debt associated with the assets. The conventional approach to resolving this issue is to change the D/E ratio into the long-term D/E ratio. This approach can help you focus on essential risks.

The overall leverage of a company still includes short-term debt, which is moderately risky because these are often settled within a year or shorter. Consider the following figures of two companies in the manufacturing industry:

Company A: $500,000 (long-term debt) and $1 million short term debt (notes, accounts payable, and wages)
Company B: $1 million (long-term debt) and $500,000 (short-term payables).

Both companies will have a D/E ratio if they both have $1.5 million in shareholder equity. At first look, the leverage risk of these two companies can be similar, but further assessment will come up with Company B as less risky.

In general, short-term debt has the tendency to be more affordable compared to long-term debt and it is less sensitive to changing interest rates. So the cost of capital and interest expense of Company A is higher. Higher debt cost would seem to make the company more attractive with more long-term debt. However, it is still at a disadvantage if the debt can be redeemed through bonds.

Dividend Coverage Ratio (DCR)

DCR is another important metric in stock investing. It states the number of times an organization is capable of paying dividends to shareholders from the profits earned during an accounting period.

You can figure out the dividend coverage ratio by dividing the net income by the dividend issued to stockholders.

Dividend Coverage Ratio = Net Income / Dividend Payout

The net income refers to the company earnings *after paying all expenses* including taxes. On the other hand, Dividend Payout refers to the amount of dividend entitled to stockholders.
There are some modified forms of the DCR that we will discuss in this book.
The first form of DCR is used to figure out the number of times that a company can issue dividends to common stockholders if the company also has preferred stockholders to consider. Below is the formula for this variation:

DCR = (Net Income - Required Preferred Dividend Payouts) / Dividends Issued to Common Stockholders

This form is also used to figure out the number of times that a company can issue dividends to preferred stockholders: Below is the formula:

DCR = Net Income / Dividends Issued to Preferred Stockholders

Example of DCR

For our example, let's take a look at a company that has reported the following numbers:

$ 500,000 (income before tax)
30% (tax rate)
$20,000 (dividend paid to preferred stockholders)
$25,000 (dividend paid to common shareholders)

In this case, you can figure out the DCR for common and preferred stockholders

($500,000 x 70%) / $20,000 = 17.5 (DCR for preferred stockholders)
($500,000 x 70% - $20,000) / $25,000 = 13.2 (DCR for common stockholders)

Remember, if the DCR is higher than 1, it signifies that the profits generated by the company are sufficient to issue dividends to shareholders. A DCR that is higher than 2 is a good indicator.
You should review your calculation or the company numbers if the DCR is below 1.5. A falling or consistently low DCR is usually an indicator that the company will lose profits in the future. The company will be incapable of sustaining its present level of dividend payouts.

Concerns with DCR

While DCR is a reliable indicator of dividend payout risk to stockholders, there are several important issues with this metric that you should consider.

First, you should take a closer look at the net income and remember that this is NOT an actual cash flow. In determining the DCR of a company, analysts often use net income in the numerator.

However, this figure doesn't mean that this is the actual cash flow of the company. Hence, a company may report high net profits but still not have the available cash to pay the dividend.

Second, DCR is not a reliable indicator for assessing future risk. Take note that net income can easily change year after year. Hence, getting a high DCR based on the record of the company's performance is not always a reliable indicator of dividend risk in the future.

Nevertheless, the DCR is still commonly used by analysts and investors to estimate the level of risk that is connected in receiving dividends from an investment.

Interesting Fact #3

Dividends have historically played a gigantic role in creating wealth for investors in the United States. In Susanna Kim's owns words from an ABC News report, "Of the S&P 500's nominal total return from 1910 to 2010, dividend yield and dividend growth comprised 90 percent [of] returns for stock holders." I've certainly come across differing figures in other reports, but the message is the same: Compounding long-term dividend growth is a key driver of wealth appreciation.

Chapter 13

Factors to Consider When Investing in Dividend Stocks

Now that you are a bit familiar with the technical terms that you will regularly encounter as you look for stock investments, it is time to look into factors that will help you to further assess the risk of a specific stock.

There are five factors that we will look at:

- Dividend Yield
- Growth Rate of Company's Profits
- The Health of the Company's Balance Sheet
- The Volume of Company's Debt and Sales Performance
- Current Dividend Tax Laws

We'll explore each factor and discuss specific circumstances that you can use to help you with your stock investments.

Dividend Yield

Issuance of dividends is one sign that a company is in good financial health. As discussed in the previous Chapter, Dividend Yield refers to the ratio that signifies the dividend income for every share dividend by the price per share.

So for example, a stock that is priced at $100 each share and issues $5 dividend, the yield is 5%.

If you are looking into stocks for your long-term investment, Dividend Yield is one of the first metrics that you should assess. You can use the dividends to purchase more shares so you don't need to commit more of your own resources just to grow your equity holdings.

Some investors depend on yields to produce a steady stream of income from their stock dividend investments. While not quite as guaranteed as fixed-income investments like bonds, dividend generating stocks could be quite valuable in this way.

But as a savvy investor, you should not only look into the Dividend Yield as this one-sided analysis can easily mislead you. There are companies that choose to continue paying yield even when they are operating at a loss. On the other hand, there are also companies that are paying very high dividends that they are not reinvesting enough to sustain their growth.

Dividend Yield and Total Return

It may be helpful in your assessment to compare Dividend Yield with Total Return. The latter is a direct representation of how much an investment has actually generated for the stockholder.
Dividend Yield only shows the actual cash dividend while the total return includes the interest and increases in share price alongside dividend and other capital gains.

By itself, this seems to provide more insight and so is a useful metric for stock performance compared to Dividend Yield. But the return is completely retrospective as the price of shares may increase for various

reasons. It is often more difficult to predict the performance of future investment from the returns of stocks compared to the Dividend Yield.
Choosing between Dividend Yield and Total Return in assessing your possible stock investments can be tricky.
Total Return is a more important metric to consider if you need to identify the stocks that have *performed better over a period of time*.

On the other hand, looking into the Dividend Yield is more important if you want to invest in stocks that will *provide you a steady income.*

It is more sensible and reasonable to focus on Total Return if you have a long-term investment plan and you are keen on keeping your equity holdings for several years.

Also, take note that the assessment of a company for possible equity investment must never be confined to these two metrics alone. Instead, you should carefully look at the income statement and balance sheet of the company and never neglect due diligence.

Relative Dividend Yield (RDY) Strategy

RDY Strategy is an important approach if you want to compare the yield of a specific stock to the yield of a sector. This way, you can figure out whether a stock is expensive or underpriced.
This strategy is not recommended for those who are looking for fast returns. This is a long-term strategy that will provide you with substantial results after a minimum of three years.
Moreover, this strategy doesn't depend on P/E ratios, forecasted profits, or past earnings to determine the valuations.

This approach will encourage you to be more contrarian, independent, disciplined and patient. These qualities will help you to concentrate on big companies who might be struggling at present but are already established organizations that are highly capable of recovering.

Employing absolute yield to pinpoint undervalued stocks in the market will leave you with several mature companies in slow-growth sectors.

Investors who are following the RDY strategy are eying for income and capital appreciation. Take note that the yield in this approach doesn't need to be very high (just a bit higher in the market). Hence, it can help you identify possible investment opportunities in both strong and weak markets.

Over the long term, RDY can help you build a portfolio with a higher stream of income (around 1.5 to 2% better total return and lower risk compared to the S&P 500 index.

RDY also signifies the sentiment of investors. A low RDY suggest that investors are enthusiastic about the current market while high RDY signifies market despair.

If you follow this strategy, you can sell dividend stocks when other investors are buying and you can buy dividend stocks when other investors are selling. You can expect the following if you use RDY:

Low Risk

The stocks you have identified through RDY tend to have lower risk than the rest of the companies in the market because these are often stocks that are ignored.

When RDY identifies a possible investment, the stock is already underperforming in the market for quite some time. There is a low possibility that the share price will fall further because it has already experienced a dramatic drop.

High Yield

Stocks identified via RDY have higher average yields. Investors who are using the RDY strategy are trained not to buy stocks until the yield is usually at least 50% higher than the market.

In using RDY, you can identify stocks that are undervalued and are expected to eventually see capital gains when it comes to price. Still, the high yield is more likely to indicate a considerable amount for returns to investors.

Low Turnover

In holding equities for an extended period, you can only sell around a third or quarter of the portfolio in a particular year. This is lower compared to the almost 100% turnover in many mutual funds.

Low turnover could lead to lower transactions costs, which will leave you with more money for investment and generation of better returns. Moreover, lower sales could mean fewer capital gains and lower tax bill.

Long Holding Periods

The usual holding period for stocks determined through RDY is 3 to 5 years. Once the share prices of these stocks recover and move higher, it can cause the relative yield of the stock to drop below the yield in the market, which triggers the sell signal.

Less Volatility

Stock portfolios under RDY usually hold big, established companies who are capable of paying consistent dividends. These stocks are less volatile compared to the general market during bear markets.

The Relative Dividend Yield Strategy can signal when to buy and sell stocks based on yield. This stock investing strategy, however, may seem a bit more complicated compared to the dividend strategy that uses absolute yield.

Growth Rate of Company's Profits

Another factor that you should look into when you are assessing stocks for your dividend investment strategy is the rate of growth in the company's profit. This is an important figure to take a closer look at so you can project future dividend increases.

The revenue and earnings of a company are among the initial metrics that you need to consider in choosing stocks for your dividend investing portfolio.

It can be difficult for a company to ensure growth if its profits are not growing. You should look for stocks of companies that have traction when it comes to increasing the amount of money they are generating in sales.

Aside from the revenue amount, the next figure to look for growth is the earnings of the company. This is also known as the net profit that refers to the amount of money the company retains after paying all its expenses (wages, taxes, and other liabilities).

The company profits are influenced by different factors such as assets, liabilities, financing, and operational expenses. To look for consistent growth in earnings you need to look into Earnings Per Share (EPS) of the company.

What is EPS?

Basically, EPS refers to the amount of net income earned per share of stock outstanding. In other words, this is the amount of money each share of stock would receive if all of the profits were distributed to the outstanding shares at the end of the year. This figure serves as an indicator of the profitability of the company.

In determining the EPS of a company, you need to first look for the weighted average number of common shares, net profit, and dividends paid on preferred shares. You can find all these figures in the income statement and balance sheet of a company.

It is better to use the weighted average number of common shares than the reporting term because the number of shares may change over time. Take note that any splits or stock dividends should be included in the computation of the weighted average number of outstanding shares.

A crucial aspect of EPS that is usually ignored is the capital needed to generate the net profits in the computation. Two companies may show the same EPS number, but one can do so with lower net assets. Such a company would be considered more efficient in using its capital in generating income and would be a more attractive investment.

Even though EPS is widely used as a way to monitor the performance of a company, shareholders don't have direct access to these earnings. A percentage of these earnings may be issued as a dividend, but a percentage of the EPS will be reserved by the company.

In order to access more of these profits, shareholders through their representatives in the company may decide to change the portion of EPS allocated for dividends.

Because stockholders cannot access the EPS allocated to their shares, the link between the share price and EPS may be difficult to identify. This is often true for companies that are not paying dividends.

Increasing Profits = Increasing Dividends

Once a company decides to enter a cycle of rising dividends, its management will be highly motivated to keep the trend. The board of directors will always pressure the management to increase the profits and ensure that the cash flow each year will be enough to pay dividends and retain sufficient earnings to fund its growth.

Without traction of increasing profits, the company may be forced to decrease or even cancel its dividend payouts. This will often cause the share price to drop sharply in the stock market. Moreover, company executives are under pressure to avoid hurting the stock price because they are usually compensated in cash and in stock options.

The company's track record of growing its dividends in the past is one strong indicator that a company has the capacity to grow its dividends in the future. Another indicator is a low payout ratio, which is the ratio of dividends to profits.

The Health of the Company's Balance Sheet

In considering an investment opportunity, stock analysts begin by assessing the balance sheet of a company. The balance sheet will provide you with a snapshot of the company's assets and liabilities in a given period of time.

Numbers don't lie especially when it comes to dividend investing. Many investors look into the cash or the top line, which is considered as the most important item in a balance sheet.

You also need to look into the accounts receivable, short-term investments, and properties, and other liabilities.

Take note that the three major categories of a balance sheet are assets, liabilities, and equity.

Assets

All company assets must be categorized under current and noncurrent assets. Assets are considered as current if the company can convert it into cash within 12 months. Net receivables, inventories, and cash are all essential current assets because they are liquid and flexible.

Cash is the top line of the balance sheet. Companies that are generating a lot of cash are usually doing a great job in delivering its products and services to its customers and collecting payments.

High topline can be worrisome, but the low top line is a sign that due diligence should be conducted. But there are companies that don't need a lot of cash to operate. Instead, they choose to reinvest the cash back into the business to improve its profit potential or issue dividends.

Liabilities

Similar to assets, liabilities are also categorized as current or noncurrent. Current liabilities are payables that should be settled within 12 months. In looking for stocks to buy, you should look for companies who have fewer liabilities, especially if compared against the company's cash flow. *Stay away from stocks of companies who owe more money than they bring in.*

The usual liabilities are deferred income, customer deposits, long-term debt, and accounts payable. While assets are often immediate and tangible, liabilities are often considered equally as crucial as debts and other forms of liabilities should be settled before booking a profit.

Equity

Equity refers to the assets less the liabilities. This represents how much the shareholders of a company actually have. In assessing a stock, you should take a look at retained earnings and paid-in capital under the equity section.

Paid-in capital represents the initial investment amount paid by stockholders for their holdings. You need to compare this to added paid-in capital to show the equity premium investors paid above the par value.

This is the main reason why equity concerns are among the top reasons when organizational investors and private funding groups are considering a merger or a business purchase.

Retained profits show the amount of profit that the firm is reinvesting or used to pay down its debt instead of distributing to shareholders as dividends.

Majority of the information you need to assess the debt of a company could be retrieved from the balance sheet. However, some debt obligations and assets are not disclosed there.

Some companies usually possess hard-to-measure intangible assets. Corporate intellectual property such as business processes, copyrights, trademarks, and patents are considered as assets today. However, these are not listed on the balance sheet of the company.

The Volume of Company's Debt and Sales Performance

If you want to invest in stocks, you should look at different financial records to check if this is a worthwhile investment. One of the most important financial metrics that you should scrutinize is the company's debt volume.

It is crucial to learn how you can assess if the debt will affect your dividend investment. But first, we need to take a look at the different forms of debt that a company usually takes.

A company can usually borrow money through two primary methods:

By taking out debt from a bank or other lending organizations such as credit cooperatives
Issuance of fixed-income debt securities such as corporate papers, bills, notes, and bonds.

Most companies are borrowing money from banks, which usually extend credit lines. Established companies usually have open credit lines from which they can draw funds to meet their cash requirement for their daily operations.

The loan that a company takes on from a bank can be used to buy new equipment, purchase additional inventory, or pay company payrolls. More often than not, loans require repayment in a shorter time period compared to most fixed-income securities.

On the other hand, fixed-income securities refer to debt securities that are issued by the company and purchased by investors. If you purchase any form of a fixed-income security, you are basically lending money to a government or business.

In issuing these securities, the company is required to pay underwriting fees. But debt securities allow the company to raise more funds and to borrow for a longer duration compared to the usual terms.

How to Evaluate Company's Debt Volume

As a dividend investor, you should look for a few critical metrics in making your decision whether you want to continue your investment in a company that is about to take on a new debt. Below are some of the important questions you need to ask:

1. How much is the current debt volume of the company?

If a company has zero debt volume, then taking on some loans can actually be beneficial because it can provide the company with more flexibility to reinvest its funds into its operations.

However, if the company you are evaluating already has substantial debt volume, then you may need to dig deeper. In general, high debt volume is not a good sign because it can prohibit the company's ability in creating cash surplus.

Moreover, high debt levels could negatively affect common shareholders who are usually the least priority to be paid when the company goes down.

2. What type of debt is the company taking on?

It is important to take note that loans and fixed-income securities that a company issues have significant differences when it comes to their maturity dates. Some types of loans should be paid within several days after issuance, while others come with longer payment periods.

Usually, debt securities that are issued to the public will have longer maturities compared to the loans offered by private institutions such as banks and large credit organizations.

Long-term fixed-income securities usually have high-interest rates and so may be difficult for the company to pay. But companies may find it hard to repay large short-term loans.

It is crucial for you to assess if the interest rate and length of the debt are suitable for funding the project that the company wants to undertake.

3. What is the purpose of the debt?

Another important factor to consider is the main reason why the company wants to take loans. Is this for a new project or venture with high potential for capital appreciation? Or the company needs to raise money to refinance or repay outstanding debts?

You need to carefully assess this area *before buying stocks in companies that have records of regular debt refinancing.* This signifies that the company doesn't have the ability to meet its financial obligations.

Companies that constantly refinance usually do so because their expenses are higher compared to their revenues. This is not a good sign if you are looking for dividend investments.

But in some special circumstances, it is a good idea for companies to refinance their debt to effectively lower their interest rates. In this case, the debt can reduce the debt volume, which should not be considered as new debt.

4. Can the company afford to pay the debt?

Most established companies are already sure of their ideas before they allocate funds for their execution. However, not all companies are guaranteed with success.

As an investor, it is crucial for you to ascertain whether the company *can still meet its repayments if the project fails*. You should check the cash flow of the company and make sure that it is sufficient to meet its financial obligations. It is best to look for companies that have diversified its prospects.

5. Are there additional provisions that may require sudden demand for repayments?

In assessing the debt volume of a company, you need to check if any special provisions could be damaging once implemented. For instance, there are banks that set a threshold ratio levels. Hence, if any of the company's ratio falls down this threshold, the bank has the right to demand immediate repayment of the loan.

A sudden demand for the company to make payment can magnify any problem inside the company and there are instances where this can lead to liquidation.

Important Financial Ratios for Industry Debt Comparison

Many financial ratios can help you in comparing the debt volume of a company against the industry. Below are the important ratios that you can use:

1. Debt-to-Equity Ratio

This ratio measures the financial leverage of the company. You can get this ratio by dividing long-term debt by the shareholder equity. This signifies what proportions of equity and debt that the company is using to fund its assets.

2. Current Ratio

This ratio in fundamental analysis shows the number of short-term assets versus short-term liabilities. The higher the short-term assets compared to liabilities, the better its capacity to pay off its short-term debt.

3. Acid Test (Quick Ratio)

This ratio will show you the capacity of the company to pay off its short-term debt without the need to sell any inventory.

Remember, a company that is increasing its debt volume must have a plan for repayment. If you have to assess the debt of the company, you need to make certain that the company is aware how the debt can affect its investors, how the debt will be paid, and how long will it take to repay the loan.

Company Sales Performance

Aside from the debt volume, you also need to assess the sales performance of the company you want to buy stocks from. In order to do this, you need to take a look into the price-to-sales ratio, which will allow you to see how the company is using its market capitalization and revenue to figure out whether the stock is worth your money.

To determine the price-to-sales ratio, you need to take the company's market capitalization and divide this by the total sales or revenue of the company over the past 12 months. More often than not, lower price-to-sales ratio signifies a good stock investment.

This metric will help you in determining the value of stocks because it will allow you to see how much the market values every dollar of sales. This ratio is ideal to use if you want to see the value of growth stocks that have yet to be converted into profit.

For instance, if you are looking into a company that is not earning any profit yet, you can take a look at the P/S ratio to figure out if the stock is overvalued or undervalued.

When the P/S ratio is lower compared to other companies in the same sector that is profitable, you may consider purchasing the stock because of low valuation. But be sure also to check other metrics and financial ratios so you can be sure that the stock is properly valued.

With highly cyclical sectors such as airlines, there are some years when only a few companies are producing profits. This doesn't mean that the airline industry is of less value. In such case, investors can use P/S ratio rather than P/E ratio (earnings) in determining how much they are paying for a dollar of their sales instead of their earnings.

When the earnings of the company are negative, the ratio can be considered as not optimal because its capacity will be limited to value the stock because the denominator will be lower than zero.

You can use the P/S ratio for verifying that the growth of a company has not become overvalued or for evaluating recovery scenarios. This will help you in assessing companies that started to suffer losses and has no earnings.

You need to consider how we assess a company that has not made any earnings in the previous 12 months. Unless the company is closing shop, the P/S can be used to determine if the company shares are valued at a discount against others in the same industry.

Let's say that the firm has a P/S of 0.6 while other companies in the sector have a P/S of 2.0. If the company becomes successful in reviving its cash flow, its shares will experience a significant rise as the ratio will become closely matched with other companies in the industry.

On the other hand, companies that are going into negative earnings could also lose the dividend yield. In such case, P/S could signify one of the last remaining metrics for business valuation. A very high P/S can be a red flag while a low P/S can be a good sign.

But you need to take note that turnover is only valuable if you can convert it into earnings. For example, property development firms have high sales turnover but usually takes modest profits.

Meanwhile, a tech company can easily generate $5 in net profit for every $12 in sales revenue. This discrepancy shows that sales dollars cannot always be considered in the same way for each company.

Some investors perceive sales revenue as a more dependable sign of a company's growth. Even though earnings are not always a good indicator of financial wealth, sales revenue metrics are not always reliable.

Evaluating sales performance should be done with a careful assessment of profit margins and compare the findings with other companies within the same sector.

Role of Debt in P/S Ratio Assessment

You should take note that the P/S ratio does not account for the debt on the balance sheet of the company. A company with no debt and a low P/S ratio is a better investment compared to a company with high debt and the same level of P/S.

At this point, the debt can be paid off and the debt will have an interest expense that is associated with it. The P/S ratio as a method of valuation doesn't consider the fact that firms with high debt levels will eventually require higher sales to pay the debt.

However, companies that are on the brink of insolvency and have high debt can rise with low P/S. This can happen if their sales have not experienced a fall while their share price and capitalization breaks down.

So how can you make a better assessment? Some investors are using a method that is effective in figuring out the difference between less healthy, high-debt companies and cheap firms.

You can use the enterprise/value instead of market capitalization/sales. This metric involves the long-term debt of the company. In adding this figure to the company's market capitalization and subtracting any cash on hand, you can determine the enterprise value of the company. The enterprise value is then considered as the total cost of buying the company including the debt and leftover cash.

Like in the case of all valuation techniques, sales-based metrics are only a small part of the assessment. You must consider several metrics to properly value a company. Low P/S could signify unrecognized potential in value as long as other criteria are in places such as high growth prospects, low debt levels, and high-profit margins. Otherwise, using the P/S ratio may result in false value assessment.

Current Dividend Tax Laws

According to the American Shareholders Association, the number of companies distributing dividends to their stockholders had been falling for a quarter of a century before 2003.

This significantly changed after the passage of the Jobs and Growth Tax Relief Reconciliation Act of 2003 (JGTRRA). Alongside other tax reforms introduced to help the economy, the JGTRRA decreased the rate of individual income tax on corporate dividends to 15% and also decreased the rate of the top individual income tax rate on long-term capital gains to 15%.

But this piece of legislation has a sunset provision, and this already expired on 2011. As an investor, you need to take a look at current tax dividend laws to determine how much you need to pay in receiving income from your stock dividends.

JGTRRA had a critical role in the current tax dividend laws as well as ongoing changes. After this passage, around 240 companies had increased the volume of their dividend payouts. This trend continued to rise from 2004 to 2007. This rising trend abruptly ended with the credit crisis and mortgage meltdown in 2008.

Important Provisions of the JGTRRA

The changes in the dividend tax rates caused by the JGTRRA were applied to dividends from "qualifying foreign corporations" and domestic corporations. This involves companies that are incorporated in a country where specific treaties with the US are applicable, companies that are incorporated in a US possession, or US securities exchange.

However, the changes in dividend tax rates do not apply to dividend payouts of the following companies:

- Securities owned through employee stock ownership arrangement
- Companies that are exempted from paying federal income tax
- Stocks owned for fewer than 60 days during the 120 days before and after the announcement of stocks for ex-dividend date.
- Short sale investments that require a related payment in substantially similar or related property
- Real estate investment trusts (REITs)
- Tax-exempt cemetery companies, farmer's cooperatives, mutual savings banks, mutual insurance companies, and credit unions.

Brief Background of Dividend Taxation in the US

To better understand the effect of the JGTRRA, let's go through a short overview of dividend taxation before it took effect in the US.

Basically, taxation started with an initial corporate income tax, at a rate of 35% that was levied against every dollar of the profit that a company earned. After paying this tax, the company may choose to distribute dividends to shareholders. At this point, the payout was considered as income of shareholders and so should be taxed again. For the highest tax bracket of taxpayers, the income tax could reach as high as 39% from every dollar of profit they receive from dividend payouts.

Companies have long expressed their concerns about this double taxation. Remember, the primary objective of corporations is to increase the shareholder value. If companies generate revenue, there are limited number of ways for these profits to be issued to shareholders or reinvested back to business.

Because dividend payouts are considered as inefficient use of capital, companies originally prefer to invest in activities that can generate capital gains, on which investors also paid tax, although at the remarkably reduced rate of 20 per cent.

This encouraged corporations to spend their profits on stock buyback programs, new equipment, acquisitions, research and development, and other activities that can help them build and strengthen their operations. Ideally, these efforts could boost the share price of the company and ultimately could lead to a bigger ROI if investors choose to sell their shares.

This situation significantly changed after the passage of JGTRRA. The decrease of dividend tax rates was one crucial development. Another major change was the decrease in tax on long-term capital gains from 20% to 15% for taxpayers in the highest tax brackets.

JGTRRA equalized the field between different forms of revenue distribution available for companies that are publicly trading.

Advantages of JGTRRA to Investors

Looking for stable dividend payouts from established companies such as Coca-Cola, Johnson & Johnson, and General Electric has been a proven strategy for investors who are looking for steady income.

Investment analysts consider steady dividend payouts as an indicator of strength while stopping dividends is seen as an indicator of weakness. Hence, companies with a strong record of dividend payments have the tendency to keep those payments in the long run.

Established yet slow-growing companies are called widow-orphan stocks because they offer a high degree of safety for investors who are risk averse.

Through JGTRRA, companies that are issuing dividends have become even more enticing for investors, especially for those in the highest tax brackets.

In general, the 15 per cent tax rate on dividends is a good bargain considering the income generated by bonds and other fixed-income securities are taxed at rates of up to 28 per cent.

Investors in the lower tax brackets also take advantage of lower tax rates on dividends with the dividend tax rates falling to only 5 per cent for investors in the 15 per cent or 10 per cent tax categories.

Even though lower taxes are direct and immediate benefits, these are not the only advantage for investors. Just consider the effect on share prices if a firm declares a new dividend payout or approves the increase of their current dividend payout. With these announcements, the share price of the company will become more enticing for investors, and so, the stock prices are more likely to increase. This trend could result in bigger capital gains for investors when they sell their shares.

Aside from the financial benefits, dividend payouts also have advantages in the market psychology. Even though we cannot measure this in a monetary perspective, the increase in the number of companies that are issuing dividends could serve to calm the nerves of the investors in a time of financial crisis.

Advantages of JGTRRA to Corporations

From a corporate perspective, dividends are part of the cost of capital of a company. Decreasing the tax on dividends make it less expensive for companies to do business by making it more affordable for them to give back money to shareholders.

This can also encourage them to invest company profits more efficiently seeking the most profitable business opportunities as opposed to looking for an opportunity that can allow them to avoid issuing dividends.

Company executives gained a lot of benefits from the passage of JGTRRA. Majority of business executives received substantial rewards because they basically rank among the biggest stockholders in the companies that they are running.

Although they do not gain a lot of publicity, corporate executives received massive dividend payouts. Many executives received millions of dollars of dividend payouts. But with the JGTRRA they only had to pay 15% tax as opposed to the 28% tax rate that they would have paid without the legislation.

Even though JGTRRA already ended in 2010, the US Congress has approved the extension of certain provisions until 2012. As an investor, you should be cautious not to put your investments in a position where you will just rely on an income stream that could be substantially reduced.

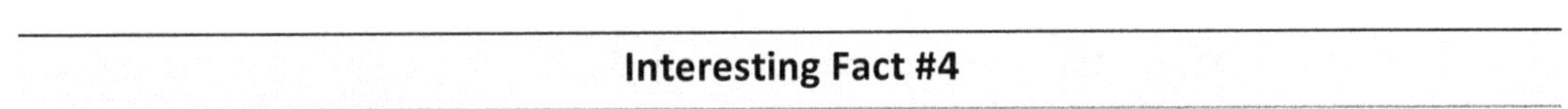

Interesting Fact #4

Ticker Tapes: Before you could trade stocks online or see which stocks and securities were trading in real time on TV, your computer or mobile phone, brokers relied on stock ticker tapes, which printed out stock price information that was transmitted over telegraph lines. The ticking sound as the paper printed is how it earned its name.

Chapter 14

High Dividend Yield Strategy

In dividend stock investing, many investors are following the high dividend yield strategy. This particular strategy could result in large cash income, usually from slow-growth companies that have a substantial cash volume to finance dividend payouts.

However, the unnecessary focus on income alone often obscures the important reality that long-term stock dividend investment is based on the total return of a portfolio, which includes both capital and income growth.

This scenario raises two important questions:

1. How does its total-return performance compare to the profits of other potential stock-option strategies?
2. With a focus on income, how has the total profit of a high-dividend yield strategy fared in comparison to the overall market?

Take note that a high-dividend yield strategy is a systematic approach in buying and holding stocks wherein the dividend is high relative to the share price. As such, this is a strategy that prefers stock valuation because this it's actually the low price of the stock in relation to the dividend, which mainly causes the high yield.

But a high-dividend yield strategy is just one form of strategy in dividend investing, which can help you in selecting stocks. There is also considerable proof and theoretical foundation that value stocks can outperform both market and growth stocks in the long run. In this perspective, the "yield" premium that is linked to high-dividend strategies really refers to the value premium.

Other strategies focus on stocks based on high earnings or high cash flow relevant to price as well as the high book value of equity that is relevant to market value.

One possible explanation for the minimal return of the high-dividend yield stocks compared to stocks chosen via other value metrics is that dividend stocks are usually sourced from bigger companies.

Companies that are not issuing dividends are not included in the list. Therefore, a high-dividend yield strategy foregoes to a higher degree the available return premium available from investing in smaller companies.

Stocks that are chosen on the basis of high profits often demonstrate strong performance. This value strategy could purchase non-dividend-payment of growth companies that are not included in the list and also companies that are generating enough revenues but have reduced their dividend payouts or they are temporarily suspended.

It is important to take note that no single value strategy could outperform consistently over shorter time frames. Therefore, the diversifying strategy can be beneficial at this point, especially for investors who are a bit impatient.

One major advantage of choosing high-dividend stocks is that they are less volatile in the market. But value stocks based on either cash flow or earnings had modestly higher risk-adjusted profits compared to high-dividend yield strategy.

A high-dividend strategy could result in less stock turnover compared to a strategy that is based on earnings or cash flow and in this case, it can drastically lower capital gains taxes.

But a strategy that is based on high book-to-market can also decrease turnover and potential capital gains taxes. In general, with a focus on consistent and significant taxable income generation, a high-dividend strategy is not tax efficient, especially in countries with higher dividend tax rates compared to the US.

Remember, a high-dividend yield strategy has several advantages for dividend investors. This is easy to understand and usually attractive to the innate desire of investors to hold on to their shares. Stocks selected using high-dividend yield strategy are often powerful enough to outperform the market with less volatility.

But if we base this on absolutes, its returns have affected other value strategies. Using the risk-adjusted perspective, the lower volatility can come at a cost of lower returns.

High-dividend yield strategy may not be applicable to wealthy investors or high-income earners. This strategy could trigger unnecessary income that created unnecessary tax drag on the accumulation of wealth.

In summary, investors, especially those that are subject to taxes, might be better off creating a cash flow stream using a systematic withdrawal program from an investment portfolio that attracts higher returns from other values strategies instead of depending solely on a high-dividend yield strategy.

The Advantages of Selecting High-Dividend Yield Stocks

Majority of dividend-paying stocks are in defensive sectors that are poised to sustain economic crises with less volatility. More often than not, dividend-paying companies have significant amounts of cash. Hence, these are established companies with better prospects in the long-term.

Dividend Yields as Regular Cash Stream

Bear in mind that the dividend yield is a financial metric that will help you figure out how much per share a company is paying out per annum in the dividend. This is expressed in percentage.

As a review, you can calculate the dividend yield by taking the yearly dividend per share divided by the price for each share. This will provide a percentage as the dividend yield, as the majority of companies are issuing dividends every quarter.

Dividends can provide a regular source of income for stock investors. You can use this passive revenue to spend or reinvest back in stocks. This is a common practice in the industry.

Investors who are about to retire or are already in retirement usually choose dividend stocks as a source of revenue as long as these stocks are less volatile.

Dividend-paying stocks will allow you to make money in two methods:

- Stock price appreciation
- Distributions issued by the company

Majority of the companies that are issuing stocks have dividend reinvestment plans, which allow investors to use dividends in purchasing more shares in the company.

This will allow you to gradually build a bigger position in a company in the long run. Many companies are not taking commissions for these added shares. Some are even offering discounts.

Companies are offering reinvestment plans because they take advantage of having a base of long-term investors who are actively involved in the future of the business.

Dividend Stocks Are Based in Defensive Sectors

Majority of the companies that are paying dividends are in defensive industries, which are seen as non-cyclical. These companies are not dependent on bigger economic cycles.

Defensive stocks can withstand economic instability and they are generally less volatile compared to the overall market. This can be a great thing for investors who are risk-averse. These stocks can pay more than investors can receive from conservative securities such as bonds. Hence they are great additions to investment portfolios.

Typical defensive sectors include healthcare, pharmaceutical, utility and housing, and food industries. Even during financial uncertainty, people still need to buy food products and keep the lights on.

Regardless of the status of the economy, people still get sick and require medical care. Healthcare stocks such as Pfizer are usual favorites of investors who love high-dividend stocks.

Established Companies

Majority of companies that are paying dividends are already established companies with well-performing stocks. They have the capacity to distribute dividends to investors because they have a substantial cash reserve. For this reason, they are good stocks to include in your portfolio. Examples of such companies are Coca-Cola and Procter & Gamble that pay 3.5% and 3.95% dividends per year.

In the long run, established companies perform better. Based on a stock analysis published by Forbes in 2015, dividend-paying stocks have shown better performance since 1927. The average growth of dividend-paying stocks is 10.4% compared to the 8.5% annual growth of non-dividend-paying stocks.

Dividend-paying stocks are also less volatile. The average deviation for dividend-paying stocks is 18% while non dividend-paying stocks are at 30%.

The Downsides of High Yield Dividend Stocks

The primary risks of high yield dividend stocks include interest rate risk and inability to make dividend payments. High yield dividend stocks could be remarkable opportunities for savvy investors who can earn a substantial amount from their investments while waiting for the prospect of stock appreciation. Hence, it is crucial to perform proper and deeper due diligence to make sure that dividend payouts are possible.

Remember, high yield dividend strategy works by choosing stocks that have *strong balance sheets* and managed by a well-experienced and skilled management team. There are instances that companies with great records of issuing payouts encounter short-term problems or poor market conditions that cause temporary hiccups. This can temporarily raise the dividend yield, which creates opportunities for savvy investors.

Remember, stocks are often affected by the performance of the underlying business as well as the interest rates. If interest rates increase, dividends could become less attractive to investors, which result in equity outflows and selling of stocks.

Many high dividend stocks are in consumer staples, master limited partnerships, utilities, and real estate investment trusts (REITs). Huge cap indexes such as S&P 100 and Dow Jones also contain a lot of high dividend stocks.

High Dividend as an Indicator of Company Distress

Although high dividends are typically attractive to investors, some are actually considered as fool's gold. In some instances, a high dividend may indicate that a company is experiencing distress. You may lose your investment during dividend cuts or stock price falls if you only choose stocks solely on the basis of the dividend.

The stock market is a forward-looking market and usually doesn't account for the underlying problems of a company. This can make the dividend more enticing for investors.

Let's say that CGF Inc is trading at $50 and issues $2.50 yearly dividend. Hence, we have a 5% dividend yield. Some movement in the market could result in a loss in earnings capacity, and the share price of the company falls to $25. This is a 50% loss. In the case of dividends, they are not automatically ceased. Hence, on the surface, some investors may see that the yield on CGF stock is now at 10 per cent.

But this high dividend yield is only temporary as the same factors that caused the fall of the share price would most likely lead to a decrease in a dividend. In other scenarios, the company may choose to keep the dividend to reward loyal stockholders. Hence, you should not ignore the need to look into the operations and the financials of the company. This will help you determine if the dividend payouts are sustainable.

Some important factors to scrutinize are the status of the company's overall financial health, management's strategy, increases and decreases, historical dividend schedules, historical payout ratio, and free cash flow.

Many of the best dividend paying companies are usually blue chips in the sector with a stable record of generating revenue and income growth over several quarters and years. This reputation and credibility usually lend itself to the stable underlying fundamentals that are associated with most companies that are paying dividends.

With this, there will always be new players entering into the mix and companies who are starting to struggle with their dividend payout. Hence, it is crucial to maintain steadfast due diligence.

Risk of Interest Rate

Dividend yields are often being compared to the risk-free rate of return that typically increases in scenarios where the government is implementing stricter financial policies.

As a result, many investors assess dividend and dividend investments in relation to this metric instead of absolute basis. If the interest rates increase, it could lead to outflows in high dividend yield stocks and may also cause stock prices to decrease. Significant changes in interest rates could be a catalyst for some market movements and possibly result in a bear market. Hence, this is a crucial factor to follow for different investing decisions.

The US government has been increasing interest rates since 2015. The stricter policy is affecting the nearly a decade of bullish returns of the stock market. This has also been aligned with increasing inflation, improving the economy and recovery of the labor market.

The year 2019 may be a good time to consider some of the best high dividend stocks and reallocate some investments. This will allow you to take advantage of a higher risk-free rate in liquid cash savings as well as short-term bonds.

Interesting Fact #5

Opening Bell: Since 1903, the start of every day's trading session on the NYSE starts with the ringing of an actual bell at 9:30 a.m. Eastern Standard Time. Originally, the signal was a gavel, and then a gong. Many high-profile people have been invited to participate in the tradition of ringing the opening bell, including singer Usher, former President Ronald Reagan, actor Robert Downey, Jr., firefighters and Star Wars villain Darth Vader.

Chapter 15

High Dividend Growth Rate Strategy

High dividend growth rate strategy requires buying of stocks in companies that are presently paying lower-than-average dividends but are growing so rapidly that within 5 to 10 years, the absolute dollar amounts collected from the equity could be higher than what you can receive using the high dividend yield strategy.

Even though companies that are paying high dividends have performed remarkably well in recent years, they have become a bit expensive in terms of most valuation metrics. While they can still pay high dividends, the previous low-interest rate setting pushed many of these companies to get more into debt to expand their reach. When interest rates increased, many of these companies are now under pressure.

On the other hand, stocks with a track record of dividend growth can present a compelling investment opportunity in a setting of rising rates and potential volatility. Investing in companies with growing and sustainable dividends will provide you the opportunity to hold high-quality stocks and higher income over time. To some extent, this will allow you to buffer against market volatility and address the risk of increasing rates.

This strategy goes beyond the conventional realm of domestic large-cap stocks. This is also effective for small and medium stocks and can also be applied to global stock markets.

Why Choose Dividend Growers?

Basically, quality dividend growth stocks tend to be of higher quality compared to those in the wider market when it comes to leverage and earnings quality. In most cases, if a company is capable of boosting its dividend payout for years, this is a good indicator that it has discipline and financial strength.

Be that as it may, the high dividend yield does not always guarantee that the company is well-disciplined or has financial strength. There are instances when new or struggling companies tried to entice market investors by taking on more debt just to issue higher dividends.

Because of this, high-dividend payers with lower earnings growth, lower profitability, and higher financial leverage are more likely to cut down their dividends during a low-growth and volatile market.

Buffer Against Market Volatility

High dividend growth stocks can be enticing to investors who are looking for established companies that can withstand stressful market and economic settings. Specifically, dividend growth stocks may provide some disadvantage during bearish markets.

Increasing Rates Risk

High dividend growth stocks can easily address the concerns surrounding the performance of high dividend payers when the rates increase in the market.

Because of its concentration on increasing dividends instead of high yield, the performance of dividend growers is less powered by the value factor in comparison with the high dividend payers. As the stock market shifts toward growth, the performance of high growth stocks is less likely to suffer.

Not similar to many pure yield strategies that tend to be focused on industries such as financials, consumer staples, and utilities, high dividend growth strategy has the tendency to include more diversified industries. Hence, the industry composition of this strategy is more stable in the long run. Diversification can help during major movements in the performance of specific sectors.

Given the concentration on quality balance sheets, a high dividend growth can be ideal to investors who are worried about volatility and the possibility of increasing rates but still prefer to hold stocks that will generate them income. If you prefer this arrangement, a high dividend growth strategy is recommended for you.

According to hypothetical analysis, dividend growth stocks can easily generate more revenue over time compared to stocks with a higher yield but with slower growth of dividend.

Although the yield on a growth-oriented stocks is initially lower compared to yield-oriented stocks, an increasing dividend and an increasing share price could lead to a more stable long-term total return.

Choosing the Largest Stream of Net Present Value Dividends

Let's say you need to choose between two different dividend-paying stocks. Which would you include in your portfolio?

- Company A has a dividend yield of 3.5%. The company has a track record of increasing the dividend by 5% per year and the current dividend payout ratio is at 60 per cent.
- Company B has a dividend yield of 0.80%. It is growing at a fast rate of 20%. The current dividend payout ratio is 10 per cent.

With everything else equal, you are more likely to choose Company B if you are following a high dividend growth rate strategy. Company A may look like the better choice, but if you choose Company B, you will end up cashing in bigger aggregate dividend checks when you own stocks from Company B, as long as the growth could be sustained in the next decade.

As the dividends increase alongside earnings, the yield-on-cost begins to overtake the company with minimal growth.

Eventually, the core business will reach its full potential and majority of the surplus generated every year will support reinvestment plus dividend payout. When this milestone is achieved, stockholder-friendly business management will return the excess profits to the owners through share buybacks or dividend payouts.

Good examples are Wal-Mart and McDonald's. During the early years of their business, when these companies were conquering each state in the US, the dividends were not very high. But investors who had bought their stocks were able to collect a fairly huge dividend yield on their cost basis within five to eight years.

Investors in the 1970s and the 1980s who used the high dividend growth strategy would not miss these present-day blue chip stocks.

Growth Is an Indicator of a Healthy Business

Which scenario will give you peace of mind?

- Owning stocks of a company that is paying you huge dividend today and is seeing a slow decline in its core business
- Owning stocks of a company that is paying you a smaller dividend today but enjoys higher profits each year

If you think there is a level of extra security in the company, you may want to consider a high dividend growth strategy. This is a wiser approach.

The board of directors of a company is unlikely to increase the dividend if they think they are going to have to cut it soon. Hence, a rising dividend rate on a per share basis usually signifies a vote of confidence from the people who have seen and analyzed the company's balance sheet and income statement.

But take note that this is not foolproof. Business executives who have the skills and expertise to serve in the board of directors are still vulnerable to self-deception, especially if it falls down to their own interest. But more often than not, this is a good indicator of company health.

Financial Gravity and Dividend Growth Investing

The biggest risk to the high dividend growth rate strategy is a primary macro movement that is beyond your control as an investor. This is the rate of interest in the market.
In fact, Warren Buffet calls interest rates as the financial gravity, because it seems universal in the financial world. All financial assets that will pay you some form of income streams such as interest income, dividends, and earnings are all priced relative to the interest rates determined by the government.

In comparison to historic standards, the stock PEs today are near nose-bleed levels while the dividends are minimal. This is primarily due to the current situation where the US Federal Reserve has pushed down the yield on all federal bonds to remarkably low levels.

Basically, the short-term federal bonds are considered as representative of the risk-free interest rate that you can earn on your money. Hence, all other assets are priced relative to these bonds. If the federal bond yields plummet, many investors look for instruments that can provide higher yields such as stocks.

This has been beneficial for investors over the two decades. As the interest rates fall the share price and bonds have increased, keeping the bond and stock markets floating and even generating enough capital gains.

It becomes problematic when interest rates start to increase - as they will do eventually. While the long term trend gravitates towards lower dividend yield, the interest rates still follow a cycle. They still rise and fall to keep the inflation in check and aids in boosting the economy. With interest rates at an all-time low, there's no way to go but up.

As an example, let's take a closer look at a hypothetical federal 30 year bond that yields 2% per annum and a hypothetical company known as Riveratic with stock at $100. Let's also say that similar to federal bonds, Riveratic's profits are not growing. Meanwhile, the financial position of the company is quite solid so its stock yield stands at 4 per cent.

In making an investment decision, you need to tackle this tradeoff. If you need a higher yield, you would definitely buy stocks of Riveratic. But if you need a rock solid stream of interest payouts you would definitely choose the federal bonds.

What will happen if the yield of the federal bond increases to 4%? In this case, both the Riveratic stocks and the 30 year federal bonds will yield the same amount. Now, which would you rather invest in?

Considering the same growth rate and the higher risk in Riveratic profits, you would go for federal bonds. In this case, there is no actual benefit in investing in Riveratic stocks. However, there is significant downside risk.

Other dividend investors will see this, so if the government rates increase, investors are willing to pay less for stocks or non-federal bonds. Share prices will fall to correct the relative valuation. In this case, Riveratic's dividend yield would have to double to recover its proper valuation versus federal bonds.

As a result, the share price would be decreased by 50%. Those who invested in Riveratic stocks would have lost the same percentage of their capital. And this will not be a short-term loss. That money will not be recovered.

Federal bonds today yield at 2.35% and the dividend growth stocks are not providing higher yield. Once US government rates eventually increase, investors who have invested in stocks priced on yield or profits will also lose a lot of money.

Dividend Growth Rate Strategy Is not a Fail-Proof Strategy

Majority of growth-oriented companies have increased their share prices as investors look forward to a long string of growing dividend payouts. But there is still a risk if the company fails to deliver its promises, which is fairly common in the business world.

Many businesses, even those that are already established ones, are managed by a business executive who is still prone to commit errors. For example, Best Buy was one of the most promising growth-oriented company for many years.

Looking back at its track record, it was easy to see a remarkable record of profit and growth. The company had a stable balance sheet and was even buying back shares. This stock price increased to reflect the past record of the company. However, in 2006, there was a clear indicator that the Best Buy's stock performance is no longer sustainable.

The company's growth started to slow down and its solid performance shifted into losses. The stock plummeted from $60 in 2006 to just $12 in 2012. Shareholders lost around 80 per cent of their holdings and the Best Buy stock is yet to fully recover from its loss (as of Feb 2019).

Unfortunately, this is not an isolated case. Companies experience major declines in performance. According to research conducted by Richard Foster from Yale University, the average lifespan of a company included in the S&P 500 plummeted from 67 years in the 1920s to just 15 years in 2015.

One of the primary reasons companies are eliminated from the index is due to financial distress. In fact, in 2015, around 44 companies in the S&P Index paid more than 100 per cent of their EPS!

Stock analysts today agree that dividend growth over the years will slow down by 45 per cent. This is an early indicator of financial distress.

Moreover, there are many companies that are no longer investing in profit-generating assets. The common practice nowadays is to use cash flow to decrease shareholder equity. This could pump up reported profits, but eventually, even this strategy has its own limitations. The share price traction of companies that are cutting dividends is usually not good.

Dividend growth investing precludes strong margins of safety, which would help in protecting against performance decline. The primary focus of this strategy is on growth and not on safeguarding principle that demands a strong safety margin.

Remember, there is a limit on dividend growth, and by paying up for assumed growth, you might be putting your capital at serious risk in the prospect of increasing your passive income.

Stock Performance of Growth-Oriented Dividend Stocks

If you like to hold a decent stream of growing dividends, then you need to choose companies with strong competitive advantages. This is one of the strategies used by Warren Buffett.

Without this, the company performance is likely to go back to a more usual level of growth and profitability and the value of your stock is likely to crater as a result.

This is known as reversion to the mean and it is a common phenomenon in the financial world.

Competitive advantages (also referred to as moats by Buffet) will gradually weaken over time. Remember, moats cannot protect your castle forever. Time will come that new technology will be developed and disrupt the core business.

But let's say that you really want to focus on looking for firms with solid moats. Companies such as Google, Harley Davidson, and Coca Cola are some of the obvious ones. However, these companies are expensive today.

There is always the possibility that your gut feeling is wrong. In addition, many investors under-estimate the skills and experience needed to execute a high dividend growth rate strategy.

The dividend growth stocks that are performing well today are considered as the survivors. These are the companies that have been consistent and withstood the test of time, while other companies in the same sector already closed shop or are still struggling.

Bear in mind that the survival of a dividend growing company over a number of years could either be driven by its competitive advantage or luck. The company's previous performance has no effect on its present business.

Interesting Fact #6

Blue Chips: This prestigious nickname is reserved for companies that are nationally known and trade high on the stock market. The name is derived from the highest value poker chip, which is blue. Companies considered "blue chips" include General Mills, the Kellogg Company, IBM and Johnson & Johnson.

Chapter 16

How to Find the Best Quality Dividend Stocks for Your Portfolio

At this point, you should already understand that dividend investing is a slow and steady way of stock market investing. But this method can help you eventually win the race. Warren Buffett, the Oracle of Omaha, is popular for investing in blue-chip stocks that are paying dividends.

Dividend investing has helped Buffet to become one of the richest men on Earth. He is also popular for his strategy of reinvesting dividends. This approach is an effective tactic in stock market investing. Dividends will provide you protection from inflation, which is non-existent when it comes to bonds.

At first, this strategy may seem very easy to follow. After all, you have to look for companies that are paying dividends. Then instead of cashing out those dividends, you can reinvest them so you can gradually build your wealth.

Unfortunately, it's not that easy. You should make certain that you are investing your money in a company that has good traction and prospects. Ignoring due diligence could lead to a depreciation of share price, elimination of dividend, or dividend cuts.

In this Chapter, we will discuss the important factors that you should look for in a stock dividend:

Low Earnings, Strong Cash Projections

Consistent cash flow should be your number one criteria in choosing stock dividends for your portfolio. Stay away from companies that are not consistently profitable.

It is easy to see healthy dividend returns from companies that can deliver you profits but not profitable growth on a yearly basis. But because there are companies that are growing as well as consistently making profits, it is nonsense to select the former. Be strict in your criteria and only choose companies that demonstrate growth and profitability.

Ideally, you should look for long-term profit growth expectations between 5 percent and 15 per cent. You should not go beyond 15 per cent because of the high probability of revenue disappointments that may affect the share price.

Even though profits can drive profitable growth and are an important indicator of a quality dividend-paying business, you should always take note that dividends will be sourced out from the company cash flow. In this case, the next step is to ensure that the company has the capacity to generate cash sustainably (i.e. the company is not in a very cyclical industry, the company has shown to either maintain or improve their margins etc.)

You should also look for companies that have increased their dividend payouts in the last five years. This significantly increases the odds of sustainable dividend growth, which is a huge plus for investors. And of course, you need to buy the shares before the ex-dividend date.

Check Sector Health

Most investors often overlook the importance of checking the health of the industry. At this moment, the banking industry is suffering because of additional regulation and the emergence of disruptive technology.

The share prices have sold off, and because of weakening demand, share price appreciation and dividend increases may not happen in the future.

Meanwhile, with an ageing population, the demand for care services for the old will increase in the next 20 to 30 years. This doesn't guarantee that stocks of healthcare companies will be immune to wider market plunges, but they are more likely to become more resilient compared to other stocks. There is a higher chance of dividend appreciation as long as the industry is doing well.

The point here is that you should never choose a stock based on history because it doesn't guarantee the future. Let's consider the case of carbonated beverages. With the emergence of health consciousness among consumers, investing in soda companies doesn't guarantee success like it used to in the past.

The big players in this industry are now shifting into the alternative drink niche but it will take some time before they can catch up with the demand. Take the smoother road instead of a rough one.

Avoid Companies with High Debt

On your prospect list, eliminate the dividend-paying companies with too much debt. You can learn about the company's current debt situation by looking at its debt-to-equity ratio. Look elsewhere if the company's D/E ratio is high.

However, you may still want to consider excluding stocks with D/E ratio upwards of 2.00. The ideal ratio is 1.00, which will give you peace of mind.

This is actually quite basic. If the company has excessive debt, then it will need to pay its debt at some point. Once the debt becomes due, it will require the extra cash to settle. This may affect dividend payouts.

Be sure to check the company's net debt-to-capital. Although it could be helpful during special circumstances, financial leverage can be quite dangerous. If you have felt the pains of overpriced home mortgage or credit card debt you will understand that borrowed money could be problematic if we overextend ourselves.

The same is true for businesses regardless of size and industry. This is the primary reason why you should take a look at the net debt-to-capital ratio of the company. This financial metric will tell you how much debt the business is using for its operations.

If a business has $100 Million worth of equipment, it acquired this important asset through a combination of equity and debt. You can figure out what percentage of a company's financing is from debt if you take a look at its debt-to-capital ratio.

Let's say that the equipment was supported by 30% debt and 70% equity. The debt-to-capital ratio of the company would appear as follows total book debt ($30 million) divided by total book debt ($30 million) plus equity ($70).

These figures would lead to a debt-to-capital ratio of 30% ($30M / $100M). To put it simply, debt accounts for 30% of the capital structure of the company we are looking at.

It is ideal to invest in a company with a net debt-to-capital ratio that is not higher than 50%. However, some sectors such as utilities could reasonably take on higher debt levels because of the *stability of their revenue.*

When a business suddenly falls during an economic recession and has high debt volume and interest to pay with its limited cash flow, the stock price could be dramatically affected and the dividend payout could become much riskier. Take note that companies will always prioritize their debt obligations before they pay a dividend.

Choose Companies that Offer Real Value

You might be attracted by businesses that are "booming" based on stock price. However, there is always the risk of you chasing the market, which is not always the best move you can make.

It is ideal to consider stocks of companies that are trading below their actual value. Businesses that have products or services that are of high quality and value are more likely to succeed.

While their share price may look average or below average, the value of what they can offer to their customers could usually make certain that their performance becomes more consistent over time.

But even businesses that are seeing a sharp decline in their stock price could be a lucrative choice to add in your portfolio. You should assess every business based on merits. A lower stock price can provide you the opportunity to invest in these companies below their actual value.

At face value, investing in a company whose stock price plummets at an unpredicted market movement may look like a bad decision. However, if you could see that the core business of the company shall continue to stay in demand in the next 20 to 30 years, one small incident will not make the company a bad investment.

As a matter of fact, the best time to buy company stocks is when their stocks are undervalued. As an investor, you should know how to assess the events that could damage the company or the whole industry and evaluate and if depreciating stock prices could reflect the whole value of the product or service that they offer. On the other hand, it may be a good time to buy into them while dividend stocks are trading below their real value.

Choose Companies with Excellent Management

You should pick companies that are managed by business executives that demonstrate discipline and excellence. The company managers play a vital role in creating wealth for you as a stockholder.

At first, it could be a bit difficult to determine if a company has a good management team. But the longer back you go, the more you can see if the business has a robust and consistent track record. Go through their previous financial statements and check how true or false management projections were (i.e. do they tend to exaggerate a lot or simply say the truth).

You should compare the performance of the company in comparison to similar companies in the sector over five years or 10 years. In addition, you should also see how the company has performed in comparison to the market index. If you are confident that the market is working out the truth, then the record should be manifested in the stock price.

Try to figure out which companies have decided to buy back shares when their shares are trading below value. This can help in adding stockholder wealth if the share prices begin to rise as this could reduce the number of shares. This is a good indicator that the management is loyal to their core business.

Meanwhile, you should be wary of businesses that are buying up other businesses beyond their industry or area of expertise. This is usually an indicator that the management is overreaching to grow the company.

Stay Away from Companies with Excessive Dividend Yields

It is ideal to stay away from any company that is offering dividend yields of more than 10% especially if the market average stands at or near 4.5 per cent. This is an indicator that the market believes that the current payout ratio of the company and its dividends are not sustainable.

Take note that the yield is based on historical dividend payouts over the last 12 months as a portion of the existing stock price. Just because a business has a history of maintaining certain dividend yield levels in the past, doesn't mean that they are still capable of doing so in the future. A plummeting stock price could mirror the expectation of the market for lower dividends in the future.

This may also mean that the business is using debt instruments to finance dividend payouts for stockholders. This is known as a dividend recapitalization. It is crucial to look at the cash track record of the company going back several years. This will allow you to avoid companies that are using debt to finance their dividend payouts. By doing this, you can also figure out how much of the dividend has come from the company's own cash profits.

You should bear in mind that if the dividend payouts are constantly lower than the amount of cash flow that the business has, it will help you to assess if they have the capacity to pay the dividend in the future.

Choose Stable Companies

In general, dividend companies are considered more stable because they usually provide basic necessities such as housing, gas, electricity, water, food, and even hygiene products. Hence, the typical sectors for dividends include:

- Real estate
- Finance
- Consumer staples (food, clothing, toiletries)
- Utilities
- Energy
- Telecommunications

Regardless of the state of the economy, people will always buy these products and services. Hence, the companies that provide them are usually more stable. Companies that are less stable usually provide products and services that people can easily let go - travel, restaurants, music, cellphones, and computers.

But every rule has its exceptions. Surely, many financials shattered the norm during the 2007 stock market bubble. However, the warning signs were already visible even before the bubble peaked. Savvy investors who saw the signs and read the "writing on the wall" bailed out early.

But in general, dividend companies are considered more stable compared to non-dividend companies. As a matter of fact, paying dividends is regarded as one key factor that helped some financial companies to survive the crash, assuming they have declined government bail out.

Dividend investors usually think that established companies are paying out a big percentage of their revenue as dividends because there are limited investment options that offer decent returns. But there is a more nuanced view in reality.

One example is the case of General Electric (GE), which is a matured company that has consistently increased its dividend payouts. However, the company has invested a nice percentage of its profits into diversification and growth. It has built and currently runs a dozen primary business units from household appliances to jet aircraft engines.

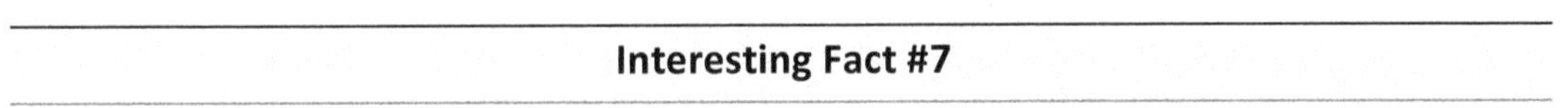

Interesting Fact #7

The Dutch East India Company, which is involved in the spice trade, was among the first companies to offer shares. Shareholders didn't have much influence – the company was controlled by its directors. However, shareholders were richly rewarded. The annual dividends were 16% on average over the first half of the 17th century.

Chapter 17

Where to Find Information on Companies

Picking stocks to buy for your dividend portfolio requires a lot of time and effort for research and analysis. Also, you need to compete with stock market professionals and fund managers who have more experience and have exclusive access to valuable insights.
But if you have the time and resources to keep an eye on the dividend market and the economy, this will be a worthwhile endeavor as dividends can provide you stable passive income and possible growth of your wealth over time.

Understand the Current US Economy and Financial Environment

It is crucial to take a closer look at the current US economy and financial setting before you start buying dividend stocks. Educate yourself about how the market and economic movements can affect your dividend investments.

You can make better investment decisions if you can access reliable information. Below are the best places where you can read information about market changes:

The Federal Reserve System

The board publishes a regular Financial Stability Report. This report summarizes the framework of the Federal Reserve Board in evaluating the status and resilience of the American financial system. The board also publishes special economic research to help investors gauge specific industries.

The research section of banks and stockbrokers

You should read expert forecasts about economic conditions in the US

Business newspapers such as:

- The Wall Street Journal
- Financial Times
- The Economic Times
- Business Standard
- International Business Times
- Investor's Business Daily

The business section of reputable newspapers such as:

- The New York Times
- Chicago Tribune
- The New York Post
- Los Angeles Times
- The Washington Post
- The Mercury News
- Credible business websites such as:
- Yahoo Finance
- Forbes

- MSN Money Central
- CNN Money
- WSJ
- Google Finance
- Bloomberg
- CNBC

High-quality business magazines such as:

- Forbes
- Bloomberg Businessweek
- WIRED
- Entrepreneur
- Fortune
- Inc
- The Economist
- Consumer Reports

Topics that you should be updated with are the following:

- The American economy
- The US economic policy
- The interest rates
- Exchange rates
- Overseas markets and economies relevant to the industry you want to invest with
- Investor sentiment

You should also get updates on sector-specific or even local influences that could affect business profits.

Finding Dividend Stocks to Buy

1. Blue Chip Companies

If you want to choose your own dividend stocks, a great place, to begin with, is the S&P 500, which is a list of top 500 companies in the USA, popularly known as "blue chip" companies.

These companies are often well-established companies that are ideal for investors who are looking for stable returns with less risk. The top blue-chip companies that are paying dividends in the US are the following:

- American Capital Agency Corp
- Southern Copper Corp
- NuStar Energy L.P.
- AT&T Inc
- STMicroelectronics N.V.
- Lockheed Martin Corp.
- Eli Lilly & Co.
- Paychex Inc
- H&R Block Inc
- United Parcel Service Inc (UPS)

2. Speculative Companies

Businesses that are relatively new in the stock market and are not in the top 100 companies in the US are called speculative companies. While there is always the potential to gain huge returns, you may also suffer heavy losses. Speculative stocks are ideal for well-experienced investors who have the resources to risk their capital to gain higher returns. Also, there are very few speculative companies that are paying dividends.

3. Invest Your Money In a Company / Industry You Know

If you are just getting started in dividend investing, it is ideal to begin with a sector or business that you understand. You will have a much better chance to assess if the business is strong or weak if you are familiar with the sector.

Take note that the US economy and the stock market are categorized into two major tiers. The upper tier (known as a sector) is a wide category of companies that have similar economic qualities. At present, there are 11 major sectors in the US that most dividend investors use in breaking down the companies.

Meanwhile, the sectors are categorized further by industry, which allows a narrower grouping of companies with similar businesses. For instance, luxury jeweler Tiffany & Company, and discount retail chain Dollar Tree are categorized in the consumer discretionary sector but they are categorized into separate industries.

Taking a closer look at industries and sectors will allow you to compare one company to its competitors. There is no way to know for sure if a specific dividend stock is good for purchase unless you assess the current competition.

Looking at industries and sectors will also help you become more familiar with how companies engage with one another. For instance, if you think that energy prices will fall, you may focus your attention on transportation shares because you think that among the largest cost inputs - jet fuel and gasoline - is about to fall. If used with long-term, low-turnover, discipline, and tax-efficient dividend investing, this knowledge can help you amass great wealth.

Stock Market Industry Sector Breakdown

In the US exchange, the stocks market has the following industry sectors:

a) Utilities

This is composed of water, gas, and electric companies including integrated providers. This industry generates stable recurring income by charging businesses and individual homes. Companies under this sector usually provide bigger dividend yields compared to other sectors.

b) Financials

This is composed of real estate firms, insurance companies, investment funds, and banks. Basically, the majority of the profits generated by the industry comes from loans and mortgages that gain value when interest rates increase.

c) Consumer Discretionary

This sector is composed of consumer durables, apparel companies, consumer service providers, media companies, and retailers. Basically, these companies take advantage of an improving economy when customer spending skyrockets.

d) Consumer Staples

The consumer staples sector is composed of food and beverage businesses and other companies that manufacture products that the majority of customers are not willing to forego from their every day living. Basically, companies in the consumer staples sector are capable of surviving and even thriving in a financial downturn.

e) Healthcare

The healthcare sector is composed of medical device manufacturers, hospital management companies, pharmaceuticals, biotechnology firms, and more. This sector is considered as both defensive and growth sector as people will always need healthcare.

f) Energy

The energy sector is composed of energy production companies, oil and gas exploration firms, and integrated power businesses. These companies are generating profits that are tied to the price of natural gas, crude oil, and other commodities.

g) Telecom

The telecom sector is composed of satellite companies, internet service providers, cable companies, and wireless providers. These companies generate recurring revenue from consumers. However, some subcategories of the industry are experiencing rapid changes.

h) Technology

This sector is composed of information technology firms, software developers, and electronics manufacturers. Basically, these businesses are driven by the general health of the economy and upgrade cycles, even though it has experienced growth over the years.

i) Real Estate

The real estate sector is composed of companies that are invested in retail, industrial, and residential real estate. The primary source of profits for this sector comes from real estate capital appreciation and rental income. Hence, this sector is quite vulnerable to changes in the interest rate.

j) Industrial

This sector is composed of manufacturing, fabrication, construction, machinery, defense, and aerospace companies. Basically, the growth in this industry is driven by the demand for manufactured and construction products such as agricultural tools and equipment.

k) Materials

The materials sector is composed of forestry, chemical, refining, and mining-related companies that are mainly focused on discovering and developing raw materials. Because these companies are at the start of the supply chain, these are sensitive to the changes in the business cycle.

When you have a list of companies, it will help you a lot to consider the current competition and how it stands compared to other companies in the sector.

You must figure out:

- The position of the company in the market
- The sustainability of the products and services that the company provides
- The growth opportunity of the company in the future

Company Due Diligence

Remember, the value of your dividend investment depends on the health of the company. Hence, it is crucial to perform the necessary due diligence before you buy shares.

Due diligence refers to an audit or investigation of a possible dividend investment so you can verify all the available facts. This includes the review of all financials on top of other necessary materials.

In the finance world, due diligence is conducted by companies who want to make acquisitions. This could be performed by investment analysts, investment brokers/dealers, fund managers, or equity research analysts.

For individual dividend investors, due diligence is voluntary yet highly recommended. However, investment brokers are legally mandated to perform due diligence before selling. This will prevent them from being held liable for non-disclosure of important information.

In the US, due diligence became a common term and practice due to the passage of the Securities Act of 1933. Stockbrokers have the obligation to completely disclose material information that is related to the financial instruments that they are offering. Without this disclosure, stockbrokers could be liable for a criminal offense.

But the authors of the Securities Act know that the full disclosure obligation could leave stockbrokers weak against unfair prosecution if they have failed to disclose materials that they did not possess.

To protect the stockbrokers, the Act added a legal defense, which states that as long as the brokers performed due diligence in evaluating companies whose stocks they were selling, and completely disclosed their results to investors, they cannot be held liable for any information not discovered during the process.

The Process of Due Diligence

Here is a step-by-step process for conducting due diligence when you are searching for a potential addition to your dividend portfolio. Aside from dividend equities, you can also use this process for evaluating real estate, debt instruments, and other forms of investments.

Step 1 - Check the Total Value (Capitalization) of the Business

The very first step in performing due diligence for your potential dividend investments is to check how big the business is. Basically, the market capitalization of the company will allow you to assess the volatility of its stocks, the possible size of the end markets of the business, and how wide the ownership could be.

For instance, mega cap and large cap businesses tend to have more established revenue streams and a diverse investor base. This translates to less volatility.

On the other hand, small cap and mid cap businesses may only cater to specific market areas, and could have regular fluctuations in their earnings and share price.

Once you begin examining profit and revenue numbers, the market capitalization will provide you better insights.

Step 2 - Take a Look at Margin Trends, Profit, and Revenue

In conducting due diligence for dividend investment, it is ideal to begin with the profit margin and revenue trends. It is crucial for any dividend investment to understand the gross revenue, profit margins, and ROE of the company. You should also check if the company is growing or downsizing.

Be sure to check the profit margins to see if they are rising, plummeting, or have simply plateaued. Many dividend investors prefer companies with profit margins equal to 50 or higher. This piece of information is crucial for the succeeding steps.

Step 3 - Benchmark the Company with Competitors and Industries

After checking the size of the company and making a sense of how much cash it can generate, the next step is to check the industries it is operating in as well as its competitors. Remember, each business is partially defined by the competition.

Be sure to compare the profit margins of two to three competitors. Checking out the major competitors in every line of business could help you in estimating the size of the end markets for the company's products or services.

- Can you consider the business as a leader in the industry?
- What is the current status of its industry?
- Is it growing?
- Could the company's position in the industry drastically change in the next five to 10 years?

You can search for information about competitors in company profiles on many research resources, often along with a comprehensive list of specific metrics filled in for the company you are looking into and its main competitors.

If you are still not certain of the business model of the company, you must look to fill the unknown details in this step before you proceed. There are instances where investigating the competitors may help you to better understand the business of your target company.

Step 4 - Study the Valuation Multiples

The next step is to take a closer look at the details of P/S ratio, PEGs ratio, and P/E ratio, and other relevant figures. Be sure to include the figures not only for your target competitor but also for its competitors.

Be sure to note any significant discrepancies between competitors for a more comprehensive review. Many investors discover more potential dividend investments in this step. But don't easily abandon your original target.

Looking into the P/E ratios will form the initial basis for studying the valuations. Even though earnings can and will affect the volatility, valuations that are based on current estimates or trailing earnings can be used as a way to measure several or direct competition.

You can compare the basic growth stock and value stock alongside the general sense on the level of expectation built into the company. Basically, it is a good idea to assess the net earnings of the company within a specific period (commonly five years) to make sure that you are looking into the latest figures (and the one you have used to compute the P/E) is more stable, and not affected by a one-time charge for adjustment.

The P/E is not a standalone metric, but rather it is used alongside revenue ratio, the enterprise multiple, and P/B ratio. These multiples underscore the company valuation as it relates to the balance sheet, annual revenues and debt volume. Because the range in these values varies from one sector to another, it is vital to study the same figures for some competitors.

Lastly, checking the PEG ratio will allow you to look into the projection for possible earnings in the future and how it compares to the actual earnings multiple in the present.

In some sectors, this ratio could be less than one, while in other areas, this could be as much as 10 or higher. Shares with PEG ratios close to one are regarded as fairly valued under normal conditions in the market.

Step 5 - Review the Stock Ownership and Management

Is the business still managed by its founders? Or has the business hired executives to professional run the enterprise? Take note that the age of the business is a vital factor here, as younger companies have the tendency to have more of the founding members still playing vital roles.

Read the profiles of business executives to check what type of expertise and experience they have. You can find this information on SEC filings and company websites.

Also, check if the founders and business executives still hold a high percentage of stocks, and verify the volume of the float held by institutional investors. This is important to check because it shows how much analyst coverage that the business can take advantage as well as other factors that can affect the volumes of the trade in the market.

Low ownership of shares among business executives is a red flag, while high ownership of shares among top managers is a good sign. Stockholders tend to be best served if people running the company also have their own stake in the stock performance.

Step 6 - Examine the Company's Balance Sheet

An entire book could be devoted just to discuss the balance sheet. However, for the initial due diligence, a light examination can do the job. Find the summarized balance sheet of the company you are looking into and check the general level of assets and liabilities.

Be sure to pay attention to the company's capacity to pay short-term liabilities (cash levels) and the volume of long-term debt held by the business.

High volume of debt doesn't necessarily mean that the business is in bad shape. This still depends on the business model of the company. But be sure to check the agency ratings for the company bonds.

Also, check if the company is capable of generating enough cash to service its debt and issue dividend payouts. Some businesses (and sectors) require intensive capital, while others only need skeletal resources to operate.

Check the D/E ratio to see if the company has positive equity, then compare this metric with the company's competitors so you can gain a better perspective. Basically, the more cash a business can generate, the better the investment.

Try to figure out the reason behind if the figures in the top line (stockholders equity, total liabilities, and total assets) changed drastically from one year to another. Read the footnotes in the financial statements so you can understand the situation of the business.

The company might be whittling away at important capital resources, accumulating retained earnings, or preparing a new product.

Step 7 - Share Price History

In this step, you should start looking into how long all shares of classes are trading including both long-term and short-term price movement. Check if the share price has been steady, smooth, volatile, or choppy. Also check the share price in different time horizons - 3 months, 6 months, 1 year, 3 years, 5 years, and 10 years. Is it falling or rising? Does the profit trends and history match with each other?
This will show you what type of profit experience the average stockholder has seen that can affect the future movement of stocks. Bear in mind that stocks that are constantly volatile tend to have short-term stockholders that could add extra risk factors to specific investors.

Step 8 - Dilution Possibilities and Stock Options

Savvy dividend investors should next look into 10-K and 10-Q reports. Check the quarterly SEC filings of the company to see all outstanding share options and the projected conversion considering a range of stock prices in the future.

You can use this to help you understand how the share count may change under various price points. Is it possible for the company to achieve a secondary offering?

Even though employee stock options are strong motivators, be wary of any formal investigations that have been launched into shady practices such as options backdating.

Step 9 - Read Expert Projections

This step requires extra effort in the investigation. You should learn the consensus of stock analysts for profit estimates, revenue, and earnings growth for at least two years ahead.

Try to make sense of the discussions involving long-term trends that affect the sector and company-specific details about new products/services, intellectual property, joint ventures, and partnerships.

Probably, news about new business products or service first attracted you towards the stock, and now could be the time to assess it more fully with the help of all the information you have gathered so far.

Step 10 - Analyze Short and Long-Term Risks

Reserving this important piece at the end of the due diligence process will ensure that investors will always remember the risks that come with investment. Make certain that you understand both company-specific and industry-wide risks.

Is the company facing regulatory or legal concerns or just a spotty record with business managers? Is the business implementing eco-friendly policies? And what type of long-term risks could lead from it following green policies?

As an investor, you must play the devil's advocate preparing for worst-case scenarios and their possible effect on the stock. How would the company survive if a new competitor brings a better product or a new product fails?

How can you manage the downside risk? For dividend bonds, how would a decline in interest rates affect the capacity of the instrument to grow money and make money?

After completing these steps, you must be able to understand what the business is doing so far, and how it could fit into your investment strategy.

Eventually, you will have your own metrics that you can follow in performing your due diligence, but following these guidelines must save you from missing something that can be vital for your decision.

Other Important Source of Information in Researching for Stock Dividends

Annual Reports

The annual report of a company is one of the best sources of information. This will provide you with vital information about the company such as:

- Core business performance
- Business strategy
- Whether the business is making profits or losing money
- Future prospects

You may find it overwhelming to read the company annual reports, so we have specified the vital things that you must look out for.

Track Record

Make sure that the activities included in the annual report are the same as what the business said it will do in the report of the previous year. Check if the current strategy is similar as described in the past statement or report. If the strategy has changed, think how will it affect the performance of your investment.

Also, consider the ultimate goals of the company. Are the activities of the company aligned with its goals? For example, did the company say it would develop technology for the insurance industry, but is now considering accounting software for the pharmaceutical sector?

Important Strategic Acquisitions

In some instances, 'strategic acquisitions' could detract from stockholder value. When the company is expanding by acquiring other companies, you should look at the effect and check if it can add value to the company.

For instance, will the new business produce new products or services, develop new technologies or provide access to new markets? This can really affect the stock price.

Profits and Loss

In reviewing the financial side of the annual report, you should carefully assess the actual profit of the company and its source. Did the business make a profit or loss?

If the company is losing money did the management give a reason for it? Established companies should be already making profits, while startup companies usually don't make money during their early years. In this case, the management may indicate in the yearly report when they are expecting the business to make revenue.

Available Cash for Operations

Don't forget to take a look at the cash flow of the company. Is the company using its own money or has it accessed additional funding through loans or through the issuance of securities that can be converted into shares later on? If the company has approved the issuance of additional shares in the current year, have these affected the shares of current investors?

Research & Development Results

Also, check if the money invested in research and development activities has resulted in tangible outcomes such as the development of high technology product or first sale of a software application. This also involves entering into partnership or understanding with another company to use the technology it has developed.

Enough Cash Supply

You should also check the expenditures of the company. Evaluate if the company will have enough cash on hand until profits start to be generated. Without enough cash supply, how will the company meet its requirements? Can it access credit offers or will it try to raise more money from investors?

Annual reports are typically available on the website of the company for download. Most businesses are happy to send you a printed copy of their annual report upon request. But this depends on the company. You can instead directly contact the company if you are not sure.

Consider the annual report as the report card for dividend stock companies. By assessing its performance over the previous financial year, you can decide if the company is worthy to be included in your dividend portfolio.

Interesting Fact #8

Stock trading in England started when King William tried to raise money for England's wars in 1693, and English stock companies followed suit very quickly. Trading first started on the Royal Exchange, but the first stockbrokers were so rude that they were banned. Because of this, they started to trade in coffeehouses along Exchange Alley, which quickly led to the establishment of the London Stock Exchange.

Chapter 18

Dividend Reinvestment Programs (DRIP)

A dividend reinvestment program (DRIP) is a program offered by a company, which allows you to reinvest their cash dividends into added shares or fractional shares.

Many DRIPs will allow you to buy shares at zero commission and at a huge discount to the present stock price. Most companies also don't allow reinvestments lower than $10.

DRIPs are offered by dividend companies that provide shareholders the option of reinvesting the amount of a specified dividend by buying more shares. Basically, when dividends are paid, they are received by stockholders as a direct deposit into their bank account or a check sent to their home or office.

Take note that shares that are purchased through a DRIP usually come from the own reserve of the company. Hence, they are not marketable through stock exchanges. Shares should be directly redeemed via the company.

While you will not actually receive the dividends, you still need to report it as taxable income. When a company is offering a DRIP, you can set it up through a brokerage as most brokers allow dividend payments for reinvestment in the shares of any stock held in an investment profile.

Types of DRIPs

Reinvestment programs are now very popular among dividend investors. Hence, more companies are setting up their DRIPs. However, not all reinvestment plans are designed in the same way.

Direct DRIPs

Dividend companies that are running their own reinvestment programs will have a specific department (usually Investor Relations) to handle all aspects of the plan. Some companies allow individuals to buy company shares (to open a DRIP account) directly via this department without going through stock brokers.

Third-Party DRIPs

While most companies choose to operate their own reinvestment plans, other companies find the cost too high. As an alternative, they tap transfer agents or third parties who usually act on behalf of the company to manage all aspects of their DRIP.

Broker DRIPs

Another way to sign up for a reinvestment plan is through a brokerage. Due to the fact that not all companies have set up their own DRIP, some broker firms fill this void so investors can avail of DRIP perks at a fraction or even zero cost.

But you should take note that broker DRIPs usually allow only dividend reinvestment and offer no cash buying option. And of course, broker firms are also businesses that need to make revenue. So they usually only provide this special service for people who are already using their account for commissioned stock trades.

Benefits of DRIPs to the Company

Companies that are paying dividends can receive several benefits when they choose to run DRIPs.

Basically, if shares are purchased from the company for a DRIP, this will generate more capital for the company.

Meanwhile, stockholders who take part in a DRIP are less likely to sell their stocks even when the market plummets. This is due to the fact that the reinvested dividends are not as liquid as shares purchased in the stock market. Moreover, most investors easily recognize the role that their dividends play in their investment's long-term growth.

Benefits of DRIPs to the Investors

There are several benefits of buying shares through a reinvestment program. Basically, DRIPs can provide you an easy way to acquire more shares without the need to pay commission or brokerage fees.

Many companies are offering shares at a discount via their reinvestment program from 1 per cent to 10 per cent off the present price. Between price cutoff and zero commission, the cost basis for holding the shares can be remarkably lower if the shares were acquired in the open stock market.

On the other hand, the impact of automatic reinvestment is the largest advantage in the long-term. When your dividends increase, you can receive an increasing amount on every share you own. You can also use these shares so you can buy a bigger number of shares.

Eventually, this can boost the potential total return of the investment. Remember, you can buy more shares if the price of the stock decreases. On the other hand, the long-term potential for bigger gains also increase.

Downsides of DRIPs

Before you sign up for the reinvestment program offered by the dividend company, you should first understand the few disadvantages of DRIPs in general.

Primarily, those who are value investing will easily see a disadvantage with the reinvestment program, which falls on the minimal discretion on the price you are paying for new shares.

Under a DRIP, the purchase will be automatic and follows a price that is established by the current market price at dividend time. Whether or not this is a disadvantage really depends on how you perceive things. Just bear in mind that the acquired shares through the DRIP will be purchased at any stage of the market cycle. There will be times that you will buy shares at a very low price, while there will be instances that they are too expensive. The sure thing is, they will not even out.

Underwritten DRIPs

For companies who need a significant amount of capital, it is ideal for the shareholders to take part in the DRIP. While this is possible, it is not practical. So, some companies arrange to set up underwritten DRIPs.

In effect, the shareholders who choose to take part in the DRIP will receive payment in form of shares. On the other hand, the rest of the shares will be sold to another group under the terms of the underwriting policy. The cash that the company raises from the sale will be used to issue cash dividend to those shareholders who don't like additional shares.

In this case, the company has declared a dividend without paying one. Basically, this is a ridiculous practice, because shareholder interest is compromised. Be sure to stay away from companies that are underwriting their DRIPs.

The Impact of DRIP to the Stock Price

In a company-run DRIP the shares are issued from the own share reserves of the firm. If investors like to sell any shares acquired via DRIP, they can only sell them back to the company. Hence, a DRIP is operated by the business so it doesn't have any significant impact on the stock price of the shares in the market.

On the other hand, a DRIP operated by a brokerage firm purchases the shares directly through the secondary market. Since these shares are both sold and bought at the prevailing prices, a broker-operated DRIP will have the same impact on share prices as a regular buy/sell transaction in the open stock market.

Starting a DRIP Account

Getting started with a DRIP will require some effort. Basically, you should find dividend-paying companies that have DRIPs. The internet can significantly help you in looking for companies that have DRIPs.

After verifying that your company has a DRIP, you should confirm who is running the plan - the company or a third party? Then, you may need to buy company shares so you can set up your account.

To be eligible for a DRIP, you might be required by the company operating the plan to have your name registered in the stock certificate.

Take note that shares held in a brokerage account are rarely registered in the stockholder's name and are rather added in the street name. This makes it easier for the company because they don't need to phone brokerage firm to verify ownership.

The specific features of DRIPs may vary from one company to another. For instance, some companies allow optional cash purchases aside from reinvested dividends, while others only allow stockholders to buy shares based on their dividends. Be sure to clarify this fine detail before you open an account for a DRIP.

How Can Taxes Affect Your Drip Investment

Some investors wrongly think that their shares acquired through DRIPs are not taxable. This is a misconception mainly due to the fact that investors are not receiving a cash dividend per se. As a matter of fact, while DRIPs are attractive because of their cost-effective approach to investing, they are still subject to tax.

Even though reinvested, there is still an actual cash dividend that is considered an income so it is subject for taxation. And like any stock, capital gains from shares acquired via DRIP are not calculated and taxed until the shares are finally sold, normally after a few years.

Managing Volatility through DRIPs and Dollar Cost Averaging

You don't need a lot of capital to begin dividend investing thanks to DRIPs. You can start with next to nothing and end up with significant holdings plus passive income. A reinvestment program makes it possible to invest as low as $30 or $50 and acquire shares directly from the company without the need to open a brokerage account and pay broker's commissions or fees.

Not so many people are aware of direct reinvestment plans because no one is advertising them. Companies are also prohibited from advertising their reinvestment programs under SEC rules.

There is no such thing as zero-risk investment. Any form of investment has a certain level of risk. However, most investors usually get burned trying to sense the direction of the market. You can manage this risk through a reinvestment program. After a certain amount of time, your conservative investment strategy already has built your wealth by consistently investing the money that you might have spent on something you didn't actually need.

Hence, DRIPs can provide you access to the same level of risk-reducing strategies that are usually reserved for the big players. You can buy shares on the market dips and get holdings from a lot of diverse companies.

Moreover, you are less likely to react emotionally to financial updates and there is no need to worry too much about your broker. The reinvestment program will keep on adding shares that you own until you increase your wealth.

Signing up for a reinvestment program will allow you to take advantage of dollar cost averaging. This will let you invest as low as $25 in every company whenever you have some spare money to do so.

Through dollar cost averaging, you can ditch the guesswork. Even when the market is down, your reinvestment strategy will allow you to buy more shares that it would when the market is following an upward trend.

Dollar cost averaging is an efficient and effective long-term investment strategy. It makes saving easy especially if you are gunning for retirement holdings and income. All you need is a small yet consistent flow of money. This will help you stand your ground despite market changes. This is how savvy dividend investors place a cap on their upside and basically lose money in the stock market.

Using this approach, the cost will be considerably less compared to the trading price of the shares during the time you are investing. This is because you are automatically buying fewer shares when the stocks are selling at higher prices and sell more when the prices are lower. Definitely, this strategy is only ideal for those who are investing with a long-term outlook, usually not shorter than five years. This will not produce results for traders who are looking for quick cash.

With a reinvestment plan, you can put the dollar-cost averaging on autopilot. You can just invest a specific dollar amount regularly. The usual outcome is that you can obtain more shares at lower prices then fewer shares at higher prices. You can do this regularly with a no-fee DRIP and you can build wealth in the most cost-efficient approach.

Not similar to the conventional way of investing that is based on acquiring a specific number of shares, DRIP investment is based on dollar amounts. A zero-fee reinvestment program makes it easy to invest even small amounts regularly. Dollar cost averaging will also impose discipline on your investment because you decide how many dollars you want to invest on a schedule that you have determined ahead.

How Dollar Cost Averaging Can Boost Your Dividend Income

The example below will help you understand how your dividend income can be significantly improved if you sign up with a reinvestment program and use dollar cost averaging. In this example, we assume that you are investing in a stock that has zero fees. Let's say you are investing $100 every quarter and acquire however many shares your investment will buy at the present share price. Take a look at what will happen over time.

Dollar-Cost Average

Invest	$/Share	Share
$100	$12	8.3333
$100	$9	11.1111
$100	$30	3.3333
$100	$35	2.8571
$400		**25.6348**

Invest	$/Share	Share
$100	$35	2.8571
$100	$30	3.3333
$100	$12	8.3333
$100	$9	11.1111
$400		**25.6348**

Invest	$/Share	Share
$100	$9	11.1111
$100	$12	8.3333
$100	$30	3.3333
$100	$35	2.8571
$400		**25.6348**

Invest	$/Share	Share
$100	$30	3.3333
$100	$35	2.8571
$100	$9	11.1111
$100	$12	8.3333
$400		**25.6348**

Average price (based on the four investment prices) = **$21.50**
Average cost (based on the amount spent and the number of shares aquired) = **$15.60**

The price of the stock fluctuated between $9 and $35 with an average price of $21.50. However, the average cost per share was only $15.60 (i.e. $400/25.6348). You can buy more shares if the price is low and fewer shares if the price is high. This is precisely how you can buy low and sell high - the classic mantra in stock dividend investing.

Interesting Fact #9

Though they have the name, 'penny stocks' usually don't cost a penny. Instead, the Securities and Exchange Commission usually considers any stock under $5.00 a 'penny stock', according to sec.gov. They categorize most stocks under $5.00 with certain rules. I say 'most stocks' because when CITI was trading under $5.00, they didn't identify CITI as a penny stock, for whatever their reason. There are penny stocks that trade for a penny, but they don't have to trade for a penny to be called a 'penny stock'.

Chapter 19

How to Diversify Your Portfolio

Diversification is a risk management technique, which includes different types of investments in a portfolio. The core concept behind this strategy claims that an investment portfolio composed of diverse forms of investments shall on average, pose a lower risk and yield higher returns than any individual investment found inside the portfolio.

Diversifying your portfolio can ease out the unsystematic risk events so the instruments that are performing well can neutralize the negative performance of others. Hence, the advantages of diversification hold only if the investments in the portfolio *are not correlated with each other.*

What is Unsystematic Risk?

Unsystematic risk, also known as residual risk or specific risk, is often described as the risk that is inherent in a business or industry investment. The types of unsystematic risk involve a new competitor in the market with the potential to take considerable market share from the business.

Even though investors may be able to project some sources of this inherent risk, it is not always certain to be aware of how or when the risk could affect your investment.

For instance, an investor in aged care stocks might be aware that a huge shift in retirement policy is inevitable. However, there is no way to know in advance the details of the new policy and how aged care companies and consumers will react.

Mathematical models and market studies have shown that keeping a well-diversified portfolio of 25 to 30 stocks could yield the most cost-effective level of reducing risk. Investing in more securities could yield further diversification benefits but in a remarkably smaller rate.

You can also maximize the benefits of diversification if you invest in foreign securities because they have the tendency to be less affected with your investments in the domestic market.

For instance, a financial crisis in the US economy may not reach the Australian economy. Hence, having Australian investments can provide you with an added layer of protection against the possible losses due to the US downturn.

Many individual investors have limited capital and so you may find it not easy to build a well-balanced and diversified portfolio. This is the reason why mutual funds are growing in popularity. Acquiring shares in a mutual fund can provide you with a more affordable way to diversify your portfolio.

Why Should You Build a Diversified Dividend Portfolio?

If you invest all of your money in one business, despite the promise of low risk and high returns, you will likely yield returns that are considerably different compared to the performance of the market in general.

Many investors don't have the stomach for such volatility, especially because there are several unforeseen events that may happen to put your investment at risk of being lost permanently.

Do you still remember Lehman Brothers? What about Enron? Placing all your eggs in one basket can have disastrous effects.

On the other hand, let's say you have the means to buy shares of each stock in the market. For each company or industry in your portfolio that is struggling, there is a possibility that there are more industries in your portfolio that are growing.

Hence, you don't need to depend on any single company to boost your investment returns and dividend income. Your portfolio can sustain a few unfortunate events because you have a diverse form of investments across several businesses.

As long as the United States continues to exist and thrive, there will be virtually no reason for your portfolio to completely lose its value. The stock market has been appreciating over the years and there are no indications that this will be disrupted anytime soon.

A diversified and well-balanced portfolio can help you diversify your risk exposure and achieve your investment goals. Building a portfolio begins with an understanding of the primary risk factors that affect the volatility and profitability of your dividend investments.

Important Risk Factors to Consider in Building Your Portfolio

Below are the most important factors that can influence the returns of your portfolio relative to the returns in the market:

- The number of holdings
- The amount of financial leverage each holding has
- The correlation between holdings
- The size of the market capitalization of each holding

These risk factor can remarkably affect the performance of a portfolio, especially during bearish markets. Many investors are usually not aware that they are betting against their portfolios until it benefits them.

As an example, let's say that around 50% of your portfolio is invested in small-cap energy stocks with high financial leverage. As oil production and prices followed an upward trend, your portfolio has received excellent returns with lower volatility as of late 2014.

Many investors would often cite their skills instead of luck when the results are favorable. But this portfolio was nothing more than a factor bet on the sector and good conditions in the market.

When the price of oil plummets and there are fewer credits available to small-cap companies, the portfolio would lose a lot of its value.

The main point of building a portfolio is to diversify the factor bets that we cannot forecast or control and concentrate our returns on the performance of individual businesses.

The Number of Holdings

Many successful investment firms are running portfolios that are considered as concentrated. For instance, the lucrative Berkshire Hathaway has several holdings that go beyond the 10 per cent of the overall value of its stock portfolio. The firm led by Warren Buffet invests with conviction behind the best stocks in the market.

Chances are, you don't have the resources, insights, and connections of a big investment firm to successfully run a concentrated investment portfolio.

As such, it is ideal for individual investors to spread their bets over a reasonable range of various stocks so you can avoid shooting yourself in the foot with stock investments that go wayward.

The fewer holdings you have, the bigger chance that your portfolio can deviate from the returns in the market. Hence, it is crucial to determine the right number of holdings you should have to maximize the benefits of diversification.

It is interesting to note that professional stock market researchers tried to answer this question over half of the century. For instance, the American Association of Individual Investors (AAII) published an article which contends:

> "Holding a single stock rather than a perfectly diversified portfolio increases annual volatility by roughly 30%...Thus, the single-stock investor will experience annual returns that average a whopping 35% above or below the market - with some years closer to the market and some years further from the market."

This institutional research went on to cite that as a general rule, company-specific (diversified) risk could be reduced by the following figures:

- 95% risk reduced when you hold 400 stocks
- 90% risk reduced when you hold 100 stocks
- 80% risk reduced when you hold 25 stocks

Another study was published in 2014 entitled "Equity Portfolio Diversification: How Many Stocks are Enough? Evidence from Five Developed Markets."

This research discovered that a higher number of stocks are required to diversify the risk during the financial downturn. In this kind of economic climate, the correlation between stocks is usually the highest.

In the US, the study concluded that to be certain of decreasing 90% of the risk, 90% of the time, the number of stocks required on average is around 55. This can however increase to around 110 stocks during times of economic turmoil.

With the findings from these studies, the sweet spot would seem in between 25 and 100 stocks. But if you throw in math into the mix, you should also consider factors that are unique to your financial constraints - trading cost, availability of resources and time for due diligence, and the size of your portfolio.

The effect of trading costs on your total returns will be bigger if your portfolio is smaller. If you have a small account, you may need to buy dividend ETFs instead of individual stocks so you can easily achieve diversification and save money on trading costs. You need less time in performing due diligence if you own more positions.

Although this is subjective, holding between 20 and 65 stocks can provide you a reasonable balance considering the factors of available time for due diligence, saving money from trading costs and the need to diversify.

Concentrating on higher quality stocks with a narrower range of possible outcomes can help in reducing risk to support a more focused portfolio. Meanwhile, a portfolio that is filled with risky stocks may choose a direction towards diversification with around 65 holdings.

Many individual investors prefer to roughly equate their positions because it can be difficult to know which holdings will perform well in the long run. Eventually, you have a unique opinion as an individual investor on how much diversification is sufficient and how much risk you can tolerate.

Diversification in the Industry Level

While adding more stocks in your portfolio can help you diversify the risk, there are still investors who end up with portfolios that are not well diversified because they follow strict investing rules (buying only stocks with P/E ratio less than 12x) or specific types of stocks (consumer products with household brands).

But holding on several stocks with the same characteristics will not help you maximize the benefits of diversification. This is due to the fact that stocks from similar industries are usually sensitive to the same factors and they usually have the same inherent risks.

Your investment portfolio could drastically underperform in the market when a shared factor like oil price or interest rates becomes unfavorable. Choosing stocks from various industries and sectors can help in diversifying the risk because if some industries are struggling, others might be doing well.

Many savvy dividend investors prefer to invest no more than 25% of their portfolio into a single sector, and try to own company stocks with minimum overlap into their actual operations.

There's no surefire way to determine which areas of the market would come in or out of favor, so sector diversification is crucial. But sector diversification must not come at the expense of contradicting principles of valuation or reaching beyond your comfort zone.

Consumer staples account for around 7% of the S&P500, but it doesn't mean you should buy stocks from this sector if you can't find one that is priced attractively. Moreover, you must not diversify into an industry or sector that is outside your circle of competence.

For instance, many conservative dividend investors have few investments in the technology sector because it evolves at a fast pace. It can be challenging to predict which companies will still be relevant for the next several years.

The takeaway here is that you must be deliberate with your diversification across business models and sectors. You still need to think through your investments. Choose market sectors that you are comfortable with and carefully evaluate each possible dividend investment as you gear towards diversification.

Financial Leverage

Using financial leverage for your investment portfolio can help you magnify your returns. This is one of the important factors that you need to understand when you are looking for safe stocks. The higher the debt volume of the company, the higher the stock price may fluctuate depending on the economic and business climate.

Hence, companies with huge debt loads and are naturally cyclical often have more volatile stocks. Some of the highly leveraged, lower quality may struggle if interest rates suddenly rise and credit conditions become stricter.

In building a portfolio, it is crucial to be aware of the general credit quality of your holdings. For many forms of investments, it is ideal to see an investment grade credit rating, strong coverage ratios, and no more than 50 per cent free cash flow generation.

Size of Investment

Historically, businesses with small market caps have shown better share price volatility compared to businesses with large market caps. Large companies are more liquid because of the availability of buyers and sellers.

If you enter into an order to sell or buy stocks of Apple, there should be someone on the other side of the counter who will agree to your asking price for the trade to proceed.

Companies with smaller market caps ($2 billion and under) could have much less liquidity in comparison to big cap companies. With fewer trades in the market, it is often difficult to move in and out of positions. Also, the spread between the buyer and the seller could become quite wide.

With less active trading liquidity, companies with small caps can easily outperform or underperform big cap stocks in various market settings. Small cap stocks also have high volatility because their businesses are usually less diversified compared to big caps.

Time Horizon and Price Volatility

Aside from the four risk factors discussed above, you should also understand price volatility or beta. This will help you take advantage of their long-term holding periods so you can enhance your dividend portfolios.

Beta will help you measure the volatility of the stock price to the market. By default, the market has a 1.0 beta, and individual stocks are ranked based on how much they deviate from the market in general.

Stocks with beta of more than 1.0 swings more than the market over time. When a stock has moved below the market, the beta of the stock is lower than 1.0.

The risk factors discussed above largely affects the beta of the stock. Smaller companies with less predictable business models and high volume of financial leverage will normally have higher betas.

It is crucial for investors to understand the different emotional tendencies and risk tolerances despite the fact that beta is backward-looking.

An investment portfolio filled with stocks that have beta values higher than 1.0 will likely move a lot compared to a portfolio that is filled with stocks with low beta.

You should also take note that beta is based on near-term price volatility that is not usually affected by business fundamentals. To put it simply, for long-term investors, a low or high beta does not indicate if an investment will be profitable over the next five years.

One advantage of individual investors is the capacity to hold stocks for a longer duration to allow strong underlying fundamentals to be reflected in the price of the stock. Building your dividend investment portfolio follows a slower pace.

Basically, it is ideal to own shares of high-quality growth stocks at a reasonable price than to stay on the sidelines trying to beat the quarterly profits game or time the market. The time horizon should be on your side and not against you.

Diversifying Your Investment through Dividend ETFs

Many dividend investors diversify their portfolios through dividend exchange traded funds (ETFs). Basically, ETFs allow you to invest in a basket of high-dividend paying stocks.

Dividend ETFs are mainly established to achieve high yields when investing in high-dividend-paying real-estate investment trusts (REITs), preferred stocks, or common stocks.

Most dividend ETFs may contain only US stocks or they could be composed of international ETFs with a global focus. Many indexes used to build the dividend ETFs contain stocks with higher than average liquidity and above-market dividend yields. But take note that these will vary based on the fund manager of the ETF and their particular style.

Dividend ETFs are managed passively, which means they are monitoring a particular index, that is often filtered based on quantitative criteria to involve companies with a solid track record of dividend increases and more established blue-chip companies that are basically regarded to carry minimal risk.

The expense to dividend ratio must be lower or at least at par to the most affordable no-load mutual funds. By definition, you can buy or redeem no-load mutual funds after a specific duration of time without sales or commission charge. In general, dividend ETFs are ideal for risk-averse stock investors who are mainly seeking income.

Dividend ETFs Vs Other ETFs

In general, ETFs will provide you the opportunity to diversify an index fund and enable minimal trades as they don't have minimum deposit requirements. Moreover, the expense ratios of ETFs are lower compared to average mutual funds for commonly available ETFs in the stock market.

Adding dividend ETFs to your overall investment portfolio will provide you robust yet safe financial strategy, but there are also other forms of ETFs that you may consider and include in your portfolio for further diversification.

For instance, an Initial Public Offering (IPO) ETF can be enticing for investors who like to try investing in startup companies who are opening their business to the public. You can diversify your investment across different IPOs from different industries and sectors.

The benefits of investing in IPO ETFs are grounded in the upsides from possible beneficial growth in the stock price. However, initial IPO success doesn't guarantee stability and growth because the value of the holdings may decrease eventually. And of course, very few startup companies will offer dividend payouts on the onset so you have to think carefully of including this in your portfolio.

Meanwhile, Index ETFs monitor a benchmark index such as the S&P 500. You can trade index ETFs all day long on a primary stock exchange and you can take advantage of exposure to different securities in a single transaction.

Depending on the ETF you are tracking, index ETFs may include both American and international markets, different asset classes or specific sectors.

Lastly, the ETF of ETFs is mainly tracking other ETFs instead of an index or an underlying stock. This special type of ETF will provide you more opportunities for diversification compared to other ETFs.

ETF of ETFs are managed actively similar to funds in comparison with other ETFs that are managed passively. Thus, they can be designed to consider other factors such as your time horizon and risk tolerance. This approach will provide you with wide exposure to strategies across various class assets, immediate diversification, and minimal charges.

Building a dividend portfolio is part science, part art. This significantly depends on your available capital, risk tolerance, and goals. Taking a closer look at the important risk factors could affect the returns of a portfolio and could help you avoid taking unnecessary risk.

Below are risk management pointers that you should bear in mind:

- Stocks must be diversified across various sectors and industries, with no specific sector composing more than 25% of the value of the portfolio.
- Stocks with high financial leverage and higher volatility usually pose a greater risk for stockholders.
- Depending on due diligence constraints and portfolio size, holding between 20 and 60 well-balanced stocks is reasonable for individual investors.
- Small cap stocks have high volatility compared to large cap stocks
- A stock beta will help you determine the volatility of the stock in relation to the market
- You are basically speculating if you invest with a time horizon in months or quarters

As an individual investor, you should review your personal goals and keep the above factors in mind.

Interesting Fact #10

While it may be true that some people get lucky and actually make money in penny stocks, these stories are rare. Remember that there are a lot of scam artists out there - if you have ever heard of the phrase "pump and dump" that's where the term comes from. Experienced people in the business of scamming others with penny stocks can easily 'hype up' a random ticker symbol and when everyone is in, they will go ahead and sell, and leave you penniless.

Chapter 20

When to Sell a Dividend Stock

Most literature about dividend investing focuses on what stocks to buy and how to build your dividend portfolio. The area of selling stocks is not usually discussed, because many investors are more excited about buying stocks than selling.

Our minds are more focused on how much profit we can make in stock investing, and how our dividend payments will grow. If you sell a stock, it is either you need to use the money in your investment or you think that there is better investment available elsewhere. This is arguably boring compared to the prospect of making profits purchasing new shares.

Two Major Reasons to Sell Dividend Stocks

There are two major reasons to help you decide if it is time to sell your stocks:

- If the stocks are selling above fair value
- If the stocks are on the verge of losing or have already lost their competitive advantage

Why Sell Overpriced Stocks?

It is ideal to sell dividend stocks with a normalized P/E ratio above 40. Historically, stocks with high P/E ratio have significantly underperformed shares with low P/E ratios. The Compustat-Faceset image below shows the performance of stocks with high P/E ratios compared to stocks with low P/E ratios in a period of 35 years.

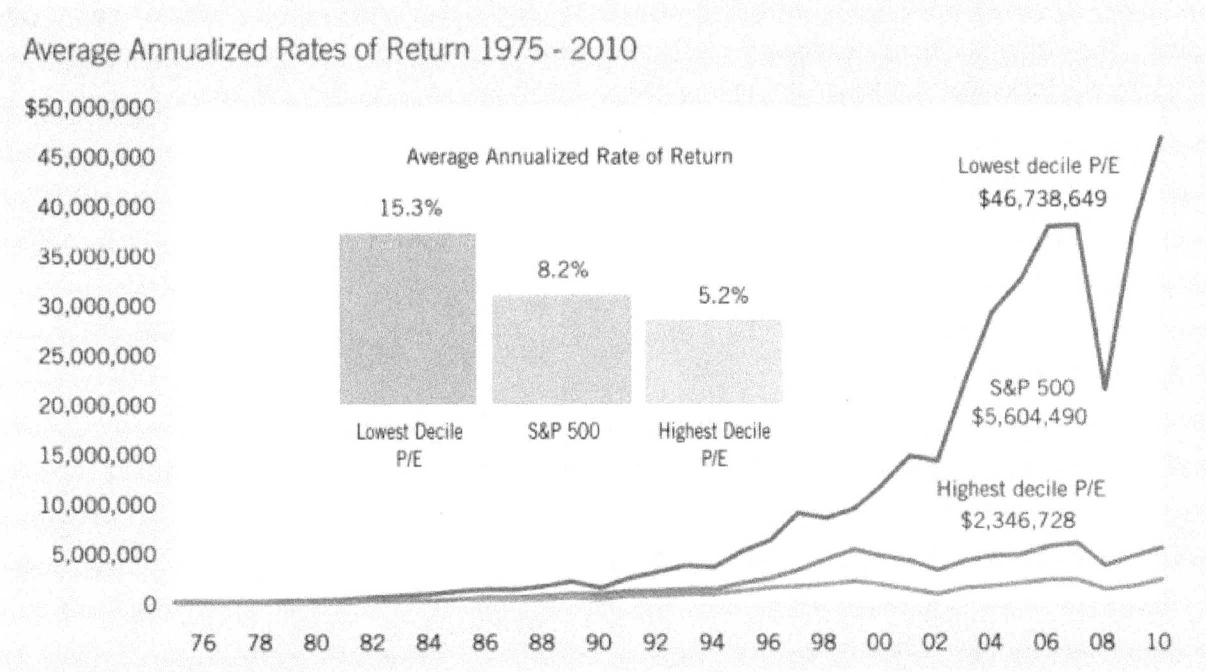

Stocks with high price tags have considerably underperformed the stock market. The normalized P/E ratio of 40 is utilized as a cut-off because this is the nearest valuation that the whole S&P 500 has achieved. A dividend stock with P/E ratio of 40 is highly likely to be overvalued.

It is ideal to use normalized profits instead of GAAP profits. You should avoid selling stocks with P/E ratio of 40 because profits are depressed 50% because of a one-time event.

In addition, it is not ideal to sell high-cycle stocks because it has a high P/E ratio because of depressed earnings from the cyclical wave. Selling your overpriced stocks will move your investments to a fair value dividend stocks that will reward you with both dividend and price growth.

Why Sell Stocks that Have Lost their Competitive Advantage?

Dividend stocks that have either eliminated or cut their dividend payouts have either permanently or temporarily affected investor dividend income. The main objective of holding onto high-quality dividend growth stocks is to ensure that the dividend stock will steadily grow over time. It doesn't make sense to hold onto stocks that cut or eliminate dividend payments.

Companies that reduce or cut dividend payouts send a warning signal to investors. This shows that the companies are not capable of maintaining its present cash flow.

This basically means the company's competitive advantage has reduced or absolutely disrupted and lost. In any case, you should move your investment into high-quality stocks that will regularly increase dividend payouts.

The strategy of holding unto stocks that have reduced or cut their dividend payouts is backed by historical data. In a 40-year period, stocks that reduce or cut their dividends generate an average returns of 0%.

Stocks that eliminate or reduce their dividend will provide reduced or zero returns. It is better to hold cash in an interest-growing bank account instead of owning stocks that have reduced or cut their dividend payouts. The Oppenheimer image below shows how dividend growth stocks have significantly outperformed stocks that reduce or cut their dividend payouts.

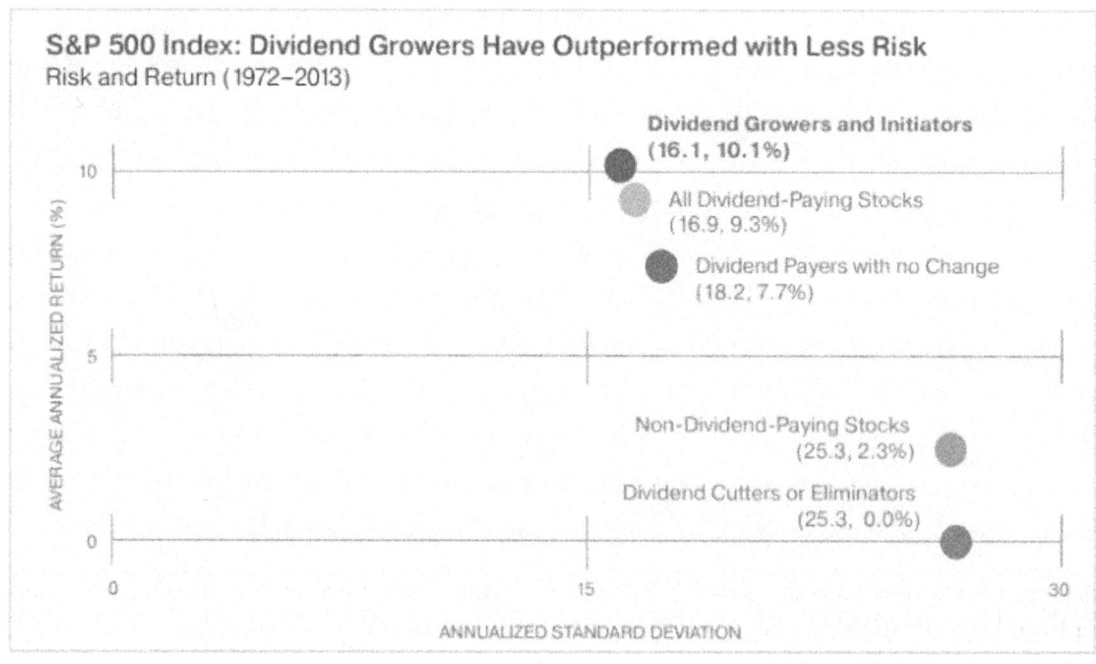

Selling Stocks Prior to Ex-Dividend Date

Bear in mind that if you sell prior to the ex-date (ex-dividend date), you are not eligible for receiving a dividend from the stocks you own.

Remember, the ex-date is the date that the company has assigned as the first day of trading in which the stocks trade without having the right for a dividend. You are still eligible for dividend payout if you sell your shares on or after this specific date.

Basically, you need to be listed on the company's date of record. This list is used to identify the company's holders of record and to authorize individuals to those whom financial reports, proxy statements, and other relevant details are sent.

If you buy shares, your name will not be instantly added to the company records. This will take around three days from the transaction date.

Hence, if the date of record is June 15, you should purchase the shares on June 12 to qualify for dividend payouts. This will make June 13 as the ex-date because this is the date directly following the last date on which you can receive dividend.

The ex-date is specified by the stock exchange or the National Association of Securities Dealers when the date of record is already set.

How Ex-Date Affect the Share Prices

Take note that a company stock will trade for less than the dividend value at the ex-date than they did the day prior. In general, if a dividend-payout distributes a huge dividend, the market could account for this dividend in the days before the ex-dividend date because of buyers still acquiring shares. There are investors who are willing to pay a high premium to be eligible for the payout.

For instance, if the stocks in a company are trading at $60 and the company announces a dividend of $6, individual investors who hold the shares past the ex-dividend date shall receive the $6, while those who sell prior to the ex-dividend date are no longer eligible for the payout.

But the company stocks might fall by around the value of the dividend, in our example, $54. There might also be an opportunity for an arbitrage in the stock market. If stocks don't fall as a result of dividend payouts, many would flock to acquire the shares for $60, receive $6, and then sell the stocks after the ex-date. So they are getting free money from the shares.

In an ideal world, investors would never have to sell their dividend stocks. Your dividend investments would continue to earn passive income as long as you hold it.

But alas, there is no surefire way to predict the future. Chances are, you will encounter and invest stocks that could eliminate or reduce their dividend payouts or become considerably overvalued.

In any case, it is ideal to reinvest the profits into stocks that are high quality but undervalued and fairly valued. Buying undervalued dividend stocks and selling overvalued dividend stocks could likely boost the dividend yield of your investment portfolio.

Even stocks with 100% payout ratio will only have 2.5 per cent yield if the P/E ratio is 40. Meanwhile, an undervalued stock will likely have better dividend yield. All things being equal, the dividend yield will be higher if the stock price of the dividend is lower.

Disposing of dividend stocks that have eliminated or canceled dividend payouts will likely increase the dividend growth rate of your dividend portfolio in the future. Savvy investors would never trust companies who decide to cut or eliminate their payouts.

You can increase the possible dividend growth rate of your general investment portfolio if you sell dividend stocks that are no longer issuing payments.

When the right time comes, investors who have a pre-established plan for selling shares can easily execute their plan. Investors who don't have a plan may prematurely sell or hold on to their shares a bit longer with the false hope that companies who eliminated their payouts will soon turn around.

A selling plan will help you prevent panic selling and will provide you with clear and solid rules on when to sell.

Interesting Fact #11

Declaring dividends without sufficient profits is illegal
Company directors issuing dividends when the company has insufficient profits don't actually have the authority to do so – if they do the dividend is illegal.
These are what's known as "ultra vires" dividends, which means 'beyond the powers'. You should ensure there are profits, and involve your accountant if required, before declaring dividends to avoid the risk of breaking the law.

Chapter 21

Dividend Investing Case Study

In this final chapter, we will take a look at the investment case study involving a middle-aged investor who has been buying dividend stocks since 2001. Let's call him Mike who is looking into the ABC Company Stocks with the following figures in 2006:

Valuation

- Dividend Yield: more than 3%
- P/E Ratio: low 20
- Forward P/E Ratio: low 20

Fundamentals

- RoE: high 15%
- EPS Growth (past 5 years): +
- EPS Growth (next 5 years): +
- Sales Growth (past 5 years): +
- Dividend Payout Ration (DPR): 33%

With Mike's experience as a dividend investor, he used different financial ratios and metrics to evaluate possible stocks for his portfolio.

Among the many available financial ratios, Mike mainly used the dividend payout ratio (DPR) to analyze the dividend stock of ABC Company. He used this metric to analyze the dollar amount of the dividend that a company is paying in accordance to its net income.

The DPR helped Mike understand the percentage of earnings that ABC company is paying to its stockholders and investors. Any money that is not paid out to shareholders or investors will be reinvested into the company operations or expansion.

While the DPR helped Mike to gain some insight about ABC company, it cannot however provide information on shareholder value. Based on his past experience, Mike doesn't use DPR as a metric to assess the viability of the company.

Mike is only using DPR if he is considering whether to invest in a profitable business that is paying dividends in comparison with a company with high potential for growth. He also used DPR as a way to compare a steady revenue or reinvestment for potential earnings in the future.

Mike's DPR Computation

Through the DPR, Mike can see how much money the business is putting back into its growth, for paying its debt, and its cash reserves. With this metric, he can compare the value of ABC company against the amount of money that is distributed to the investors and stockholders as dividends. To get the DPR, Mike reviewed the company's income statement.

To double check, Mike used a formula for computing the DPR by dividing the annual dividend paid by the net income (Dividends/Net Income = DPR).

Through this formula, Mike confirmed that ABC Company paid $1 dollar for every share in yearly dividend payouts, while the EPS was $3. Then, the DPR would be 33% or 0.33 or 1/3.

Mike's DPR Interpretation

But through experience, Mike knows that DPR interpretation is relative. In this case, ABC company has a DPR of 33%. This doesn't mean it is already a good payout or a bad one. The answer to this may vary depending on Mike's risk tolerance, personal goals, and investment strategy.

More often than not, growing companies have the tendency to retain the majority of its revenue to finance growth. Eventually, this will provide the investor with dividend in the future. However, this will come at a cost of the investor not receiving any dividend at present.

After reviewing the company profile, Mike learned that ABC Company can be considered a mature company so it has the capacity to provide higher dividends. The company has already reached the peak of its growth so it can sustain a 33% payout rate.

Mike also checked the dividend payout trend of the company over time. This helped him to know if the company has the ability to sustain its profits and thus sustain the dividend payouts.

Sustainable Growth Model for ABC Company

In looking into the financials of ABC Company, Mike also came across XYZ Company which has similar net income and ROE to the former. The only difference is in their retention ratios.

ABC Company has an ROE of 15% and returns 33% of its net income to stockholders in a dividend. Hence, the company is retaining 67% of its net income.

XYZ Company also has ROE of 15% but only returns 10% of its net income to stockholders for a retention ratio of 90%.

Mike used the sustainable growth model to do a comparative analysis of the two companies. He has learned to use this model to make estimates about the future of dividend stocks and to determine if specific stocks are risky because their dividend payouts are not sustainable.

Mike is aware that a stock that is slowly growing compared to its sustainable rate might be undervalued, or the stock market might be discounting red flags from the company. In any case, a growth rate that is below or above the sustainable rate should require more due diligence.

The result of the comparative analysis seems to make XYZ company look more attractive than ABC Company. However, this is reckless to say because it doesn't consider the benefits of a higher dividend rate that could be attractive to savvy investors.

You can modify the computation to make an estimate of the dividend growth rate of the stock that could be more important for Mike who is an income investor.

To get an estimate, Mike multiplied ROE by the payout ratio, which resulted in the sustainable growth rate that favors ABC Company.

Mike's Timing Strategy

ABC Company stocks caught Mike's attention because of the announcement of ex-dividend date where investors can receive a dividend from the company. Mike is aware that he can sell the shares a bit later after receiving the dividend.

To put it simply, Mike can choose to buy the dividend. However, Mike is also aware that this strategy is risky, since he believes the current market is relatively efficient.

In his prior trades, he learned that share prices could be pushed higher before the ex-date as investors are getting excited. On or around the payment date, the price usually plummets. So Mike made sure that before buying ABC Company stocks, he would hold on to it because of passive income and not because of the immediate dividend that he could receive.

Mike's Dividend Holding Size

Within five years of building his dividend portfolio, Mike has around 80 stocks diversified in different industries and sectors. While he has several stocks, he still investigates any stock he wants to buy like he did his first investment.

He aims to have at least 300 stocks in a 10-year time horizon, so buying ABC Company stocks is just one of the many stocks he will end up holding. So far, Mike only bought 1,000 shares of ABC Company stocks.

After buying the shares, Mike plans to monitor the performance of the stock, stay updated on news about the company, and check the daily fluctuations of the stocks. He also made sure that the commissions and trading costs are below 2% of his total purchase amount.

Mike's Dollar Cost Averaging Strategy

Mike follows dollar cost averaging for his dividend investment strategy. He is now trained in placing a specific dollar value into his dividend investments on a regular recurring schedule, which he plans to employ for his investment in ABC Company.

Mike found it helpful to follow dollar cost averaging because it allows him to be consistent and remove the emotion from investing. Because of the fixed dollar value he is investing, he can buy more ABC Company stocks if the market is lower and fewer shares if the market is higher.

Mike's Decision to Sell ABC Company Shares

After 12 years of holding ABC Company shares, Mike decided to sell all his stocks after confirming the news that the company board of directors decided to cut their dividend payouts.

As a dividend investor, Mike's primary objective is to hold onto high-quality dividend growth stocks that would steadily grow over time. Hence, ABC Company reducing their dividend payout is quite concerning.

After years of investing in dividends, Mike is already aware that companies that are cutting or even reducing their dividend payments are in some kind of distress, because they are no longer capable of sustaining their current cash flow.

Upon further investigation, Mike also learned that ABC Company already lost its competitive advantage due to a new player in the industry that is aggressively fighting for market share and making the competition more cut throat.

What's more? ABC Company's profit margins have been on the decline for 3 straight years prior to the reduction in dividend payout! This further solidified his decision to move his investment into other dividend stocks that have a high potential for dividend payouts.

Conclusion I

I'd like to thank you and congratulate you for transiting my lines from start to finish. I hope that you enjoyed this stock investing collection and it'll help you start your journey as a stock market investor and eventually master the process.

Stock market investing is a great way to grow your wealth and earn more money. But, it is also a fun and exhilarating experience. It strengthens your logic and significantly increases your analytical skills. It also allows you to earn passive income.

But, before you start your journey to great wealth and financial independence, let's review the major points of this book:

Stock market investing is one of the best ways to build your wealth. It's also a good way to earn passive income.

A stock represents part ownership of a company. When you own a few stocks of a company, you're essentially a part owner.

Companies create stocks to help raise money for business expansion. When a company was built, it's classified as private, but once it starts selling its shares in the stock market, it's classified as public.

IPO or initial public offering is the process that companies go through when they sell their shares in a stock market for the first time. It's also called "going public".

A stock market is a place where companies issue stocks and where investors buy company shares. A stock exchange is a stock market.

A stock market has two parts – the primary and the secondary market.

There are various stock market players, including the investors, shareholders, listed companies, stockbrokers, venture capitalists, investment bank, floor trader, floor broker, analysts, and clearing houses.

You can make money in the stock market in two ways – capital appreciation and dividend payments.

There are two types of stocks – preferred and common.

Common stocks are cheaper, but they are at the bottom of the payout hierarchy. This means that common stockholders are only paid after the bondholders and preferred stock holders get their share.

Preferred stocks are more rare and expensive. But, preferred stockholders do not have voting rights. They cannot decide on company's policies.

Stock prices fluctuate for many reasons, including market volatility, imbalance of the stock's supply and demand, economic policy changes, interest rate changes, economic predictions, inflation, deflation, and natural disasters.

An index is a metric that's used to measure the overall performance of the stock market.

The stock market is heavily affected by speculations. This is the reason why the bull and bear market exist.

A bull market happens when investors are so optimistic that they end up buying a lot of stocks. This drives the stock prices up.

A bear market happens when investors are too pessimistic and so they sell their stocks. This decreases the stock prices and can lead to stock market crash like what happened in 2008.

To invest in stocks, you need to first understand the difference between a stock and a mutual fund. An individual stock represents part ownership of a certain company. A mutual fund, on the other hand, is a basket made of different stocks. An ETF is a mutual fund that's traded in the stock market as a stock.

You must also identify your investing style. Do you want to be a long term investor or a day trader? This will help you pick the right investment plan.

You must set a budget. How much are you willing to invest in stocks?

Choose a trustworthy brokerage firm to work with. You also need to look at commission and transaction fees. You would want to avoid companies that charge hefty fees.

401(k) plan is a retirement plan that comes with an employer matching plan. This means that both the employee and his employer can deposit money into his 401k account.

IRA or individual retirement account is also a retirement plan that comes with tax advantages. There are various types of IRA – Traditional, SIMPLE, Roth, Spousal, SEP, and non-deductible.

A taxable brokerage account, as the name suggests, is an investment plan opened through a broker. It doesn't have tax advantages, but it doesn't have limits and you can withdraw it any time.

When you have a brokerage account, your broker will execute your trade orders. You don't have to do much.

If you do not want to work with a broker, it's best to open a direct purchase plan. This allows you to purchase the stocks directly from the company.

Dividend reinvestment plan allows you to use your dividend earnings to buy new stocks. This helps you increase your portfolio and investment earnings over time.

There are different investment strategies, including value investing, growth investing, and dividend investing.

Dividend investing is best for those who want to receive dividend checks every quarter. But, keep in mind that dividend payments are not guaranteed. The company can reduce or completely cut dividend payments when profits decrease.

Value investing is for people who want to invest in undervalued and stable companies. A lot of seasoned investors use this strategy. This is a low risk strategy, but it can cause you to lose opportunities, too.

Growth investing is great for more adventurous and risk-averse investors. Growth investors place their bets on fast-rising companies called "unicorns". This strategy can help you earn thousands of dollars in capital appreciation profit each year. But, it's also risky because most overhyped companies can't live up to all the hype.

Day trading is a process where you buy and sell a stock the same time in the hopes of earning quick bucks. It capitalizes on stock market volatility. This strategy is great for full time traders because it requires a lot of time.

Short-selling is a strategy that doesn't require an upfront investment. It's also a great strategy for those who are a bit pessimistic. This strategy helps you profit from declining prices. When you short sell, you borrow a stock from your broker and sell it at prevailing market price. Once the price goes down, you can buy back the stock and return it to your broker. The difference between your selling price and buying price is your profit.

Before you invest, you must set goals. How much do you want to earn in a year or in a five year period? How much risk can you take?

To make sure that you pick the right stock, you have to look at various factors, such as the company's financial health, debt/equity ratio, P/E ratio, profitability, market share, and dividend payments.

Look at the company's P/E and PEG ratio to see if a company is overvalued.

There are various trades that you can place with your broker, including market orders, limit orders, stop order, stop-limit order, and trailing stop order.

The market order is the most basic of all the order types and it has to be executed within the day. But, if you want to "buy low, sell high", you must do the limit order. This order type allows you to either buy or sell a stock at a specific price during a specific time frame.

A day order is an order that expires at the end of the trading day.

A stock exchange usually closes at 4 pm. But, keep in mind that you can still trade after trading hours online. You can trade from 4:15 to 8 pm. You can also trade from 8:00 to 9:15 am before the stock exchange opens.

You can use a stop order to help reduce your loss.

You can always cancel an order. You just have to log in to your account, go to your order, and click on "cancel".

A brokerage account allows you to buy and sell stocks in the stock market. It is usually opened through a broker. This account can hold different types of securities, such as stock, mutual fund, bond, ETF, REIT, and certificate of deposit.

Study your broker's statement carefully to spot fraudulent activities.

You will receive a trade confirmation each time you buy or sell a stock. You must examine your trade confirmation carefully to make sure that your broker executed your order according to your instructions.

You must invest in a company with huge profits and low debt. This is the reason why you should look at the balance sheet carefully.

Review your brokerage confirmation to see if there are errors. Call your broker right away if you see irregularities.

Do not invest all your money right away. Test the water first. Invest a small part of your investment fund and then, once you earn at least 2% capital appreciation profit, invest another small percentage of your investment fund. Repeat this process until you've invested all the money in your brokerage account.

Before you buy a stock, you must do extensive research. You must do microeconomic analysis and look at the industry as a whole. Is the industry doing well? Is the economy good? Is it a good time to invest in stocks.

After you do your macroeconomic analysis, you should do company research. You should check how the company is doing. Is it in good financial health? Is it earning profits?

To maximize your investment profits, you must manage your portfolio well. One way to do this is to diversify your investments.

Index fund investing is one of the best ways to diversify your portfolio. It's inexpensive, too.

Invest in non-correlated assets. Investing in non-correlated stocks help reduce risk and spread your wealth to various industries.

Look at the facts and the numbers. Use logic when making investment decisions. But, sometimes, you have to listen to your gut, too. If something doesn't right, just don't do it.

Do not invest in just one industry. You'll never know what will happen. An entire industry may be irrelevant years from now. Remember when CD replaced VHS? Well, Netflix may push cable into extinction soon.

Try to place a stop order with your broker to minimize your losses.

Invest in companies that pay dividends. This is a great way to earn regular income from your investments.

Do not hold on to your investments for so long. Once the price starts to go down, it's time to let your stocks go. Sometimes, investors get too attached to their stock position that they end up losing profits.

Stock market investment is a complicated animal. You're not going to master it in just a few weeks. Expect to make mistakes or make bad investment decisions. When you do, don't beat yourself up. Mistakes are part of your journey. Just keep going.

Remember that stock market investing is not some "get rich quick" scheme, so you have to be really patient.

And lastly, don't stop learning. Keep reading new materials. Connect with other stock traders and attend seminars. This book is just a "stock investing for dummies" course. There's more to learn.

I wish you the best of luck!

Book 3

Real Estate Investing For Beginners

Earn Passive Income

With Reits, Tax Lien Certificates, Lease,

Residential and Commercial Real Estate

By

Michael Ezeanaka

www.MichaelEzeanaka.com

Real Estate Business Scorecard

How would you like to download a scorecard that **neatly summarizes**, in a table each Real Estate Business Model's score across 5 areas – Liquidity, Scalability, Potential return on investment, Passivity and Simplicity? If you want it, a PDF version of the card is hosted on my **website** and can be downloaded for free. However, a password is required to unlock the download. Follow the steps below to **retrieve the password**!

Steps to take

1. The password consists of 8 characters (all lower case)
2. Here is the incomplete password: p-k-n-b-
3. The **second**, **fourth**, **sixth** and **eighth** character of the password is missing and is located in random pages of this book.
4. **Read this book** carefully to locate and retrieve them (they're so obvious you can't miss them).
5. Once you have the complete password then go to www.MichaelEzeanaka.com > Free Stuff > Ebooks/Audiobooks > Real Estate Business Scorecard.
6. Enter the password, download the business scorecard and enjoy!

Introduction III

Real estate has long been one of the most popular assets to invest in. After all, land is something that people will always need to build their homes and businesses on. As an asset, real estate provides the potential for multiple income streams.

There are many ways through which you can benefit from investing in real estate. As a direct owner, you can refurbish a building and rent it out to a tenant to generate a fairly passive income or you can resell (flip) it. But you can also make money without actually owning property.

In most cases, property values appreciate over time. This means that you can sell it for a higher amount in the future or use it to raise capital that you can reinvest.

Real estate investments can provide you with passive income. There are ways that you can make money from real estate that don't require you to exert a lot of effort and time. You don't even need to directly own real estate in order for this to happen.

Moreover, your income from real estate investments is not affected by inflation. If anything, your rental income will increase along with inflation. This means that you will be able to enjoy a higher cash flow while maintaining or improving the purchasing power of your money.

There are tax benefits too. If you have investment property, you are allowed to deduct deprecation of the building and any additional capital investments, which will reduce your taxable income. And there are other tax advantages you can enjoy based on what investment method you use.

In this book, we will describe the various methods that you can use to invest in real estate. Like we said before, you don't actually need to be a direct owner of property in order to make money from it. We will give you an overview of each investment method, including the pros and cons of each one.

Each real estate investment method will be scored using this set of criteria:

- **Liquidity** – this refers to how easy it is to convert your investment into cash if you suddenly need the money.
- **Scalability** – this refers to how easy it is to increase your investment.
- **Potential Return on Investment** – this is how much income you can gain from the investment considering your costs and expenses.
- **Passivity** – this refers to how easy it will be to earn money without much time and effort.
- **Simplicity** – this refers to how easy it is to get started with an investment.

Most, if not all, of the *basic information* that you need to examine and evaluate your real estate investment options are in this book. There are also tips for success at the end of each chapter to guide you in your investment activities.

Without further ado, let's get right into it!

Interesting Fact #1

Most people don't realise it but McDonalds is not a burger flipping-restaurant chain; it is one of the worlds best real estate portfolios. Franchisees do the burger flipping and McDonalds gets paid handsomely for owning the best commercial real estate all over the world!

Congratulations!

The second character of the password required to unlock the *Real Estate Business Scorecard* is letter m.

Chapter 22

Real Estate Investment Trusts

Real Estate Investment Trusts (REITs) are companies that invest in commercial real estate properties, and allow investors to buy shares in them. They are designed to make investing in real estate **more accessible** by making the amount of money needed more affordable. For instance, a shopping mall costs millions of dollars to build, making investing in them prohibitive for most investors. However, by buying shares in an REIT that specializes in shopping malls, you can have exposure to this type of investment for a relatively small capital outlay.

A Short History of REITs

REITs were first created in 1960 via Public-Law 86-779 under President Dwight Eisenhower, as a way of making investment in large-scale real estate more accessible to the ordinary investor with limited funds. The first REIT to be established under the new law was the American Realty Trust in 1961.

Initially, REITs mostly invested in mortgage companies, which helped fuel the growth of the real estate industry in the sixties and seventies. The funds invested by the REITs were used to invest in construction and land development.

In 1992, Retail REIT Taubman Centers expanded the scope of REITs by creating the UPREIT. UPREITs allowed REITs to enter into an "operating partnership" with an existing partnership. Under this agreement, the partnership contributes properties that the REIT is the majority owner of. In exchange for the properties, the partners have the right to exchange these for cash or shares in the REIT.

At present, over 30 countries have their own REIT regimes. A global index to track both REITs and the global property market in general, the FTSE EPRA/ Nareit Global Real Estate Series, was created in 2001. According to this index, there were 477 real estate companies from 35 countries that listed in the stock exchange, accounting for a $2 trillion equity market capitalization, as of December 2017. REITs accounted for around 78% of the total capitalization.

Types of REITs

There are three general categories of REITs:

- Equity REITs are those that directly invest in real estate, either by financing their development or by purchasing already existing properties. The REIT generates income by renting out to tenants and distributes these to shareholders as dividends.
- Mortgage REITs, on the other hand, invest in real estate mortgages, either by lending money for real estate loans or by buying mortgage-backed securities. They generate income through the interest they earn from the loans, less the cost of funding the loans (net interest margin).
- Hybrid REITs. These are REITs that invest in real estate and mortgage loans. Hybrid REITs are generally in the minority, although they generally are weighted on one investment type over the other.

In order to qualify as a REIT, the company must be an entity that is taxable as a corporation and meet the following requirements:

- It must have at least 100 shareholders
- It must distribute at least 90% of its taxable income annually to shareholders
- No more than half of its shares should be held by five or less shareholders
- At least 75% of its gross income should come from rents, sales of real estate or interest on mortgages financing real estate
- It should be managed by a board of directors/trustees

Equity REITs

We are focusing our discussion on equity REITs, since these are the most-commonly invested in. Thus, whenever we refer to REITs, we are talking about equity REITs. Mortgage REITs will be referred to as mREITs.

The majority of equity REITs focus on a particular type of property, although there are some that have a diversified portfolio. The most common types of REITs are:

- **Retail** - These REITs invest in retail properties such as shopping malls and freestanding outlets. One example is Realty Income, whose portfolio focuses on freestanding, single-tenant properties that are rented out to warehouse clubs, drugstores and other retail businesses. Realty Income has 5,326 properties in its portfolio and its major tenants include 7-11, FedEx, Walgreens and AMC Theaters.
- **Healthcare** - These REITs invest in properties that are rented to tenants that provide health care services such as hospitals, skilled nursing facilities and elderly housing facilities. An example is Ventas, which has a diversified portfolio that consists of both real estate leased on a net-lease basis and run through operating partnerships with companies like Altria Senior Living.
- **Hotel** - These REITs invest in luxury hotels, budget motels or destination resorts. An example of a hotel REIT is Apple Hospitality, whose portfolio focuses on properties that are operated under the Marriott and Hilton brands.
- **Industrial** - These REITs are focused on factory and warehouse properties. An example is STAG Industrial, which specializes in single-tenant properties and has 360 properties in 37 states.
- **Residential** - These REITs focus mainly on apartments. One example is Avalon Bay Communities whose portfolio of apartment communities is mainly centered in leading metropolitan areas such as New York/New Jersey Metro, New England and the Pacific Northwest.
- **Data centers** - These REITs operate and own facilities that lease to companies that provide data protection and storage services. An example of a data center REIT is Equinx, which is the largest publicly traded REIT of this type, and operates close to 200 data centers in five continents.

It should be noted that the dividends you receive from REITs are called distributions. The reason for this is that distributions are treated differently than dividends for tax purposes. REIT distributions are divided into three categories:

- **Dividends**. These are taxed as ordinary income, up to a maximum 39.6% rate plus a 3.8% investment income surcharge.

- **Return of capital.** This portion is nontaxable in the year you received it and will also reduce your taxable income. However, you will have to pay tax on it when you sell your shares. They will be taxed as either long-term or short-term capital gains, based on how long you held on to the shares.
- **Capital gains.** If you receive this as part of your disbursement, you will be taxed at the short-term or long-term capital gains rate during the year you received it.

The REIT will make it easy to declare your distributions on your taxes by sending you IRS Form 1099-DIV, which breaks them down for you.

Mortgage REITs

Mortgage REITs are an alternative to equity REITs that provide higher yields, but also require you to accept higher risks. MREITs actually make up only a small percentage of total traded REITs but they are popular among investors who are willing to accept the risks they entail in exchange for the high dividends they generate. As of 2017, there are 222 REITs listed, of which 181 are equity REITs and 41 are mortgage REITs.

Instead of buying real estate, mREITs purchase mortgages and mortgage-backed securities. By doing so, they provide mortgage credit for individual homebuyers as well as businesses that want to invest in commercial real estate.

To raise capital, however, they rely on equity and leverage. They can raise equity by making secondary stock offerings. Using leverage, however, can be a double-edged sword. Using high amounts of debt allows the mREIT to increase its holdings and the potential profits it can earn. However, if market conditions are unfavorable, higher leverage can increase potential losses since the cost of paying loans will be more than what it earns from its holdings.

MREITs are vulnerable to changes in both long-term and short-term interest rates, and thus you have to be prepared for the volatility they cause in order to remain profitable. If interest rates fall, more homeowners may pre-pay their loans, reducing the amount of income the mREIT generates. But if interest rates rise, the mREIT's holdings may lose their value, and its share prices may fall.

Non-Traded REITs

These are a type of REIT that does not list in the stock exchange and shares must be purchased through brokers. Since they are not publicly traded, their shares do not suffer from the volatility that REITs traded on exchanges experience. This essentially means that investing in non-traded REITs is similar to investing directly in real estate since the price of the shares are driven by the net asset value of their portfolio.

However, the reason why these REITs do not experience volatility is because of their lack of liquidity. Investors cannot simply sell their shares the way they could with a public REIT since there is a holding period of eight years or longer. Although some private REITs do allow for early redemption, this may be at a discount, meaning that the investor could lose part of their investment.

Thus, the shares of private REITs tend to hold their value. According to research published in the University of Texas's research publication Texas Enterprise, in 2009 the share value of non-traded REITs declined by only 15% while that of exchange-traded REITs fell by some 67 percent

However, there are a number of drawbacks and risks when investing in non-traded REITs. For instance, they are known for charging high fees due to broker commissions and other upfront fees, which can be as much as 15% of the offering price. The initial distributions may also come from the proceeds of the offering, which includes the principal of the investors, since the REIT may not yet be generating significant income in its early stages.

In addition, many non-traded REITs are structured such that they must either go public at the end of a certain period or must liquidate. If it goes public, the investors' shares are replaced with new ones that may have a lower value than the original. If it liquidates, then the investor may end up with the value of their investment greatly decreased.

Thus, if you are considering investing in non-traded REITs, you should be sure to do your homework by finding out as much as you can about it. You should acquire the REIT's prospectus, which is an offering document in which they provide information such as the offering terms and investing strategy. These are available through your broker or from the EDGAR database of the SEC, which usually identifies them as a 424B3 filing.

REIT ETFs

These investment instruments are alternatives to directly investing in REITs. These exchange-traded funds invest in REITs that are designed to mirror the performance of REIT indexes such as the Dow Jones US REIT Index and the MSCI US REIT Index. Since these ETFs represent a diversified portfolio of REITs of different types of real estate, there is less risk that their profitability will be affected by market shifts.

The largest REIT ETFs include:

- Vanguard Real Estate ETF. This fund tracks the performance of the MSCI US REIT Index and its holdings include some of the largest REITs in the market, such as Crown Castle International, Simon Property Group and American Tower.
- Shwab US REIT ETF. This fund mostly invests in REITs included in the Dow Jones US Select REIT Index, although it may also include others not listed as well.
- iShares US Real Estate ETF. This fund mostly invests in REITs that are included in the Dow Jones US Real Estate Index. Although its holdings emphasize large cap companies, they may also include medium and small cap companies.

In addition, more adventurous investors may consider REIT ETFs that invests in real estate outside of the US. One example is the Vanguard Global ex-US Real Estate ETF, which tracks the performance of the S&P Global ex-US Property Index, including real estate stocks from over 30 countries.

Pros and Cons of Investing in REITs

When you are considering investing in REITs, the main thing to remember is that you are essentially becoming a real estate owner, with the advantages and disadvantages that brings. Here is a quick overview of the pros and cons of buying REIT shares.

Pros

- REITs are required to distribute the bulk of their earnings as dividends. This is one of the main reasons that investors are attracted to REITs, particularly those that are looking for an income-generating investment.
- The REIT is able to avoid being double taxed. A corporation is taxed on the profits it earns, and when it pays out part of these as dividends, the recipients also have to pay tax on them. But since REITs don't report a profit and distribute the majority of their income, they are not charged corporate income tax. This means that the after-tax dividends you receive on the REITs will be higher compared with those from stocks issued by corporations.
- REITs are managed by real estate professionals. This means that the properties will be professionally managed, maximizing the amount of revenue they generate.
- REITs are easy to liquidate. Unlike physical real estate, which can be difficult to turn into cash since the process of finding a buyer and completing the paperwork to finalize the sale can take weeks or even months. On the other hand, you can easily dispose of your REIT shares if you should suddenly need cash.
- Real estate is the underlying asset of the REITs. Of course, the value of real estate can fluctuate based on market conditions. But in general, the value of real estate, particularly commercial properties, goes up over the long term. This means that your investment will retain its value.
- REITs make it easy to diversity your portfolio. If you bought a property, your money would be tied up in it until you could resell it or it started to generate income. On the other hand, by investing in REIT shares, you can own a diversified portfolio of properties that would already start earning you money. In addition, REITs allow your portfolio to be exposed to another asset class apart from the traditional stocks and bonds.

Cons

- REITs are vulnerable to market downturns. If there is an economic slowdown, for instance, occupancy rates for retail properties may decline, affecting the income they generate. Thus, the dividends you receive from your shares will also fall
- The value of the REIT shares themselves may also decline. This can be due to factors related to the property market, but share prices can also fall as a result of the decline of the overall stock market.
- REITs are still subject to taxation. Although the income generated by REITs are exempt from corporate tax, the company still has to pay real estate taxes. When real estate prices rise, this can significantly increase tax expenses and reduce the revenues available for distribution.
- REIT dividends do not enjoy preferential tax rates. REIT dividends are taxed as ordinary income rather than as dividends. This means that they will not be taxed the 15% dividend rate, but a much higher one.
- There is little money available for further investment. Since the majority of the REITs income is distributed, there is little left over that can be reinvested in the business. This may require the company to borrow money if it wants to purchase additional properties.

Scoring REITs

A. Liquidity

Since REITs are traded on major stock exchanges, they are very easy to liquidate, compared with actually owning physical real estate. As of 2017, there are 222 REITs with total market capitalization of over $1 trillion. Only physical cash at the bank is more liquid than this!

9/10

B. Scalability

REITs are very scalable since you only need to buy more shares if you want to invest more. On the other hand, if you want to buy more real estate, it is a cumbersome process that requires a lot of time, money and potentially more land.

10/10

C. Potential Return on Investment

When it comes to return on investment, REITs on average provide higher returns than rental income from direct real estate investment. According to data from the NAREIT REITwatch, REITs have returned over 12% a year from 1977 to 2010, compared with private real estate funds, which had returns of 6% to 8% over the same period. In addition, from 2012 to 2017, REITs had a 9% average annual return compared with direct real estate investment, which was at an average annualized rate of around or below eight percent.

As far as taxes go, REIT dividends are taxed as ordinary income and the shareholder has to pay at their highest marginal tax rate. Rental income is taxed as personal income, although you can deduct the expenses related to refurbishing it in preparation for being rented out, as well as maintenance costs.

Most importantly, you can **depreciate the cost of your residential property over 27.5 years**. The depreciation deduction is tax-free, meaning that you can subtract this amount from your rental income and only the difference, if any, is taxable.

In addition, when the shareholder shares their REIT holdings, they are taxed based on whether there has been a capital gain or loss. However, if they have held their shares for more than a year, they can be taxed at long-term capital gains rates, which are smaller.

The same reduced tax rates are applied for those who hold their properties for longer than a year. However, if you flip in less than a year, your profits will be considered short-term capital gains and taxed at the regular income tax rate.

However, REITs are vulnerable to interest rate increases, which can cause dividend yields to decrease. This is because, as interest rates rise, all else being equal, the income produced by REITs at the current stock price is worth less, and so prices generally fall in order to increase the yield of those stocks relative to other income producing instruments. Thus, the accepted wisdom is that investors should sell their REITs when the Fed is raising interest rates.

But real estate is also susceptible to market downturns, which can affect their rental income if they cannot find tenants. And there are costs such as property taxes and maintenance costs, which you will have to shoulder whether or not your property is generating income.

Overall, however, you will enjoy a higher rate of return on REITs compared with direct real estate investment.

8/10

D. Passivity

REITs are a great source of passive income compared with being a property owner (which requires you to be more hands on). Your dividends will be sent to your home as soon as they are paid out, usually in the form of a check or a direct deposit to your account. The only thing that is potentially more passive than this is the interest you earn on your money in the bank - this is why REITs received a passivity score of 90% in this book as well as in the book Passive Income Ideas – 50 Ways to Make Money Online Analyzed.

9/10

E. Simplicity

This criterion refers to how easy it is to get started with this investment. All you need to do to invest in REITs is simply to buy shares in the one you've chosen. Most REITs do not require a minimum investment although the broker may require that you buy shares in blocks of 10 or 100. The broker may also require you to maintain a minimum amount in your trading account.

In addition, many REITs also give you the option to automatically reinvest your dividends in additional shares, although you will still have to pay taxes on them. Reinvestment will allow you to compound your returns over time, substantially increasing the value of your investment. In addition, since the value of the REIT shares can also increase over time, they will pay out higher dividends.

The only difficulty with investing in REITs is choosing which ones to invest in. This will require you to have some knowledge of how to analyze them.

7/10

Ten Tips for Successfully Investing in REITs

1. Stick with equity REITs unless you develop a higher tolerance for risk. If you are an ordinary investor who is just looking for high returns, REITs are a good choice particularly if you are willing to hold on to them for the long-term. But unless you are willing to accept a high level of risk, you should not be tempted by the high returns promised by mortgage REITs.

2. Be forward thinking when you are choosing your REITs. Instead of simply considering where the real estate market is now, look at **where it will be in the future**. For instance, ask what the real estate trends will be in the medium-term, and buy REITs that invest in them. What will be the most popular types of real estate?

3. Consider what the economic conditions will be since these can affect the real estate market. To illustrate, in a recession the income from REITs that focus on industrial and office properties may suffer as their tenants go out of business. On the other hand, retail and residential REITs may be more resilient to hard times.

4. Avoid buying into newly established REITs. These REITs have not yet established a track record so there is no reliable way for you to determine how they perform. For instance, you cannot determine how the REIT maintains its payouts over time. You also cannot tell how the REIT manages changes in interest rates.

5. Avoid buying REITs when the prices are on an uptrend. The reason for this is simple: if the REIT suffers from price volatility, the price could go down below the level you bought it at, resulting in a loss. Instead, look for REITs whose prices have hit their floor price and thus, are on an upswing. This advice is applicable not just to REITs but also stocks.

6. Learn to assess the REIT using the income statement. Net income figures can be deceptive since they may include depreciation expenses, which reduce net income. However, property values often appreciate, which makes it inferior for evaluating performance. Instead, look at funds from operations (FFO), where depreciation is excluded. FFO can be found in the footnotes.

7. Hold your REIT shares in your retirement accounts. If you are planning to save for retirement, REITs are a great way to do so. If you have an IRA Roth account, you will pay taxes on the dividends up-front, but enjoy tax-free disbursements when you reach retirement age. In the meantime, the dividends you placed into the account compound on a tax-free basis. You can also enjoy some tax benefits with traditional REITs, since you may be in a lower tax bracket when you retire.

8. Check the REIT's growth potential by looking at its portfolio of holdings. You can usually find this information on their websites. In particular, look at who the REIT's top tenants are and how many properties they are renting, as well as where they are located. Try to avoid REITs whose tenants are too concentrated in one industry and focus on those whose properties are located in areas with flourishing economies. This will **help you predict what the cash flow and stock price of the REIT will be in the future.**

9. Look at the price of the REIT shares relative to its funds from operations (FFO). If the price-to-FFO multiple is too high, it may indicate that the REIT is overvalued, and the price may experience a big drop. You can compute this multiple by dividing the price by the FFO. How high is too high? You can look at the average multiples from the particular sector the REIT is in to see if the multiple is higher or lower.

10. Make sure that you get help from financial professionals. The tax implications of REITs can be very complicated so to make sure that you are able to fully benefit from your investments, you should consult with an accountant. Of course, you should still do your due diligence on the accountant's advice since your tax returns are ultimately your responsibility.

Interesting Fact #2

The famous Las Vegas strip is for the most part not located in the city of Las Vegas. To avoid tax, it's in a city known as "Paradise" – which is completely surrounded by Las Vegas!

Chapter 23

Real Estate Investment Groups

Real estate investment groups (REIG) have become a popular alternative in recent years to real estate investment trusts. Both allow you to enjoy the benefits of investing in real estate without the effort and time required for direct ownership. They also allow you to start investing without requiring you to have a lot of knowledge about real estate.

However, joining a REIG provides you with an opportunity to learn the ins and outs of real estate investing. This knowledge can be valuable to you later on should you decide to buy your own investment properties.

REIGs are associations of investors who pool their money to invest in real estate, buying, and/or developing properties. They then rent these properties out to generate rental income from them. This income is shared among the investors.

These groups usually specialize in a certain property type, such as commercial or residential real estate. They may also focus on finding properties nationally or concentrate on local real estate investments.

REIGs usually hire professionals to manage and maintain the properties as well as to find tenants. Mortgage payments come from rental income. If there are vacancies, the group may put aside a certain portion of their earnings to cover the shortfall.

REIGs are not the same as real estate investment clubs, although some people use the terms interchangeably. A real estate investment club does not invest in properties. It is simply a networking and educational group that allows members to share expertise about real estate investments. They also help each other find investment opportunities.

These groups are formally incorporated as legal entities, with each member listed as a joint owner. When the group makes a purchase, its official name is what is listed on the deed. Although there are no legal minimums or limits on membership, these groups usually only accept a manageable number, which may be around five to ten members.

They are run based on formal operating rules that the members have agreed on. Like any organization, most of them elect members as officers with specific responsibilities in the running of the group. Members will also jointly make investment decisions, voting on which properties to buy or to sell.

Pros and Cons Of REIGs

The main advantage of joining a REIG is that it allows you to invest in properties for a relatively small amount, although your investment will be larger than when you buy into real estate investment trusts. In exchange, however, the potential earnings will be higher.

Another advantage is that, collectively, the group is pooling its investment capital. This gives them the ability to place bids for properties that, as individuals, they may not be able to bid for.

In addition, REIGs also allow certain underrepresented groups to benefit from property investing. For instance, there are women's real estate clubs and clubs that are designed to teach minorities how to invest in real estate and to accumulate assets. This is to empower them to actually get into the market themselves.

Some groups may also provide education for their members by hosting events in which speakers talk about various investment topics. This may be useful to members who want to learn more about the subject and improve their skills. These gatherings are also invaluable for networking purposes as it allows members to meet and interact with other potential investors.

However, members may be asked to pay an entry fee in addition to their initial investment. They may also be asked to pay recurring annual fees. These fees may ultimately affect your net earnings.

In addition, your investment is not liquid. If you suddenly need to get your money back, you cannot just sell your share. You have to follow the guidelines of the organization as to how to liquidate your investment. This might require that another member buy you out. When this happens, you will have effectively withdrawn from the group since you no longer have any investment in it.

The collective way that decisions are made may also pose a problem. The various members may vote on their decisions based on emotional factors, and this could affect the profitability of the group. For instance, one member may convince the others to vote to hold on to a property that is not generating sufficient income, for sentimental reasons.

How to Choose a Group

Before you decide to invest in a REIG, you should be familiar with what your investment goals are. A REIG holds on to property over the long term in order to generate income from it. If you are expecting to see quick returns on your investment, i.e. by flipping the property, you should not invest in this group.

On the other hand, if you are preparing for retirement, then you should definitely consider investing in a group. This investment will provide you with a recurring source of income for when you are no longer earning income from employment.

When you contact the group, ask about their history. Have they been operating for some time, or are they just getting organized?

If they are a new group, ask about the other members. What experience do they have? If they are all new investors, who is guiding the group as to what investments they should make?

If they are an existing group that is looking for new members, ask about their record. How successful have they been with their investments over time? Ask if you can talk with former members about their experiences with the club.

Ask them about their portfolio of properties. They don't have to give you specifics, just what type of properties they generally invest in. Find out how much you can potentially earn by investing in the group and how often the returns are paid out.

Also consider: who are the members? Is the membership focused on a certain demographic, i.e. older adults, or are they open to anybody? How does the composition of the group affect its investment decisions?

Next, look at the costs of membership. How much does it cost to invest in the group? After your initial investment, do you have to make additional investments?

Also ask about the fees the group charges. Are there entry fees? Are there any recurring fees such as service fees? How are they charged? Are they fixed amounts or a percentage of the profits? Can you offset these fees from your earnings or do you have to pay them separately? Or do you have the option to choose?

What are your obligations as a member? Are there certain duties and responsibilities that you have to fulfill as a member of the group? Does the group meet regularly? Do you have to participate when it has to make investment decisions?

Another important consideration is the group's investment goals. Does the group invest in the type of real estate properties that you are interested in? What is their investment strategy? Is it an aggressive or a conservative one?

If the group offers you access to invest in wholesale properties, do they have documentation attesting to the quality of these assets?

What about exiting the group? What if you want to withdraw your investment? How long do you have to maintain your investment before you can exit? Are there fees and penalties for early withdrawal?

Now that you know what to look for, how do you find a group? Before you start, keep in mind that, generally, REIGs are not regulated in the US unless they have more than $25 million in assets. So, you will have to do your homework to avoid signing up with a group that is not reputable.

The best way to find a trustworthy group is to look for a trade association of investment groups. For instance, there is the National Real Estate Investors Association, which includes investors' groups among its membership. The websites of these groups usually allow you to do a search to find a group in your area.

You can also do a Google search for real estate investment groups, but this is more time-consuming. In addition, the results usually also include real estate investment clubs. But if you have the patience and the search engine skills, this can also be effective.

If you are doing your own research, you might want to check out if the group has a listing and ranking at the Better Business Bureau website. For your own security, go with a group that has the highest A+ rating.

If you know any realtors or real estate dealers in your area, you can also ask them to recommend a group. This is the best way, since you can talk to them about your requirements so that they can suggest a group that best meets them.

Forming Your Own Investment Group

If you can't find a real estate investment group in your area that suits your requirements, you might want to consider forming your own group. Of course, this will take a lot of time and effort on your part, but the potential rewards will be substantial.

Unless you already have some prospects in mind, you should start by joining a real estate investment club. This will allow you to network and find potential members of your club. You can also start to learn about how to invest and what properties to invest in.

Joining a club may also provide you with the opportunity to meet with members of existing investment groups so that you can get an idea of how they work. You can also learn from their mistakes so you can avoid them in your own investment activities.

When assessing potential members, some of the considerations to keep in mind include:

- Do you feel comfortable entrusting them with your money?
- Do you feel that they are responsible enough to pay their contributions on time?
- Will they be able to meaningfully contribute to the group?
- Are they decisive enough to 'pull the trigger' when it comes to making investment decisions?

Aside from looking for potential partners, you should think about how your group will be run. For instance, how much will you need as an initial investment so that you can start buying properties? How many members will you accept and how much will you require them to invest?

You should also consider your investment goals. What types of property do you want to invest in? What investment strategy are you going to follow? You should look for members whose investment outlooks reflect yours.

Once you have identified potential members with similar investment goals who are willing to join your club, invite them for an organizational meeting. Discuss with them how the group will be run and will be organized. For instance, what officer positions will the organization have (President, Vice-President, Treasurer, et. al.)?

You should also discuss how much each person will invest, how withdrawals or reductions of investments will be handled and how the group will be dissolved. Can a person make an initial investment and then pay smaller monthly amounts?

You should also decide how and why to accept new members. For instance, if one of the founders withdraws, will you accept a new member or just increase the remaining members' investments? Under what circumstances will you accept new members?

In addition, if you already have an investment property in mind, you can propose it to them. Make sure to provide details such as the cost of the property, how much is the down payment and how big the mortgage will be.

When you have decided on policies regarding how the group will be run, these should be written down. This document will serve as your operating agreement. All members should agree with its provisions and sign the document in order to make it binding.

Having a binding operating agreement means that you have a formal set of rules that dictates how the company will be run. Thus, you can avoid misunderstandings since you already have written specific guidelines for how to deal with particular issues. Keep this in mind when you are drafting the operating agreement.

Here are some of the things that should be covered:

- What is each member's ownership share (in percent)?
- What are the responsibilities of members?
- What are their duties?
- What are their voting rights?
- How will profit and loss be allocated?
- How will meetings be held?
- How will the company be managed?

- What are the provisions if a member wants to sell his share? What if a member wants to buy out another's share? What if a member wants to sell his share to an outsider?
- What happens if a member dies?

Once you have created an operating agreement and an organizational structure, you can start preparing to register your group. Generally, investment groups are organized as general partnerships, under which all partners will equally share the assets and profits of a business as well as its legal and financial liabilities.

For the purposes of investing, it is best that you register your group as a limited liability company or LLC. Under this type of corporate structure, the partners are not personally liable for the company's debts. This means that creditors cannot sue to seize your personal assets so they can be paid back.

Another advantage of the LLC is that you will enjoy taxation benefits. Since the LLC is considered a pass-through entity, it passes on its profits and losses to the members. Each member is then required to report his profits, paying taxes at personal federal tax rates, rather than as corporate tax.

The LLC thus allows you to avoid double taxation on the rental income. In addition, if you were to dispose of the investment property after a year, it would be also be taxed at the lower capital gains rate.

Another benefit of an LLC is that it allows you the freedom to distribute profits, unlike in a corporation where they have to be given out based on the amounts invested. Thus, you can have a partner who does not make a direct financial investment, but who has agreed to handle the running and maintenance of the properties in exchange for a share of the profits.

It should be noted, however, that the LLC does not exist in perpetuity unlike a corporation. If a member dies or goes bankrupt, the LLC has to be dissolved. In this case, the partners will have to create a business continuation agreement, which will transfer the member's interest to another party to ensure that the company can continue.

Although it is possible to file your own LLC documents, you might want to consult with a lawyer or legal service to help you. This way, you are assured that you will not miss anything that could make your LLC registration invalid. There are many low-cost and reputable legal services, such as Nolo, that you can find online.

In addition, you will have to apply for an Employer Identification Number (EIN) with the IRS. The EIN is a unique nine-digit number that also indicates in which state the business is registered. You can apply for one at the IRS website by filling up an application form. You do not have to pay for anything as registration is free.

All businesses need to have an EIN as this allows the IRS to identify them for the purposes of filing business taxes. Financial institutions such as banks and brokerages will also not allow you to open an account if you do not have an EIN.

When you register your LLC, you should include your operating agreement in the registration papers. It is not mandatory in most states, but if you do not file one, it is construed to indicate your agreement to run your group based on your state's default rules. These are very broad since they are not tailored to a particular business and may not be appropriate for your particular requirements.

Another thing you need to do is to open a bank account in the name of the business. You will have to designate people who will have direct access to this account – usually the treasurer or other officer. The company's money will be deposited into this account and disbursed as needed.

One of the keys to the success of the group is keeping accurate records. By doing so, you can account for each members' share of the equity as well as their returns. This will help you avoid misunderstandings that can result in conflict within the group.

You can prepare your records using a Google spreadsheet with the relevant data on it. You can even make it accessible to the other members to ensure the transparency of the group's financial affairs.

If you are inexperienced, you might want to consult with a professional accountant. They will show you how to keep records, what documents you need to keep, and most importantly, how to file your tax returns. The cost of hiring one will be more than offset by the potential penalties from the IRS that you will be able to avoid.

Unless one or more of the members are willing to take on the job of managing and maintaining the property, the group will have to hire somebody to do it. You and the other members will have to decide how much to pay them and how they will be paid. If the property is not yet generating income, you will have to shoulder their salary out-of-pocket. The members may have to make donations until the rental income starts to come in.

Once there are candidates, the members will have to approve them, unless a particular member is designated with the power to hire. Either way, once a particular person or persons are hired, there will have to be a meeting so that the members will be familiar with them.

Scoring REIGs

A. Liquidity

Your investment is not liquid since it is not easy to withdraw it if you suddenly need money. Unlike REITs, you cannot simply sell your share. Depending on the bylaws of the group, you may need to ask another member if they are willing to buy out your share.

2/10

B. Scalability

This depends on the rules of the group. Usually, however, you cannot just increase your investment unless the group decides to buy another property. If you want to increase your investment in real estate, you may have to join another group.

2/10

C. Potential Return On Investment

As with real estate investment trusts, the ROI earned with REIGs comes from both rental income and your share of the proceeds if the property is sold. Thus, the return on investment can vary depending on how much income is generated.

There are other factors that may affect your profitability. For instance, the group may impose other fees and charges, such as your share of management and maintenance costs.

On the other hand, it should be noted that real estate investments are still among the most profitable. Provided that the group chose its investment well, then you should still enjoy a high ROI even after expenses are removed. You will also be able to pay fewer taxes if you organize your group as an LLC.

5/10

D. Passivity

Investing with a real estate investment group is not passive income since it requires some effort. The amount of effort required depends on whether you join a group or form your own. However, it still requires less effort than direct ownership since you can share duties with others. In addition, once the property has started generating income, the effort required to continue earning income will be sharply reduced.

5/10

D. Simplicity

How easy is it to get into investing through a group? Again, it depends. If you are setting up your own group, then it is not simple. But if you are just joining one, it may be as simple as just attending meetings and making your investment.

Be that as it may, you do not need a high level of expertise when you invest with a group. In fact, it is designed for people who are not that knowledgeable about investing, since you will have the benefit of more experienced investors working with you.

5/10

Ten Tips for Successfully Investing in REIGs

1. Make sure that you feel comfortable with the other members of the group. Whether you join a group or form your own, keep in mind that you are ultimately entrusting the success of your investment to other people. So it is very important that you trust them and feel comfortable with them handling your money. This way, you will have peace of mind that your investment is in good hands.

2. Take a long-term viewpoint. As mentioned earlier, REIGs follow a buy-and-hold strategy that involves holding on to the investment property to generate income from it. It may take some time before you start earning the maximum returns from your investment. So you should be patient. Don't expect to start earning a lot from your investment at once.

3. Keep learning. Real estate investment clubs should never be just about making money. They should also provide an opportunity for members to constantly learn new things about investing. If you run the group, make sure that you provide educational opportunities such as inviting speakers and holding workshops. This will help them to make better decisions when you have to vote on your investments and ultimately make them more profitable.

4. Build a network. One of the most important functions of joining a REIG is not just being able to pool your money to invest, but meeting people who can help you. Through the group, you can find a mentor who will help you learn about investing and avoiding common mistakes. You can also build a support group with whom you can brainstorm ideas and talk over your problems.

5. Be disciplined with your commitments to the group. You should not view your participation in the REIG as simply a way to make money. Make sure that you allocate time to meet your duties and responsibilities. Keep in mind that the success of the group would ultimate result in greater profitability of your investment.

6. Periodically assess the strategy of the group. Take time to meet with the other members and discuss investments. Are you maximizing your investment with this property? Should you add another property or sell the one you have? Should you shift (i.e. pivot) to another type of property? Is the management strategy maximizing the returns the group gets from the property? Does the group need to change or adjust its strategy?

7. Work with an accountant. Unfortunately, our tax laws are very complicated and there is a possibility that you may miss something that will result in severe penalties later on. A qualified accountant can help you avoid these pitfalls. And the costs of hiring one will be more than offset by the savings you can enjoy long-term.

8. Make the meetings enjoyable. You should not treat your group meetings as if it was a board meeting of a corporation. Of course, there are serious parts, such as reporting on the state of the investments. At the same time, you should remember that you are also networking with the other members. Make sure that you provide snacks and refreshments. You can also schedule social activities for the members, such as going golfing.

9. Don't be afraid to leave if you have to. If the group no longer fulfills your investment requirements, you should not hesitate to exit. Of course, this can be difficult, particularly if you have already become fond of the other members. But keep in mind that there are other ways that you can support the group, such as becoming a mentor to new members or by being a regular speaker.

10. Have an exit strategy. There may be times when the group decides that it is better to sell the property to a bigger investor rather that continue to run it. You should already have prepared for this possibility by creating a plan for wrapping up the group. How will you wrap up the group's affairs? How will the proceeds of the sale be divided among the members?

Interesting Fact #3

The primary purpose of a Castle's moat was to prevent attackers from digging tunnels under the walls.

Chapter 24

Real Estate Limited Partnership

Partnership is a form of business entity that exists in numerous industries, not just in real estate. It has two classifications: general and limited. In general partnerships, two or more parties join together and contribute their resources for a venture. These resources include, but are not limited to, skills, labor, money, equipment and land. All the parties involved (known as partners) have their own roles and can exercise control on the various operations of the business.

If they have no written agreement about unequal profit and role distribution, they would share the gains and losses together. Every partner also has the same limitless personal liability for debts and litigations involving the venture.

In contrast, limited partnership, as its name implies, have definite boundaries regarding the contribution of each partner and the distribution of profits and liabilities. In this setup, the one party that does more gets more and has more power compared to the other party. However, the other party can gain from the venture without spending much time and effort. His personal liabilities are limited and risk exposure is low as well.

Each partner in general partnership should be knowledgeable in operating a business. On the other hand, limited partnership doesn't require everyone to be familiar with the nature of the business. This makes real estate limited partnership (RELP) an ideal investment choice for anyone who wants to invest in the real estate industry despite not having sufficient knowledge or training on property development and management.

Overview of Business Model

Limited partnership is more common in the real estate industry than in any other industry. It's mainly because property development and management require significant amount of capital investments. Other businesses can be financed through loans because they have securities to offer. The real estate can be used as securities for loans, but doing so usually complicates property management. The interests can eat up the potential profits as well.

RELP is similar with REIT and REIG in the sense that it raises capital by getting investors. Unlike the two, however, limited partnership is less complex. It may also be restricted to a small group. One family or group of friends can even pool their money, select a property manager, and set up a RELP.

In RELP, there are at least two parties involved. They're classified as either general or limited partner. Real estate developers and property managers are the ones who serve as general partners. Limited partners, on the other hand, could be any person or business.

The General Partner

Purchasing raw land, developing properties, converting lands, financing real estate deals and selling developed lands are among the functions of real estate developers. They usually start with planning what kind of property to develop; it could be a condominium building, an apartment complex, a planned community or a shopping center. If the developer gets capital investments from limited partners, the properties they tend to develop are those that can be sold.

Before making proposals to would-be limited partners, developers scour the state or country for raw or developed lands where they can turn their plans into reality. Upon making a shortlist, they make an offer to buy the lands from the respective owners. The sale rarely happens overnight. It may take numerous negotiations which involve adjusting the proposed amount and adding offers such as relocation.

If the negotiations fail, the developers go for the other options in their shortlists. They'll keep going until a landowner accepts the offer. Prior the transfer of ownership, the developers get capital investments from limited partners and use a portion of that to pay the landowners.

Once all the paperwork regarding the ownership is done, the developers will then start the construction in a raw land. If the land they bought has an existing building, they will begin with demolition. Before the construction gets completed, the developers will market them to potential buyers. The sale of properties determines the amount that each limited partner will get as ROI.

Before the sale of developed properties, the developers hold ownership over them. This is their main difference with property managers. Developers may or may not manage the properties they own. Conversely, property managers may not own the properties they're supposed to rent out or sell.

Independent property managers don't have to buy and develop properties, but they may do some renovation. They're hired by developers, building-owners and homeowners to oversee the sale or lease of properties. Property managers are in charge of dealing with the buyers and tenants directly. They're expected to be familiar with the properties and the surrounding environment because they have to answer queries from prospects. If the buyers and tenants have issues, property managers are also tasked to resolve them.

In RELP, property managers can also get financial investments from limited partners and use such to purchase properties. The limited partners could be deemed as the collective owners of the properties before they get sold. However, they can't live on the said properties or use them in any other way because there's no definite distribution of the properties beforehand.

Between developers and property managers, the former deals with greater risk. Property development involves several steps that take years to be completed. The negotiations alone can take months. Disputes with the owners of neighboring properties may also arise, which will further cause delays and losses. The construction, along with the demolition of existing structure, may be finished within a year provided that the developer has sufficient capital investments.

As a general partner, however, developers are better in offering higher ROIs especially if they handle every aspect of property development (like construction, property management and marketing) instead of outsourcing the services of other companies.

In contrast, independent property managers may only take months to renovate, market and sell properties. But because they didn't have much control over the construction of the property, they have to settle with the existing design. This limits the potential worth of the property.

The Limited Partner

As for the role of a limited partner, it's basically providing capital investments to finance the purchase, development and marketing of properties. In the process, as a limited partner, you're also indirectly paying management fees to the general partner.

Depending on the size of the real estate, there could be one or more limited partners. For limited partners, the number of limited partners shouldn't affect their ROIs. It's the amount of their capital investments that matter. The number of limited partners affects the general partner in different ways, though. If there's only one limited partner, the amount of capital investment may not be that sufficient for the real estate deals.

On the other hand, having more limited partners mean more financial help for the general partner. But this also means that the general partner is financially and legally accountable to more people in case there are violations in the written agreement regarding the RELP.

Limited partners and stockholders are both regarded as investors, but unlike the latter, limited partners have no direct control on the selection, conversion, marketing and other management aspects of the real estate. Stockholders may not have control as well, but because their investments can be liquidated easily, they can influence the management to bend down and heed their demands. Limited partners, on the other hand, don't have such influence.

There are two ways to become a limited partner: the first one is buying limited partnership (LP) units and the other is dealing with a general partner directly. Buying LP units is a lot like buying stocks. You can do it online with the help of brokerage firm or through the stock exchange itself. It's less time-consuming and less risky than setting up a RELP with a general partner. If you choose to buy LP units, you can also benefit from property management involving real estate in different states or even in another country.

Brokerage firms can be strict, though, when it comes to accepting limited partners. They usually set a minimum amount of capital investment. Additionally, you might be required to undergo some training.

If you intend to get LP units from the stock exchange, make sure you are buying the right securities. Otherwise, you won't be able to enjoy the tax benefits for limited partners.

Forming a RELP along with a general partner offers you a chance to suggest properties to manage especially if real estate opportunities abound in your district. A general partner could be any individual, but as much as possible, you should choose someone who has experience in property management. If you opt for this instead of buying LP units, you're not just investing money; you're also investing trust in the general partner. If a problem arises, both your investment and relationship could be affected.

For managing family estates, the members of the family can form a RELP as well. Once the family estate is rented out or sold, the gift and excess taxes that the limited partnership has to pay are lesser compared to the taxes when managing the estate as individuals. Moreover, a RELP offers transparency and helps reduce the possibility of conflicts between family members regarding the distribution of profits. To further ensure fairness, the family can hire a third-party as property manager.

Formation of a RELP

To form a RELP from scratch, you and your would-be general partner should discuss the properties that the latter will manage. You may or may not partake in the researching and planning stages. However, you have the chance to participate in discussing the goals of the limited partnership so you should make the most out of it.

When the business goals and plans are determined, you and your general partner can then decide the name and logo of your RELP. The next step is to set up an office for your general partner. As the registered agent of your venture, an office address is necessary partly because this is where the authorities can send summons to and where prospective buyers can visit.

In most US states, another requirement for registering a RELP is a written agreement between the partners. The written agreement should detail the rights and responsibilities of each party. There should also be information regarding legal and financial sanctions in case one party fails to do his task.

These sanctions should protect the general partner if you, as the limited partner, don't give the amount required for capital investments. Such sanctions should also provide protection for you in case your general partner doesn't give your supposed dividends or allow you to review the venture's accounting records.

The distribution of profits and liabilities should be included in the agreement as well. There should be a target date indicated in the written agreement about the start of putting the properties on sale. This will give you an idea on how long you have to wait before you can get your investment back and earn profits.

To protect himself from unlimited personal liability, the general partner can apply for a limited liability partnership. If the general partner does all the work while you're the only one financing, you may opt for an equal distribution of profits. However, the general partner has the upper hand in altering the distribution after a certain period of time.

Another important component of the written agreement is the clause regarding the process of dissolving the RELP. This one will be useful in mitigating losses in case the property management doesn't work out the way the general partner has planned. The written agreement should be reviewed by a certified public accountant and notarized by a lawyer to prevent loopholes and to make sure it's legally binding.

This may not be necessary but it helps if you include information regarding a possible change in ownership structure. This will become useful when you're not satisfied with your general partner's management style. You may choose to take over some of his roles and rights as general partner based on the clause on changing ownership structure. Doing so, however, entails that you're no longer a limited partner so you'll be no longer eligible for the tax benefits, lower risk exposure and limited personal liability.

Aside from the written agreement, the general partner has to secure the necessary permits, licenses and certifications required in the state where the office is located. Once settled, the general partner can then file for a certificate of limited partnership in the office of the local secretary of the state. This involves paying for filing fees. Registering for business tax is the next step.

Some RELPs opted to register in another state instead of where their office is. This is a strategy to avoid costly filing fees especially in states where there's a real estate boom. Tax incentives are also better in some states which serve as their way of attracting investors. To apply your RELP in another state, though, you and your general partner need to comply with the foreign qualifications set by the state.

Before you get the certificate of limited partnership, you can still make suggestions to your general partner. However, once there's a certificate, you shouldn't meddle with the tasks of the general partner in one way or another. Doing so can serve as violation of your written agreement.

Depending on your agreement, the general partner should provide weekly, monthly and yearly updates regarding the gains and losses of your venture. Other than the gains and losses, he has the option not to divulge information about the daily operations of your partnership.

Being the sole limited partner means you'll shoulder the majority—if not all—of the capital investments needed to be raised for your venture. This is a great risk on your part. To minimize such risk, one option is to look for additional limited partners. You can let your general partner do this on your behalf. But if you do so, you shouldn't stop your general partner from accepting or rejecting certain people or business entities.

Ideally, all limited partners will get the same percentage of dividends. However, when a general partner talks to another limited partner, he may offer a deal that's better than the one he has with you.

After a certain period of time, you may re-negotiate with your general partner. He might make additional proposals to entice you to re-invest your dividends to the partnership. It may also be his way of encouraging you to increase your capital investments. If you no longer want to take part in the partnership, you can get out and take your investment elsewhere.

During negotiations, the general partner usually presents projected values of the properties. Instead of focusing on the projections, you should ask about the bases for such. Political and economic crisis in the local communities can affect the real estate market.

If the general partner can't justify that the local political and economic scene will maintain its status quo or improve in the future, it might not be better to invest in the said properties. But if the status quo could be maintained or if the prospects are good, the property development and management are ideal investment options.

Pros and Cons Of Limited Partner

One pro of being a limited partner is that it doesn't require your active involvement in managing the properties. On the other hand, general partners handle many things. It's not surprising that not a lot of people would like to be such. The same goes with being a stockholder in a real estate company or being an owner of a rental property. Thankfully, being a limited partner enables you to earn passively from real estate.

It's also a pro that you don't have to find and convince buyers when you are in a RELP. Not everyone is cut out to be a property manager because such job requires people skills. If you're not too keen on dealing with investors, contractors, landowners, buyers, tenants, and maintenance technicians, being a property manager may not be for you. Nevertheless, you can still gain from RELP thanks to a skilled property manager.

Your personal liability in a RELP is limited. As a limited partner, you still have personal liability over the venture's debts. This means that the authorities and creditors can go after your personal assets. **However, your personal liability won't go beyond the amount of your capital investment**. Plus, the authorities and creditors usually go after the general partner's assets first. You might still have a bit more time to prepare if they start seizing.

Another good thing about RELP is that the limited partner doesn't have to deal with litigation. Only the general partner has personal liability in case the company gets sued.

You're also not in charge of paying business taxes. The general partner will be the one paying business taxes. The payment may come from your capital investments but at least you won't have to deal with tax preparation and filing.

RELP is less risky compared to other real estate investment options. In RELP, there's always a property to be sold which means that there's a greater chance that you'll be able to get your investment back. After the sale, you can invest elsewhere or re-invest in your partnership which will cover new properties.

It's easier to track your profits and expenses as a limited partner.

A general partner can enjoy management fees and shared profits from the sale of the real estate. However, such advantages come with the complexity of tracking personal gains and losses. As a limited partner, you'll find it easier to identify and compute your profits, making your tax preparation less stressful as well.

You can learn from your general partner. Even if you aren't directly involved in the way the property or your capital investments are managed, you can still observe and learn from your general partner's marketing strategies. You might be able to score some connections for your next investments as well. Being a limited partner can also serve as your training ground in becoming a general partner.

On the downside, you have little to no control on various aspects of the business in a RELP. In a general partnership, the parties involved can make compromises whenever they have disagreements. That can't be said about limited partnership. Limited partners are also referred as silent partners because they don't have a say on how the property is managed. Nevertheless, you won't feel the need to control the business operations if you have a dependable property manager.

As a limited partner, you can't force your general partner to buy a property you like or market it in a certain way. You can't stop him from buying certain properties either. If you're quite close to your general partner, you might be able to recommend properties and marketing strategies. However, the other party still reserves the right to accept or reject your suggestions. In case you just have LP units, your ability to make suggestions is further restricted.

It will take years before you can make some profits. Unless your general partner has plenty of connections to close sales and unless the properties are already developed, you shouldn't expect to gain significant ROIs right away. You're lucky if you get your investment back and earn 15% ROIs after five years.

If the real estate gets sold at a much lower price, you might not be able to recoup your initial investment. Most of the time, the properties involved in RELPs are sold in one way or another. However, the expected value of the property doesn't always turn out to be true.

If this happens, you won't be able to get your investment back. Worse, you might even have to pay for debts in case the sale didn't generate enough money to pay back the venture's debts. The general partner may get debts in case the real estate deals require re-financing. As a limited partner, you can't advise him to avoid such.

The general partner can re-schedule the distribution of dividends. As if the years of waiting aren't enough, the general partner can postpone the distribution of dividends. This won't be much of a disadvantage if the general partner makes a counter-offer such as bigger percentage in the succeeding sales. But if you badly needed that ROI, this will become a major disappointment.

In case the property is sold at a much higher price than the projected one, the general partner may keep the excess for himself. It's a good thing if your general partner is able to meet the expected sale of the property. This means that you'll get your expected ROIs as well.

As for the excess, the general partner can opt not to share it with you. But instead of considering this as a disadvantage on your part, you should think of it as an incentive for the general partner for doing a great job.

There's a risk that your general partner will abandon your venture. Trust is an important element in RELP. Even if your general partner is someone you know personally, there's still the possibility that he will spend all your capital investment and run away without giving your money back. The risk is greater if you're dealing with a general partner you just met for the sake of the venture.

The best way to reduce this risk is get to know your general partner well. Even if you're buying LP units from a brokerage firm, you should still research about the developer or property manager that will use up your capital investments.

If you have doubts about the integrity and/or competency of a potential general partner, it will be much better for you to avoid partnering up with him. Making a deal with them, despite having trust issues, will only result to stress in the long run, whether your doubts are proven right or wrong. If your doubts are proven to be true, your capital investment is also at risk.

Scoring RELPs

A. Liquidity

One of the criticisms with RELPs is that it takes time for every partner to get their investment back. For limited partners, their investments are practically illiquid. It's possible for them to opt out, but getting the exact capital investment right away is another story.

3/10

B. Scalability

Property developments may need re-financing at one point. This will be a good chance for limited partners to increase their investments. However, scaling may not be that easy if there's a certain period of time stated in the written agreement before re-financing and re-negotiations will be entertained.

5/10

C. Potential Return On Investment

The earnings of limited partners in RELPs can be substantial and they are considered as securities. Thus, if you're a limited partner, you have to pay for the appropriate taxes for such earnings. Nevertheless, the tax isn't as burdensome as business and estate tax.

8/10

D. Passivity

Of all real estate investment options, nothing can beat RELP in terms of earning passively. Your only task is to buy LP units or provide cold cash. Once you're done with this, you can leave everything to the general partner. You can simply look or ask for updates every once in a while.

9/10

E. Simplicity

Whether you buy LP units or form a RELP with someone else, being a limited partner is simpler than being a property manager, stockholder or landlord. The major challenges with this investment option are to find a reliable RELP and be accepted as a limited partner.

8/10

Tips for Successfully Investing in RELPs

1. Choose a general partner who has a proven track record of selecting and managing properties that offer high ROIs.

2. Start investing in a RELP that focuses more on developing residential properties.

3. If you want quicker returns, invest in properties that are already constructed. If you want higher returns, look for properties that are still in the process of getting completed.

4. Diversify your RELP investments. Make sure there are short-term and long-term RELPs.

5. Avoid "handshake" agreements even if the general partner is a family, friend or colleague. Always have a written partnership agreement that's properly accounted and notarized.

6. Prioritize buying LP units from a reliable brokerage firm instead of giving cold cash and setting up a RELP from scratch.

7. Never step out of your boundaries as a limited partner. If you try to get involved in any of the daily operations of your partnership, you might lose your status as limited partner and incur additional liabilities in the process.

8. Partner up with one general partner and several limited partners for one venture.

9. Never invest more than what you can afford to lose.

10. If RELP is just a single investment opportunity for you, you can do it with a small group like your family or friends. If you intend to make it as a recurring investment, go for an established firm.

Interesting Fact #4

In Japan, most houses *depreciate in value*. Half of all houses are demolished within 38 years and there is virtually no market for pre-owned homes. Per capita, there are nearly four times as many architects and more than twice as many construction workers in Japan as the U.S.

Books In The Business and Money Series	
Series #	**Book Title**
1	Affiliate Marketing
2	Passive Income Ideas
3	Affiliate Marketing + Passive Income Ideas (2-in-1 Bundle)
4	Facebook Advertising
5	Dropshipping
6	Dropshipping + Facebook Advertising (2-in-1 Bundle)
7	Real Estate Investing For Beginners
8	Credit Cards and Credit Repair Secrets
9	Real Estate Investing And Credit Repair Strategies (2-in-1 Bundle)
10	Passive Income With Affiliate Marketing (2nd Edition)
11	Passive Income With Dividend Investing
12	Stock Market Investing For Beginners
13	The Simple Stock Market Investing Blueprint (2-in-1 Bundle)
The kindle edition will be available to you for FREE when you purchase the paperback version from Amazon.com (The US Store)	

Download The Audio Versions Along With The Complementary PDF Document For FREE from www.MichaelEzeanaka.com > My Audiobooks

Chapter 25

Tax Lien Certificates

Many real estate investors allocate a portion of their investment portfolio to tax lien certificates. They find it wise to invest in these instruments owing to the relatively low entry point and safety.

Tax lien certificates are issued on properties with unpaid property taxes. They can be acquired through auctions. Depending on the rules, a bidder wins by offering either the lowest interest rate or the highest premium over the amount of the lien.

The winning bidder pays the government in cash for the amount of tax liability on the property. He receives his tax lien certificate and can expect to be paid by the property owner an amount equivalent to the lien plus the interest before a specified expiration date.

This investment instrument is favorable to the government and to the investor. The government is able to effectively collect on property taxes by offering lien certificates to willing investors. For investors, on the other hand, these are simple and safe instruments that can give them modest returns over a term of 3-5 years.

How Tax Liens Work

Property taxes are used to fund the salaries of school teachers, policemen, firemen, and other public officials and employees in many counties and territories. Tax revenues are also used to build infrastructure.

When property owners do not pay their taxes, it follows that the government will not have a source of funds for all its essential expenses. This is why the government needs to issue tax liens on properties whose owners go delinquent on their tax obligations.

Liens are issued by the government and tax lien auctions are held periodically. There are on-location auctions and online auctions. Investors bid on these liens either in terms of interest rate or of premium top up. The government issues tax lien certificates that indicate the amount of tax to be settled, the interest due, and the expiration date.

It is important to note that not all states offer tax liens. There are some states that sell the property straight out. In states that do issue tax liens, the government offers investors a chance to earn when the taxes are paid by the property owner or future buyer on or before a specified date.

The property owner is obligated to pay the tax lien within the stipulated period. Otherwise, the property may be foreclosed. Either way, the tax lien certificate investor does not have to worry about as he is assured of payment.

The security of a tax lien certificate comes from it being higher in priority ranking in terms of payments. Even in a mortgage foreclosure, the holder of the tax lien certificate is paid first before payments are applied to other financial obligations and expense lines.

Investing in Tax Lien Certificates

One of the factors that make tax lien certificates appealing to investors is their affordability. The purchase amount can be as low as a few hundred dollars for small properties to thousands of dollars for bigger and more attractive properties. Investors buy tax lien certificates from auctions by placing bids on:

1. **Interest** – the maximum interest rate is set by each county. They can be as low as 12% to as high as 50%. The interest rates are printed on the tax lien certificates and are considered to be binding.

2. **Premium**– the bidders may ask to pay a specified amount of premium on top of the tax lien. This may or may not earn interest to be paid back to the investor within the redemption period.

The certificate also indicates the redemption period within which the property owner should settle the full amount of his financial obligation. This is usually about 2 to 5 years.

The Auction Process

The tax lien auction is a fairly simple process, but you have to be prepared for it. You need to understand what you are getting into as well as the various factors that affect the market. As yields on tax liens certificates are pretty much set in auctions, you do not have to worry about market fluctuations and valuations.

You need to do due diligence to make sure that the tax lien certificates that you are considering are worth investing in. It's not always about buying the property with the lowest liens. While future property values do not directly affect how much your tax lien certificates are worth, they do affect your chances of being paid back.

Find out what you need to do so you can evaluate your potential yield versus your risks accordingly. Also, be ready with a fall-back position in case things do not go your way during the auction.

Check the auction details in advance to know what is required of you on the day itself. This will also allow you to make quick decisions on properties that you are particularly interested in. For instance, you might have to be prepared to pay up right there and then when you win a bid. Some auctions require full payment within 24 hours while some require upfront payment.

Don't be worried about walking away empty handed. That's alright. Learn from every experience and take each auction as an opportunity to network with other investors. Perhaps these could lead to mutually beneficial partnerships in the future.

Earning From Tax Lien Certificates

There are two possible ways for you to get a return on your investment in tax lien certificates. The first one is, of course, through interest payments. If all works out well and the property owner is able to pay off the lien, you get your money back plus interest.

If, on the other hand, the property owner is not able to make his payments, you can gain from your investment through potential property ownership. However, there are risks and unexpected expenses that could arise out of this scenario. In this case, your gain would depend on how well prepared you are for the risks.

- **When the property owner pays** – you will receive a check within 5 to 10 business days for your investment plus the interest rate. The lien is erased, the property remains with its owner, and you collect on your investment and earnings.
- **When the property owner does not pay** – you may have the property foreclosed and take the amount representing the lien and the interest. Or, you can also take ownership of the house. Your lawyer and the assigned county officials can assist you throughout this process.

Pros and Cons of Tax Lien Certificates

Tax lien certificates are profitable investments. Tax revenue authorities give taxpayers a specific time period within which to settle their obligations on the tax lien certificate. If the taxpayers end up not paying off the debt, then the investor will receive the property deed.

If the owner redeems the property by settling the unpaid balance during the set redemption period, then the investor will receive a profit. You'll get whatever you invested plus the interest earnings. At the very least, you gain a modest amount in interest earnings. At best, you get to own property without paying for its actual market value.

You don't need a huge capital to begin investing in tax lien certificates. Compared to other investment methods, investing in these certificates do not require a huge amount of capital for buying in.

You do not have to fork out thousands of dollars to invest in these certificates as you would for mutual funds and other investment instruments. For just a few hundred dollars, you can already purchase tax lien certificates and look forward to more substantial potential yield.

You can diversify your investments. Because your initial capital is smaller compared to other kinds of investments, you can easily diversify and spread your capital across various multiple tax lien certificates.

Diversification can be done by buying certificates found in various housing markets. Do not limit yourself to just one county. There are various auctions held all across the country. It would be good to do some research on the most profitable areas for investing in tax lien certificates.

It could serve as a source of passive income. While you would have to do some ground work before you invest in this instrument, you can just leave it to earn for you once you've finished setting it up.

There are no market values for you to watch or bids and trades to place to profit from your investment. If you are investing in several certificates, you simply need to get organized and track the redemption periods and expiration dates.

You'll be able to familiarize yourself with the real estate market and take advantage of other investment opportunities it offers. Going to auctions and investing in these certificates is a good way to get your feet wet in the real estate market. There are many other real estate investment instruments for you to put your money in and earn from.

The real estate market is a lucrative market. Aside from tax lien certificates, you can learn all about buying and selling properties, renting out residential and commercial spaces, providing accommodations to transients and long-term tenants, flipping houses, and other similar income-generating activities. Eventually, you can move to other kinds of real estate investments and grow your income earning potential.

Beginner investors should be cautious about plunging into this kind of investment. Although it is relatively safe, it is easy for those who are just starting out to make bad decisions when it comes to which properties to invest in.

Do your homework and learn as much as you can about this instrument. The prep work and the decision-making required for this investment requires deeper understanding of the market and the possible outcomes of investing in tax lien certificates.

For instance, you have to be aware of the risks that you may face if the owner doesn't pay for the taxes and fails to redeem the property. You can end up paying for expensive court costs just to obtain the tax deed and you won't even get profits from your original investment.

Also, if the property owner ends up filing for bankruptcy, you might not be able to push for the foreclosure of the property while the decision on the bankruptcy case is still pending.

Tax liens aren't everlasting instruments. You cannot buy a tax lien certificate and hold on to it for a long time. You cannot expect it to appreciate in value over the long term. It has an expiration date. After this date, any unclaimed and unpaid balances cannot be collected by the investor anymore.

It is also possible for the property to go into foreclosure and the investor could find out that there are other liens issued on it. This means that there are others who can lay claim on the property and it would be difficult to get the property deed or title.

To put it bluntly, you might not get anything from your investment when this happens. Your certificate will not be worth more than the paper it's printed on after its expiration date.

The amount of capital can vary. You need to have cash on-hand to invest in this instrument. Those who are short of cash might not be able to take advantage of this investment instrument even if it only requires a small amount of money to get into.

Be careful not to put in all your cash into this investment. These are not liquid assets that you can convert to cash when you need it. Follow the basic rule that you are not supposed to invest money that you are not prepared to lose.

You could end up spending more on repairs and other related expenses. If you buy a tax lien certificate on a property without checking it out first, you could end up with a property that requires considerable repairs. With such a property, the owner would probably not have any interest in making any more payments at all and could easily 'abandon' it.

This could leave you with a piece of property that's worth less than what you expected. You might have to spend more for the repairs just to get the property marketable again. Even worse is when the property turns out to have been permanently damaged by some natural catastrophe or environmental conditions.

You can prevent this from happening to you by doing your research and due diligence. The extra time and effort you spend check out the properties will be an advantage for you.

The competition can get fierce. You'd find other investors and money managers looking at the best tax liens to purchase. These seasoned market players already know the market well and have a keen eye on which properties to target.

It could be intimidating when you are faced with competitors with more experience and resources. Don't get fazed. You just have to make sure that you exert more effort in learning the ropes. There are actually experts who can guide you in preparing for the auction and planning your investment strategy.

Scoring Tax Lien Certificates

A. Liquidity

A tax lien certificate is not a liquid investment unlike other financial instruments such as stocks, bonds, and bank deposits that can easily be withdrawn, redeemed, or sold.

Once you've bought a tax lien, you've said goodbye to your money. You can't really demand to get your cash back. You can only wait for the property owner to pay the tax lien off, and sometimes it can take a long time for them to settle the amount.

The tax lien will stay in your portfolio until the owner redeems the property or if you foreclose it. Sure, you can sell your tax lien certificate or assign the rights to another party, but it would also take time before you can find a buyer for it. You may even have to sacrifice the interest you've earned if you want to get your principal back.

1/10

B. Scalability

Tax lien certificate investments are quite scalable, as you can just stock up on these certificates, provided you have the funds to buy more of them. It's not impossible to have multiple certificates, especially if you're closely watching the calendar for auctions in the areas you are interested in. You can build your portfolio if you regularly go to these auctions and buy more certificates.

7/10

C. Potential Return On Investment

Investing in tax lien certificates can be financially rewarding, especially if you came in prepared with enough capital to spend on investments. If you perform the necessary research, then you have bigger chances of bringing home profits.

This kind of investment involves taxes, simply because it all starts with the property owner not paying for the right amount of taxes to the government. When you buy the tax lien certificate, you pay the office the necessary amount of taxes owed by the property owner. In this manner, you're paying taxes owed by somebody else.

6/10

D. Passivity

Investing in tax lien certificates take some amount of work especially if you plan to add new ones to your portfolio periodically. This mean always being on the lookout for properties with tax liens that are going to be auctioned soon, going around to 'investigate' the properties that you are interested in, and preparing bids.

You also have to keep track of redemption periods and expiration dates to ensure that you will get your money back. You can choose to partner with someone else to co-manage your tax lien certificates especially if you are new to investing in real estate.

If you are only interested in investing in a few certificates, you can just sit back and see what happens to your investment after you have done your prep work and have set up this portion of your portfolio, you can pretty much just sit back and wait for the property owners to make their payments.

5/10

E. Simplicity

Investing in tax lien certificates is simple enough for those who already have experience in the real estate market. The process is fairly straightforward, but some groundwork needs to be done before the auction date. Novice investors can learn about this investment instrument, but would benefit from advice and guidance from more experienced investors.

It also does not take a lot of cash to invest in tax lien certificates. You can choose to put your money in only a handful of properties that fit your criteria. Even receiving the payout on the certificate is simple as the investor just has to wait for the check in the mail within a few days from the owner's settlement of his obligations.

5/10

Ten Tips for Successfully Investing in Tax Lien Certificates

As you've realized, like any other investment, there are risks that come with tax lien certificates. You may have been promised a good deal of returns, but you still have to be careful in investing on these. To increase your chances of gaining from your investment in tax lien certificates, here are 10 tips to keep in mind:

1. Be aware of the laws of the area you will be operating in. Laws involving real estate vary across jurisdictions, so you cannot assume that what works when investing in tax lien certificates in one location will be the same in another. Check local laws on liens and real estate investing.

Laws can be very specific to each state and even counties can have their own specified rules as well. You don't have to look far, as most laws are found on the county's official website. If you need qualifications, then you can reach out to the county executive office and they'll assist you further.

2. Have the necessary knowledge and connections. If you're going to invest in tax lien certificates, or in any other real estate investment for that matter, you need to study the market and the competition. You can do this on your own by doing research and taking classes or short courses. You can also find an expert to guide you as you 'learn by doing.'

Establishing connections with those who are already in the industry is a good way to familiarize yourself with the real estate market. If there are local trade groups in your area, it would be good to join them and actively participate in their activities. In the process, you pick up tips and benefit from the sharing of experiences and practices among the members of the group.

3. Understand the auction process. If you could, prior to your first bid, you should attend first an auction just to have a feel of the atmosphere. You may have seen one on TV, but the real process can be scary especially to those who are just starting out. It'll be good to see how it looks like before you get into the real action just yet.

All bids are binding, so don't even attempt to go for one just for experience. Some auctions are held at the property itself, while some are held at a courthouse or even at a specific disclosed location. If you know of a foreclosure lawyer, you may consult with him about the auction process.

4. Be familiar with the property you're going to buy. You don't just buy tax lien certificates without knowing the property associated with it. This is to ensure that you're going to collect the money from the property owner.

What if you're going to be sold a dilapidated property in the slums? That's probably not a good idea regardless of the offered interest rate – the property owner probably wouldn't be able, or even be unwilling, to settle the tax owed.

Stay away from properties that have been hit with environmental damage (e.g., hazardous materials, chemical deposits, storm and flooding, etc.). These properties are generally undesirable.

The more you know about the property, area, and condition, the more confident you will be in placing your bids. It would be a gamble to bid on a property that you are not familiar with or that you have not checked out. When you place your bids, remember that you are not there to win your bids at all cost. You want to go for good deals.

5. Understand that you won't always end up owning the property on which the tax lien certificate that you bought was issued. You shouldn't be investing in tax liens if your intention is to own the properties after the redemption period.

The homeowners still have a chance to retain ownership of their property if they pay their financial obligations before the end of the redemption period. In this case, your gain will only be in the form of interest earnings as dictated by your winning bid.

6. Research, research, research. The fact that you have to research can't be emphasized enough. You should do your due diligence and perform research to succeed. Not doing so could cost you a fortune, so you have to be careful. You wouldn't want to purchase a property just to realize that what you've bought is pretty useless and worthless.

You should also study the market you're interested in so that you'll be aware of the price range at which tax lien certificates in this area are usually sold. It will also give you an idea of the competition among other investors.

7. Work with a professional. Investing in tax lien certificates is not recommended for novice investors, but that doesn't mean newcomers can't entirely invest in them. If you're new but you still want to invest in this real estate instrument, ask for the help of a professional. This way, you'll have someone to guide you through the process and to advice you on the best investment moves.

8. Some people consider tax lien certificates as unacceptable, so you have to be prepared to deal with them. As investing in these certificates is a personal decision, it should not matter what others think. While other people might view the act of taking over someone else's debt as immoral, the other perspective presents it as beneficial to both the homeowner and the investor.

You have to be prepared to be the bad guy in case the homeowner cannot pay his obligations and you are forced to file for foreclosure. If you do not have the heart to do this, perhaps you should look at another real estate investment instrument.

9. Understand the responsibilities that come with your investment. Upon receiving the certificates, the property owner should be informed, in writing, of the purchase within a specific amount of time. Another letter of notification should be sent to the property owner once the redemption period is almost over. You should also be aware of the foreclosure laws. Pay attention to provisions that govern the handling of the property when the owner fails to pay his debt.

10. There are risks associated with this kind of investment. There will always be risks associated with investments, and this isn't an exception. Tax lien certificates may not be related to the markets, making them a somehow predictable and stable investment, but there still are factors to consider especially in this field where interest rates are rising. You'd also have to face tough competition, especially when it comes to auctions.

The risks often come with the properties being bought. Again, choosing unwanted properties, or those with little value, can leave you with a land that you'll find hard to make money from. You wouldn't want to lose your principal and not receive interest just because nobody wishes to redeem the property you bought.

Interesting Fact #5

The Buji Khalifa (in Dubai) is so tall that you can watch the sunset from the base of the building, take an elevator to the top, and *watch the sunset all over again*!

Congratulations!

The fourth character of the password required to unlock the *Real Estate Business Scorecard* is letter s.

Chapter 26

Land

Investing in a vacant land is often the most misunderstood and overlooked real estate business model. Many real estate investors would tell you that this is a high-risk real estate investment strategy, and they have some valid arguments.

Basically, a vacant land will not provide you an outright regular income, and you can't just sell it overnight. Buying a vacant land is also not as sexy as buying REITs or investing in REIGs. But once you drill down the intricacies of this business model, you can transform a boring piece of land into an asset that will become a source of your regular cash flow.

For some investors, investing in a vacant land is boring, but for those who know the business, they love the fact that the land is just sitting there. The stability and simplicity of owning the land purchased at the right price could really override the multitude of problems that you have to face with other forms of real estate investments.

It is best first to understand the business model of vacant land investment including its pros and cons so you are equipped with the right knowledge once you encounter this viable real estate opportunity.

Land Investment Business Model

Purchasing a vacant land is just one of the many ways to make money in property investment. However, this form of investment does not actually involve any property at all because you are purchasing only the land. In this form of real estate investment, you are buying a land and holding it for a while in the hope that its value will increase in the future.

Why Does Land Value Increase Over Time?

There are several factors behind the growth of land's market value, which is also known as capital value appreciation. These factors include supply and demand, fiscal inflation, bank interest rates, area development, and population growth.

Supply and Demand

If a demand is increasing for certain types of land in an area, such as residential, agricultural, or industrial, the prices will go up when the volume of real estate projects being developed to sustain the demand doesn't catch up. For example, companies purchasing vacant lots in an area deemed ideal for factories are willing to pay more for lands because establishing factories in the area is great for business.

When it comes to residential areas, the demand from end-users can also attract the attention of investors who are buying residential properties with the perspective of placing them in the market again once the supply in the area decreases and the prices increase.

Fiscal Inflation

Inflation happens when there is a high volume of money in circulation, which causes the value of money to decrease. In this case, the prices of commodities increase including construction materials and the cost of acquiring land. Certainly, fiscal inflation will not lead to increased property prices in an area if the location itself is not sufficient, which means it has poor accessibility, civic and social infrastructure, or there is an oversupply of real estate projects already.

Bank Interest Rates

The variable movement of bank rates has a direct effect on the value of land. If the cost of borrowing increases, the demand for properties slows down because few buyers are willing to purchase lands through bank financing. Similarly, if bank interest rates decrease, more investors are willing to buy properties and so the market sentiment also appreciates. These factors result in a higher demand for land purchase.

Area Development

Especially for residential areas, the value of land could significantly increase if there are current developments in an area such as shopping malls, schools, public transport facilities, government offices, commercial buildings, and more. You should also check the zoning regulations in the area to see if there are limits on excessive development.

Population Growth

Obviously, the more people who are willing to live in an area the higher the demand for housing and industrial buildings. Higher demand will significantly boost the price of real estate in an area.

Farm Rental

Many real estate investors are into purchasing agricultural lands and renting them out to farmers who don't have the capacity to buy the land or the eligibility for a bank loan. This investment can be tricky as you need to find the right farmer and learn effective lease agreement. There is no generic business model for a farm rental as the strategy you need to use will largely depend on the status of the land and the needs of the farmer.

This business model is usually ideal for those who have the know-how in agriculture such as retiring farmers or those who have inherited farms but don't want to cultivate the land so they opt to just lease out. There are also government organizations, non-profit entities, and private companies who are also into this business model.

The common end users for farm rentals are farmers who are starting a new farm business, expanding their farm, or those who are relocating their business. Many of these end-users are starters who don't have the working capital to buy their own farm and purchase the required equipment.

In this real estate model, the land could be a currently cultivated farm or has been cultivated a long time ago but has been abandoned. However, there are also ideal lands that were never farmed but can be converted into an agricultural type. Just be sure to check the land use restrictions to know if the land is under conservation or has been zoned as agricultural.

If you are interested in this form of real estate investment, you need to understand that you may have to provide the infrastructure needed by farmers such as water supply, fencing, electricity, housing, greenhouses, barns, and access to roads. Your tenant may also require added infrastructure during the lease.

Lease Agreement

Basically, your lease agreement for a farm rental should specify the important details of the landlord and the tenant on top of the clear description of the land and the facilities you are leasing and how the agreement will be terminated. Be sure to clarify liability and other forms of insurance.

In this form of real estate business, you need to specifically include the prohibited farm practices, the process for future capital investments, and responsibility for the land and the structures built before and during the lease agreement.

Lease Types

The common type of lease for a farm rental is a yearly lease in which the lease is renewed every year, so it is a short-term agreement. Other forms of lease include multi-year lease, renewable lease, and lease with the right of first refusal. You need to decide whether you want a short-term lease or a long-term lease.

Short term lease is more appealing to starting farmers, but be wary because they can easily move their business to a new location with better infrastructure. Hence, you may need to deal with several starting farmers instead of a successful business in the long-term.

Take note that a farm rental business is highly variable. As a landowner, you need to consider the requirements of various farming activities and their impact on your land. Grazing animals or haying is considered as low cost and low impact farming. High cost and high impact farming such as corn or wheat require more investment and calls for more land security for the farmer.

Finding the Right Farmer

To find the right farmer for your agricultural investment, it is ideal to specifically point out what your land is offering, what you are expecting in return, and which terms are negotiable and non-negotiable.

You can reach out to nearby farmers looking to supplement their own land for grazing or growing new crops. You can also get in touch with farmers in surrounding areas who might be interested to relocate their business. A review or an application process before meeting the potential tenant can save you time.

The vetting process could be very informal but you should regard it as a serious interview. A basic conversation over the phone or in person is a traditional approach when you are recruiting farmers for low impact farming such as haying. You need to use a more formal process if you are looking for farmers for high impact farming or if you prefer a long-term lease.

You need to screen out the farmers who are not a good fit with your goals. In this way, you can also identify issues that you need to think about before meeting the prospective tenant. There is no need to complicate the application. Just make sure that it will be able to provide you with insight on the agricultural experience of the farmer, the farm activities that he is interested in doing on your land, the support they need, if they have a written business plan, and possibly some references.

How Much Can You Charge for Rent?

The lease will vary depending on the farming activities and the benefit to you as the owner of the land. You may agree on a 100% rental fee or you may arrange a lower rental fee then a share of the profits of the farm.

Car Park Business

Some say that investing in car parks is no longer a lucrative real estate investment mainly because of the increase in research and investment to initiatives such as self-driving cars and the growth of car sharing economy. On the other hand, major cities are now trying to solve air and noise pollution by reducing the number of cars allowed.

However, buying a vacant land and transforming it into a car park will continue to become a lucrative business in the next 15 to 20 years. In spite of the technological advancements with self-driving cars, the growth of the car industry will not be significantly disrupted. These innovations will continue to gain traction but not at the speed that we expect. There are also challenges when it comes to regulation, which is the main reason why there is still demand for spaces where people can safely park their personal vehicles.

The Ideal Land for a Car Park

Location is crucial when you are starting a car park business. There are things you need to consider such as:

- **Convenience** - Is the location accessible for people to park their cars?
- **Zoning limits** - Does the city allow you to convert the land into a car park?
- **Traffic** - Are there enough cars in the area to make the business lucrative? Lands that are near convention centers, airports or shopping complexes are usually ideal places to look
- **Area Demand** - How much parking space does the area require? You may try talking to people in the area about parking, and check if your local government has available research for parking requirements
- **Land Price** - Check if you can afford to purchase the lot and then convert it into a car park

In looking for a location, don't filter out land with abandoned buildings. Take note that the location is more important than looking for empty lots. A perfect site could have abandoned structures, although you may need to add the cost of demolishing the building to your startup expenses.

Pavement Expenses

An important requirement for a car park is to have a smooth asphalt pavement. You can save a lot of time and money if you hire skilled professionals to do the job. Basically, the bigger your land is, the lower the price per square foot of developing it. For instance, a 50,000 sq. ft. parking area may cost around $1.50 to $2.00 per sq. ft. Take note that this is just an estimate.

Also, check with your local government office on the standards for constructing a parking lot. You need to follow the local rules so you can be granted a construction permit. Usually, you will be required to provide a drainage plan so the rain will not flow off the lot and flood the surrounding areas.

Nitty Gritty

There are three primary ways to design the entrance to your parking lot. First, you may choose a car park with no gate, in which you can trust your patrons to pay based on how long they park their vehicles. Second, you can have a gated car park that requires you to hire a cashier who will collect the parking fee. Third, an electronic gate equipped with an automated payment system.

The first option is most affordable but it carries the risk of people abusing the system. Hiring personnel to collect rent will cost you more over time compared to installing an automated system. But take note that an actual person will provide your business with the flexibility because machines cannot resolve complaints.

You may also need to consider if you like your customers to pay on the go or set up a membership service where they can pay each month so they can get a guaranteed parking space. You can choose one system or follow a hybrid model.

Security

Aside from the personnel who will collect the parking fee, you also need to consider the cost of the security and maintenance of the car park. If you want a big parking space that can accommodate hundreds of cars, you may add a valet service. This will add more to your operational expenses.

Security personnel are also crucial to make your space safe. You may also need to install a Closed Circuit TV (CCTV) and enough lighting that will discourage attackers and thieves.

Pros and Cons of Investing in Land

As you should know by now, there are many opportunities you can explore when you purchase a vacant lot. However, you should always do your due diligence whenever you are considering a business opportunity, especially when it comes to land investments. Below you will find the pros and cons of investing in land.

One of the main advantages of purchasing vacant land is that you have the freedom to create the property that you like. While this may require foresight, as you have to determine what is the best use for the property will be in a specific area, it provides you with a great window to be creative. Certainly, you need to consider various zoning restrictions, so you should comply with the rules.

Vacant land is a lot easier to remotely manage compared to rental properties. With vacant land, you don't have to concern yourself with electricity, plumbing, security and other concerns.

Investing in vacant land is a lot cheaper as a long-term real estate investment. Basically, the property fees and taxes are usually lower compared to a developed lot. Moreover, sellers of vacant lots are normally more willing to dispose of the property, so you could gain a lower price. You can even be eligible for financing. Its affordability could become your competitive advantage in the real estate game.

For example, when you buy the vacant lot for your second home, the value of the land may increase between when you purchased it and when you are developing it. You can use the land as collateral for a construction loan, which you can use to convert to a conventional mortgage without the need to refinance. Upon the completion of the project, the total cost for the land and the development is much lower compared to the retail value of the property.

Because vacant lots are a lot cheaper, you can even buy them with cash. This will enable you to have direct or full ownership. Owning the land directly can provide you peace of mind, especially because this is a tangible asset that will not depreciate. In the process, you can get rid of additional cost such as loan origination fees and mortgage interest that are usually charged by the bank.

There are also potential downsides to consider if you want to invest in vacant land. For one, you will not realize income right away. While you will not have any mortgage to pay, you will also need to pay other expenses such as association fees, the cost of improving the property, and property taxes.

Without rental income, you have to be creative so you can cover the expenses. Aside from renting out the land to farmers or converting the lot to a car park, you can also sell parts of the lot for rights such as gaming or mineral. You may also find another use (short-term) for the lot while you are still looking for a buyer or waiting for the value to increase.

It can be a challenge to secure bank financing to buy a vacant lot. Hence, if you develop it and then you can't sell it right away, your investment will be idle while you are waiting for your strategy to become successful.

There are instances that the lot can have physical issues. Many real estate investors caution purchasing flat lands mainly because of water runoff issues. Similarly, if you are looking into mountainous terrain, you may find it difficult to build properties. You also need to be clear on the situation with road access, water source, and sewer quality.

While you can still depreciate specific improvements like a new sewer system or roads, a vacant lot will leave you without any structure that is subject to depreciation. There is also no mortgage that is tied to a structure so you will not be eligible for deduction on mortgage interest.

There are required permits and approvals when you invest in land. The local zoning can determine what you can do with your vacant lot. In addition, the timetable for your project approved by local regulating bodies may also vary. You also need to check how many lots you are allowed to develop. This dictates how much you can make in this investment. In this real estate business strategy, you may need to add contingencies to your plan, which also includes your permit approvals. Do not buy the land if you are not able to acquire the approvals for what you are trying to build.

Scoring Land

A. Liquidity

Investing in a vacant land is basically regarded as high risk because it has higher liquidity risk. This means that a vacant land may take time to be purchased or sold in the market. If you want to sell a vacant land quickly, you may need to lower down the price. Take note that in a real estate investment, it is ideal to consider those properties that you can easily convert into cash at a reasonable cost, at a reasonable price, and at a reasonable period of time.

Just a few years ago, real estate is generally considered as a liquid asset, but this is not much the case today. The lack of liquidity for vacant lots is aggravated by the situation wherein very few real estate investors are comfortable in investing in vacant land. Hence, the potential market for investors is not that active. But with such risk, you can also expect higher returns. You just need to be comfortable with the risks.

3/10

B. Scalability

A real estate business involving raw land is difficult to scale as you can't just buy a vacant land and convert it overnight. This is in high contrast with REITs, which are very scalable because you can just buy more shares in a matter of hours. Purchasing raw land is a lot harder because you need to first do your due diligence, get the necessary permits and approvals, develop the property, and do other laborious steps before you can scale up the business.

2/10

C. Potential Return On Investment

In exchange for the high risk, the potential earnings you can gain from raw land investing can be substantial. This is possible if you know the strategy such as the buy and hold. For example, you can purchase a vacant lot today for a lower price, then walk away with the original price increasing to a hundred fold 20 years later. And while waiting for capital appreciation, you can choose to lease the land to a farmer as discussed earlier or convert it into a car park so you can start earning regular income.

7/10

D. Passivity

Once you have already converted the vacant land into a business that can provide you with regular stream of income, it becomes easy for you to earn money without directly exchanging your time for it. However, you still need to take care of the needs of your tenants or make sure that the car park is properly maintained. You can easily solve this by hiring a property manager so you can free yourself from the responsibilities of operating the business every day.

6/10

E. Simplicity

Investing in a vacant land is a bit harder than it looks. While the business model seems simple, entry to this investment should not be taken lightly. You need to do your due diligence first before you purchase any land to make sure that it is aligned with your goals. You also need to gain a lot of capital and study the market well to ensure your investment has the potential to be profitable.

4/10

Ten Tips for Successfully Investing in Land

1. **Have a plan** - Before you buy a vacant land, you should first figure out precisely how you want to use the property. Careful planning can help you choose the lot that is right for your real estate investment goal.

For example, land purchased for farming would require accessible water and roads to market. Moreover, you need to consider at what point you can call your investment a success.

2. **Understand the downsides** - While investing in vacant land can be profitable, there can also be disadvantages. Land is not subject to depreciation, and there are several tax advantages that are associated with it.

But, this form of real estate investment is considered as illiquid and ideal for long-term. Even if you start developing it days after your purchase, it may take several years before you can gain ROI. Selling it immediately is often not an option.

3. **Understand the factors that affect the land's value** - It is often hard to determine value although there are specific factors that can affect it. For instance, a land that is sloped could make development difficult and expensive. Hence, be sure that you review the depth, width, shape, and exact size of the property that you want to consider.

Location is an important factor. The prime candidates for development are usually corner lots with easy access to parking and roads. Other factors to consider are access to telephone service, electricity, natural gas, drinking water, and sewers.

4. **Be ready to face possible problems** - Look beyond the aesthetics of your vacant land. An abandoned lot could be even profitable than a sunny meadow. You need to check for hidden problems such as old septic tanks, buried toxic wastes, sinister history, and more.

And even though you may not see rocks on the ground that you need to get rid of, you should also check if there are huge boulders buried in the ground. This will significantly limit your plan for developing the land.

5. **Consider the environment** - Regardless of how you want to develop your vacant land, you need to know if it has the minimal necessities and the environment is pleasing. A flood-prone area can heavily damage your potential car park business. A nearby subdivision may impede your plan to rent out the land for farming.

6. **Know the total cost of your purchase** - Remember, the cost of purchasing the vacant land is not the same as the price you pay, because the sales price is just a portion of the cost. You need to consider the yield or what you can gain from the land once you developed it. This will demand more capital outlays for soil tests, engineering services, permits, fees, surveys, and more.

7. **Do your due diligence -** It is always ideal to do your research and uncover more information about the raw land that you want to purchase. Secure a survey of the parcel and personally locate fence lines, trails, streams, or ponds. Capture photos and look for the boundaries of the lot. Make certain to look for any signs of toxic wastes that can drastically lower down the price of the property. A closer look at the vacant land is well worth it. The more research, the fewer surprises you need to manage later.

8. **Love the land** - Before buying the land, be sure that you follow your gut and you are positive about it. You can ask the current owner of the land about the property and his reason for selling. Be sure to ask about financing options and taxes. You should also visit the neighbors and ask about the property and what they want about the area.

9. **Trust the experts** - Buying a vacant land is an extensive process, which can be easier if you have a team of experts to help in facilitating the sale. Ideally, you need to seek assistance from a real estate agent, a realtor, and a real estate attorney to iron out all problems before you buy the property.

10. **Know your timetable** - Time is an important element in developing a vacant land. You should consider uncontrollable factors such as the economy or the changing demographics in the area.

Interesting Fact #6

Monopoly was originally designed to teach players about the broken nature of capitalism. It's inventor, Elizabeth Magie, would have sent herself straight to jail if she'd lived to know just how influential today's twisted version of her game turned out to be!

Chapter 27

Industrial Real Estate

The thriving real estate industry doesn't just revolve around residential and commercial properties. The management of industrial properties has significant contribution as well. However, some starters and small-time investors tend to disregard industrial real estate because it seems not as glamorous as its residential and commercial counterparts. (Think of condominiums, hotels, resorts and malls.) There's also a misconception that only institutional investors can afford to put capital on it.

Industrial properties are sometimes deemed as a form of commercial real estate. It's regarded as the biggest; other types of commercial property include office and retail. Due to its market size, industrial real estate is treated as a category on its own.

Overview of Business Model

Industrial real estate is a key aspect of the global supply chain. It covers properties such as warehouses and factories. An industrial property is intended to be a place for making or storing goods. Some properties are flexible enough to be used for displaying and selling supplies. Others are even utilized for events, car washes, art exhibits, data hosting centers, and TV and movie productions.

Unlike residential and commercial properties, there's no alternative to industrial properties. If buying or constructing a house is too costly, prospects may rent or live with loved ones for a while. As for offices, users may be allowed to work from home. With the rise of e-commerce, some brick-and-mortars may close. But when it comes to factories and warehouses, manufacturers, wholesalers and suppliers have to make or rent industrial properties.

The demand makes industrial real estate as an ideal investment option. You can invest by being a stockholder or limited partner of an entity that manages such properties. Another option is to become the property manager. You may either buy or develop industrial properties. After buying or developing, you can lease or sell the property.

Types of Industrial Properties

Industrial properties are generally classified into three: factories, warehouses and flexible centers. The property type determines the kinds of potential tenants or buyers. Compared to factories, the demand for warehouses and flex centers is greater. However, factories lead in terms of quality of tenants.

Factories are built with production in mind. Thus, they are roomy enough to accommodate big machineries or a fleet of equipment. Aside from that, they have spacious driveway and parking area near its main doorway. These speed up getting truckloads of raw materials and shipping processed goods afterwards.

Manufacturers are the top seekers of factories. Those that are planning to expand their operations sooner look for properties to rent instead of constructing a new one. They usually go for long-term lease. Additionally, landlords don't usually deal with property maintenance because doing so might affect the production of goods. The tenants will handle property maintenance, along with monthly operational expenses.

Warehouses are made for storage of various things. They can accommodate shipping containers, big boxes, and vehicles. They can also serve as temporary storage place for production machinery while the factory is still being constructed. Individuals, manufacturers, suppliers, wholesalers, e-commerce sites operators and even some government institutions may rent a warehouse.

Flex buildings can be used for either warehousing or light manufacturing. They can also be utilized as car washes, show rooms and filming location, among others.

Depending on their building specifications, industrial properties could also be categorized as standalone, strata title, distribution centers and industrial parks. A standalone building is made up of one unit while strata title is composed of two or more units. An industrial park is an area in a city that are designated and developed for the industrial sector's use. A distribution center is intended to house shipments of goods that will be delivered to retailers.

Building specifications and zoning regulations prevent owners from changing the use of their industrial property frequently. In the US, zoning categories are referred to as industrial 1 and industrial 2. Industrial 1 covers real estate used in toxic manufacturing. Each town or city may also have a list of other areas that fall under the said category. In contrast, industrial 2 focuses more on warehousing and light manufacturing. When it comes to compliance and paperwork, going for industrial 2 is easier than opting for industrial 1.

Factors that Improve Industrial Real Estate Market

The recession hurt the industrial real estate market in the past. However, government intervention, economic improvements and technological advancements drove the market to stability.

Advancements in robotics and 3D printing are among the noteworthy factors that are helping the industrial real estate market, albeit indirectly. It's no secret that small to big companies outsource services outside the US for cheap labor. This prompted the closure of many factories.

In recent years though, there has been an increasing demand to keep all aspects of production in the country. Quality control issues, political rifts, high shipping costs, and extensive waiting period contributed to the demand for total on-shore production. The increasing affordability and flexibility of tech advancements help manufacturers meet such need. But due to the closure of many industrial properties before, someone has to make new ones to accommodate the growing on-shore productions.

The expansion of the Panama Canal is also beneficial to the country's logistics. The ports in the west coast have been carrying much of the US shipping trade for years. As the Panama Canal widens, more ships can deliver on ports in the east coast. This entails increase in truckloads of raw materials and finished products shipped to more parts of the country.

To help keep running costs low, manufacturers have their factories near ports. The closeness of their factories reduces waiting period and fuel costs. Because of the demand to be so near to ports, the market value of the properties increased. This is a boon for those that already have buildings in the area. However, beginner investors and tenants will find it hard to meet the needed capital to invest, buy or rent such properties.

With the accessibility of more products on the other side of the country, there will be more undeveloped lands where industrial properties can be constructed. The number of existing industrial properties is also lower than those near ports in the west coast. Small competition entails more affordable properties.

The rise of e-commerce came with advantages and disadvantages as well. The increase in online shopping activities makes many brick-and-mortar stores obsolete. This, in turn, lowers the demand for distribution centers. However, delivery of goods won't be efficient without fulfillment centers.

Every major manufacturer owns or rents distribution centers. These are the initial destination points of big boxes or wholesale products before they get shipped to retailers.

But in the field of e-commerce, middlemen like wholesalers and retailers may no longer be necessary. Consumers can just buy directly from the manufacturer through the latter's website or through an e-commerce site. Fulfillment centers make this possible. You can learn more about this whole process in the book: Dropshipping: Discover how to make money online, build sustainable streams of passive income and gain financial freedom using the Dropshipping e-commerce business model

The increasing need for fulfillment centers is one of the advantages that resulted from e-commerce's growth. Fulfillment centers are similar to warehouses in terms of function. However, they also play a role in ensuring quick delivery of goods. Recent studies suggest that majority of the US states enjoy delivery period of one to three days.

Right now, the use of drones in delivery is being explored. This is expected to speed up delivery to few hours to one day. If this practice goes operational, e-commerce sites will need more fulfillment centers. Delivery drones will adversely affect trucking businesses though.

Buying versus Building

If you want to make the most out of the industrial real estate market, buying or building will be your best choices. Your savings may not be enough to finance either option. To finance your purchase or construction, you may search for limited partners or take loans.

As mentioned previously, many industrial properties were closed down due to the various factors. These properties were built to withstand harsh weather conditions and minimal maintenance. It's not surprising that some of them are put on sale.

Such properties are cheaper than buying a relatively new property or building a new one. The problem with old industrial properties is that they don't meet the updated standards. They might fall under Class B building or lower. This classification will hurt your marketing and limit your potential tenants. The ROI from resale will be low as well. Even if you repair and upgrade the property, there won't be significant increase in the resale value.

If there's one redeeming quality about such buildings, it's their ideal locations. More often than not, they are near densely populated areas. Demolishing them and building a new industrial property in their place may be worth considering. But you need to weigh the time needed to complete the construction and the demand for the property.

The best way to get a Class A building is to build it from scratch. Building requires extensive research. You're going to study ideal locations, possible tenants, marketing strategies, and industry standards, among others. Moreover, it may be hard to find a contractor who focuses more on industrial real estate.

Despite the difficulties, the high ROI makes building a more ideal choice than buying and repairing an old property. It's also less expensive and less time-consuming than demolishing an obsolete property to construct a new one.

Planning and getting building permits may take weeks. Meanwhile, the construction period may range from several months to a year. If you add demolition in the process, it may mean an additional month. The biggest challenge with building from scratch is getting enough capital.

If you choose to build, you should know the **three key elements of industrial property: an office, a wide room and a sufficient parking space**. Even factories require some office space. It can be as small as 10% of the entire usable space. The wide room is for production or warehousing. As for your parking needs, make sure there's ample space for trucks and for the employees' cars.

The Most Important Factor to Consider

The marketability of industrial properties depends a lot on the location. Areas near ports and train stations are ideal in many cases. Densely populated areas are good locations as well. But this doesn't mean you can build any industrial property in these locations.

In the US, one of the ideal locations for industrial property is the San Francisco Bay Area. It's near ports. It's densely populated. However, the prices of properties are sky-high. Denver and Chicago are also among the good locations. For international trade, Shanghai and Tokyo are the top destinations in Asia, while Paris and Prague are representatives of Europe.

For densely populated areas, consider the age distribution of the members. If the majority of the population is 40 years old and below, fulfillment centers are more suitable in their locations. Such young population is more likely into online shopping than older ones. Thus, there'll be a high demand for fulfillment centers in them.

Factories are still best situated near ports or near the sources of raw materials. In industries such as food and drugs, many of the raw materials needed are time-sensitive. To avoid spoilage, they should be delivered and processed as soon as possible.

Industrial parks in top cities are naturally expensive. But to have an advantage over this competition, one option is to buy or set up an industrial property in the neighboring town or city.

Constructing industrial properties in less known towns may be helpful to the local economy. If there are many unemployed individuals in the area, you can help provide jobs. The initial cost of the property is also far lower than those in major cities. However, the marketability and resale value of the property won't be that good.

During the lean season, you can turn your warehouse or factory into a seasonal storage center. If your industrial property is located near bodies of water, storing boats during the winter season will be advantageous. You may also rent out your parking space if the property is located near event centers and tourist destinations.

Offering unique services can also improve your chances of getting high ROIs. In an industrial park where most properties are into warehousing, you might want to create a factory. Or, if the warehouses in the area are mostly for dry goods, consider cold storage buildings. This will be a hit in cities where there's shortage of locally grown produce.

You can also take advantage of the west coast's IT hubs. With some upgrades, your warehouse may serve as a data hosting center. Two of the upgrades you'll need are backup heating, ventilation and air conditioning (HVAC) system and reinforced flooring.

Despite having an ideal location, your management skills can either make or break your venture. The first step to better management is to know and understand the purpose of your industrial property. Moreover, keep in mind that industrial property can be obsolete in just a span of 15 years. Thus, your occupancy should be less than 15 years. You should resell the property afterwards.

Pros and Cons

It's an advantage for investors that the demand for industrial properties remains high. Year after year, the outlook for the industrial real estate market remains positive. The growth is even expected to be better than that of residential and commercial markets.

With subtle trade wars not easing anytime soon, manufacturers are expected to boost their on-shore production to meet the local demand. This will drive a greater need for manufacturing plants.

There's also the unending need for storage facilities, especially in countries like the US. A lot of people are materialistic as evident in the number of possessions they have that could no longer fit into their homes. Self-storage and storage containers are usually the go-to options for these homeowners. However, those who prefer lower storage costs tend to look for subdivided warehouses.

Tenants often go for long-term leases. Short-term leases come with higher risk of vacancies. Finding new tenants and re-cleaning your property can eat up your time. The re-leasing costs are higher as well. Re-leasing costs cover marketing, cleanup and repair expenses. Having long-term tenants greatly minimize such problems. But if you subdivide your industrial property or offer seasonal rental, you might not reap this advantage.

Tenants and buyers are also less picky. If you're looking for a home or for a commercial space, your personal preferences often come into play. Your emotions can make it hard for you to decide which one to choose. In contrast, tenants and buyers of industrial property approach their search with their business in minds. Their biggest considerations are usually the location, condition and facilities available at the property.

With less picky clients, you shouldn't stress about aesthetics in your industrial property. The things you should focus more on are security, accessibility, safety and durability. It also helps to emphasize flexibility.

Unlike prospective tenants and homebuyers, the clients of industrial real estate don't usually negotiate prices. If they see the property as a great asset due to its location and facilities, they won't mind the high rent.

You'll only have to deal with one tenant at a time. If you have an apartment or a commercial building, you're going to find and manage different tenants at once. It's time-consuming and stressful. With a rental industrial property, you just have to worry about one tenant as long as you don't turn it into subdivided rental spaces.

Industrial real estate properties can withstand months or even years with only minimal maintenance. Maintaining a warehouse requires specialty equipment and safety gear. The good thing about this is that it's not needed for months or even years.

The owner of an industrial property doesn't have to do maintenance when there's a tenant. This is especially true in cases where the tenants are into manufacturing, assembly or packaging. In these production processes, the tenants prefer to take care of the cleanup to prevent security and contamination problems.

There are fewer market fluctuations in the industrial real estate market compared to their residential and commercial counterparts. Economic and political issues can affect various industries. However, they won't cause outright closures and vacancies. They won't also influence the prices to go higher or lower in a span of hours. If you opt for annual payment of rent, market fluctuations won't bother you and your tenant.

The resale value of used industrial property is still great. Manufacturers, wholesalers, retailers or e-commerce companies don't usually buy a brand-new industrial property. They'll rent first and wait for used properties to become available. Used industrial properties are more affordable, but they remain suitable and safe for production and storage.

The bad thing about investing in industrial real estate property is that getting a long-term tenant isn't easy. Studying the recent business strategies of major manufacturers, wholesalers and e-commerce sites can help you in your quest for potential tenants. However, making a proposal will require much of your people skills. You have to be knowledgeable on the advantages and challenges associated with the location of your property.

Setting up an industrial real estate requires a lot of paperwork. To make your property more marketable, it should have building compliance certificates from leading organizations in numerous industries. It should also comply with local zoning laws.

The leasing agreement can entail a lot of work as well. Finalizing it may take several negotiations. For this process, always hire a lawyer to draft your leasing agreement and spot loopholes early on.

Compared to residential and commercial real estate, their industrial counterpart is at a higher risk of being the target of a corrupt government. Such government will make it harder for you to get the needed business licenses and certifications.

There's a binary vacancy risk. Like other wide real estate properties, you'll have to rent the entire industrial property to one tenant at a time. When that tenant doesn't want to extend the lease, you'll end up with a single yet significant vacancy.

Subdividing the spaces in your property can help resolve this problem. With subdivided storage space, you can allow individuals or small-scale entrepreneurs to store their things in your property. But doing so entails costs. Aside from buying the materials, you'll need to hire people who will install them. The management of multiple tenants can be an issue as well.

Environmentalists may question your venture. Environmentalists are never tolerant of industrial waste. Even if you're not the one using your industrial property for production, you may get dragged into the conversation because of your tenant's improper waste disposal. You can prevent this from happening by planning the waste disposal right from the start. Consult your contractor and the local authorities about the proper disposal. Furthermore, you have to make sure your tenant is compliant with environmental laws.

It's important to be as environmentally-friendly as possible. However, you shouldn't go as far as using green practices as part of your marketing strategies. It might backfire big time. Implement eco-friendly facilities such as energy-saving HVAC systems and glass panels. Glass panels allow more natural light into the industrial property. This can reduce your tenant's dependence on electricity for lighting.

Institutional investors and corporations impose risks to the stability of the industrial real estate market. Institutional investors are well-aware of the potential of the industrial real estate market. It's not surprising to know that they are increasing their investments year after year. Their contributions are a boon for tenants, but for starters and small-time investors, they are a hard-to-beat competition.

Many corporations also opt to set up their own facilities. They won't rent forever. You may offer to sell your property, but just like you, they might not want to deal with the costs and time required for demolition and construction of a new building.

With the aforementioned competitions, it might affect the stability of the industrial real estate market. Institutional investors can drive the prices high. Meanwhile, when manufacturers create their own facilities, it may reduce the demand for industrial properties.

Scoring Industrial Properties

A. Liquidity

It may take months before you can earn your first few dollars from your industrial property. Getting back your entire investment and paying all your loans may take years to happen. When managed right, the ROI will be high but you have to wait for years, especially if you put the property on a rental for a few years.

For many investors in industrial property, rental is their initial source of gains. However, a big chunk of the ROI will materialize once the property is sold. After the initial rent, the reselling period may take at least a few months up to a year.

4/10

B. Scalability

Physical assets like warehouses and factories are never easy to expand. You can't just use your parking space to widen your building. Buying the neighboring properties can resolve the issue of limited space. However, there are instances when this is just impractical.

In case your property is located in an industrial park, there's a great chance that other real estate investors in the area won't just give up their properties easily. If your current tenant has no plans of increasing production, storage or distribution in the area, offering additional space may not be worth it. The additional paperwork is discouraging as well.

4/10

C. Potential Return On Investment

The construction materials, industrial facilities and large-scale property require high capital investments. The good news is that the ROI can cover these expenses. Moreover, you won't have to worry about operational expenses such as repairs, replacements, security, maintenance, property taxes, property insurance, HVAC costs and utility costs. Your tenant will be the shouldering these.

9/10

C. Simplicity

Managing industrial real estate requires knowledge in building specifications and industry standards. Once you have handled this, though, the management part tends to be simpler because you'll only talk to one tenant at a time.

Having a contractor helps simplify the steps. But, there are costs involved. Hiring is still more cost-effective and time-saving though. It also spares you from the stresses of buying materials and subcontracting for other jobs.

6/10

D. Passivity

Once you're able to rent out your industrial real estate property, you can start earning passively. Before that though, you'll need to spend time, effort and money studying what property to set up, where to build it and how to market it.

If you want to capitalize on industrial real estate with minimal efforts, being a limited partner or stockholder will be your best options. However, you'll need to find a general partner or investment institution that's knowledgeable and well-connected in the field.

7/10

Ten Tips for Successfully Investing in Industrial Real Estate

1. Hire a contractor who specializes in industrial real estate. Building specifications and industry standards aren't the same with residential or commercial properties. It's only advisable to get help from someone who understands the terms and knows what's right for the venture.

2. Do a background check of the local government before buying a property and getting building permits. A committed government can see you as a potential driving force of economic growth. In contrast, a corrupt government can target you and your venture.

3. Screen your tenants thoroughly. Make sure your leasing agreement specifies what kind of goods the tenant is going to create or store in your industrial property.

4. Months before your tenant's rent ends, start negotiating for extensions. If you can't agree on new terms, plan for the upcoming vacancy by looking for possible buyers or tenants.

5. Apply value added strategies such as increasing doors, widening parking spaces, subdividing spaces and modernizing facilities. Modernization includes increase of CCTV cameras, motion sensors and glass panels.

6. Stick to properties under industrial 2. You and your tenant will face less environmental concerns than engaging in a property under industrial 1.

7. Maximize the cubic space of your property by increasing the floor-to-ceiling height. The ideal height ranges from 32 to 36 feet. Anything lower than that range is deemed obsolete and relegated to Class B building status.

8. Make sure there's a clause in your leasing agreement regarding the penalties in case your tenant fails to pay for a certain period.

9. To lessen your management duties, indicate in your leasing agreement that the tenant has to prepare and clean your property before and during occupancy.

10. The liability should be equitably distributed between you and your tenant. In case poor construction or the use of substandard materials caused injuries or damages, you should be held liable. If the accidents are related to the operations of your tenant, he or she should be responsible.

Interesting Fact #7

When Apple was building a new server in North Carolina, they paid one elderly couple $1.7 million for one acre of land. The couple had purchased the property 34 years earlier for $6,000.

Chapter 28

Commercial Real Estate

Commercial real estate refers to real properties built, developed, and used to generate profit. It is the umbrella term that includes industrial properties, office buildings, medical centers, hotels, farmlands, malls, skyscrapers, apartment buildings, and warehouses.

Real estate properties are considered "hard assets" or investments that have inherent value because they serve a basic need. Land can be thought of as a commodity in limited supply. The value goes higher the scarcer the land is. When the price of raw materials used to construct a building structure increases, the entire property becomes more valuable.

This makes investing in commercial real estate enticing. But what really makes it a worthwhile investment is that the value of real estate properties rises when the general price levels of goods and services rise. As such, they are used as a hedge against inflation.

The fact that commercial properties can preserve their value even during periods of high inflation makes investing in them even more desirable. They are a legitimate income-producing investment vehicle that not only pays dividends, but also serves as a protection against the potentially damaging effects of high inflation on investments.

There are two ways to make money in commercial real estate. The first is to lease the property and charge the tenants for the use of the property. The second is through the appreciation of the value of the property over time.

In the first case, investors earn a rental income for the lease of office buildings, warehouses, and skyscrapers. The lease agreements would vary depending on the type of property and tenants. Typically, an office building would have different types of companies as tenants. It could be a start-up company, a law firm, a publication, or a tech company. The company can opt for short-term or long-term lease depending on the need. Usually, companies opt for a five-year or a ten-year term lease.

In the second case, the potential income comes from the appreciation of the value of the commercial real estate being held by the investor over time. The increase in value is determined by the demand for the property or the area around the property. Strategic locations can demand higher rent and prospective buyers are willing to meet the price if they see the earning potential for their businesses or if it gives them prestige to boost their brands.

Another way to increase the value of the commercial property is for investors to take an active approach to add value to it. This means making cosmetic improvements, redesigning, and modernizing. This allows investors to charge higher rent prices for the increase in the property's intrinsic value. Any renovation made to the office building can boost the rental or selling price in the foreseeable future.

Pros and Cons

There is a lucrative earning potential to look for when you invest in commercial property. Commercial property rentals edge out residential rentals when it comes to the rate of annual return. Depending on the location, commercial properties have an annual return of 6% to 12%, which is significantly higher than the 1% to 4% of residential properties. With better returns, commercial properties are a worthwhile investment.

Another advantage of commercial property investing is economies of scale. This may not be obvious at first glance because of the significantly higher investment capital, but economies of scale in commercial real estate do exist. The acquisition cost and the operating expenses can be substantially lower on a per-square-foot basis, especially for larger properties.

The cost of large capital items like heating and cooling system wouldn't be as high if there are more tenants, compared to just one tenant in a residential property. With economies of scale, commercial property owners are able to reduce cost and increase profitability.

Investors in commercial properties can also take advantage of triple net leases.

Under a triple net lease agreement, the lessee will shoulder the real estate tax, the building insurance, and the maintenance expenses. The property owner will only have to pay the mortgage for the building. This kind of agreement is optimal for large businesses that want to maintain a certain look or brand prestige.

There's also flexibility in lease terms. Unlike residential real estate, commercial leases are not governed by numerous consumer protection laws that have stipulations on security deposit and termination.

To those who are short on cash, alternative financing arrangements are available. Evidently, a higher capital is needed to purchase a commercial property. Typically, lenders would require an investor to make a 25% to 30% down payment plus the closing costs. Many investors who had their start in residential investments may not be aware that many lenders offer an alternative financing arrangement that is more flexible and with less constraints.

This kind of arrangement is commonplace in commercial transactions than in residential deals. With this kind of flexibility, the investor's cash can be stretched a little more, which can yield a better cash-on-cash returns (i.e., better cash flow).

Evaluating the price of a commercial property is less "emotional" compared to residential property because there is transparency when it comes to the financial records of the current owner. Particularly, the income statement can be requested and from there, the price can be assessed using the figures. The rule of thumb is that the asking price should be within a threshold where the investor can earn the prevailing capitalization rate (cap rate) for an office building. This way, the potential return on investment can be calculated or estimated.

This investment instrument is quite rational as well. Investors can easily gauge more reliably if a commercial property has a high potential for success because the variables to which decisions can be made are grounded in rationality.

For example, the desirability of an office building or skyscraper is a function of its suite size, proximity to transit, accessibility, ease of loading and unloading, etc. The commercial property's viability hinges on certain variables that can easily be measured or determined.

Tenants and investors of commercial property generally have aligned interests. They both have a vested interest in upholding their good reputation, so they would go to great lengths to ensure that they maintain their business storefront or corporate offices. This is advantageous to the owner because the convergence of their interests makes maintaining and improving the property easier and less costly to do.

Tenants of office buildings and skyscrapers are typically corporations with a reputation to uphold. They have the financial means to pay long-term leases and they have their own property maintenance team to ensure that the property meets or exceeds the quality standards. This is one less problem that a property owner has to contend with.

The biggest disadvantage of investing in commercial real estate is the high initial investment requirement. A commercial property is evidently more expensive than a residential property that's why the barriers to entry are high. A single investor would have a difficult time securing financing and would most likely partner with other investors. Acquiring a commercial property requires a higher initial capital outlay and possibly more capital expenditures to address maintenance issues like fixing furnace and renovating.

A large commercial property with huge foot traffic from customers and visitors means there are more facilities to maintain or fix. When the expenditure is too large, it can eat up the investor's profits. The investor could only hope that the revenue would be high enough to cover the recurring costs to maintain a busy commercial property.

There's also increased competition as investors all look for the same things, whether they be the commercial property's desirability to potential clients or red flags that previous owners tend to hide in the most subtle of ways. Whatever the case, one investor would always be competing with other investors. Competition is high for commercial properties that meet investors' criteria. An investor must be able to have excellent negotiation skills or at least the business acumen to close the deal.

Investors need to express time commitment as well. Operating a commercial property like an office or retail building with more than five tenants can be challenging. It not only requires money, but it also demands time and energy. Dealing with multiple leases means that there are more potential issues to face on a daily basis. The element of uncertainty requires a proactive attitude towards certain issues such as maintenance, emergency response, and public safety.

Often, there is a need to contract professional services. A single investor may try to do things by himself to cut down on costs. This may be viable in residential properties, but it is not possible in commercial properties. Maintenance issues in a commercial property can be overwhelming for a "do-it-yourselfer". Emergency repairs are best left in the hands of professionals if an investor wants the property to be in tip-top shape. The odds that an investor is ill-prepared to handle maintenance issues are high.

So, at the onset, it is best to factor in the property management expenses when evaluating the price of a commercial investment property. Generally, a property management company charges 5% to 10% of the rent revenues to handle the job including the lease administration. This is something that needs to be considered when thinking of outsourcing certain responsibilities to a third-party.

One of the biggest disadvantages in commercial property investing is the risk of long vacancies, particularly when the market conditions turn sour and the economy is sluggish.

Additionally, commercial properties have more public visitors and there is the risk of them getting hurt or some people damaging the property. Also, these properties have parking lots where car accidents can occur. With a higher volume of people going in and out of the premises, there is always the risk of incidents occurring.

While accidents are beyond the property owner's control, a system must be put in place to mitigate the risks. Doing so entails additional costs that must be included when estimating the value of the commercial property. Risk-adverse individuals may find it difficult to handle such undertaking.

Scoring Commercial Properties

A. Liquidity

In any investment venture, liquidity is a crucial consideration. This truly matters especially when an investor wishes to exit the business or wants to convert physical assets to cash to pay off a debt. In general, real estate investments are non-liquid because of the difficulty to which the properties could be sold. It would take a significant amount of time to complete the process of selling, which includes finding an investor, negotiating, and closing the sale. Real estate properties cannot be easily converted to cash.

For commercial real estate property, specifically, office buildings and skyscrapers, liquidity is low because of the significantly higher price tag compared to residential real estate. As such, there are a limited number of potential buyers because only large firms have the financing capabilities to negotiate and close such a multi-million-dollar deal.

Skyscrapers such as the Trump International Hotel and Tower, Aon Center and One World Trade Center fall under the category of Institutional Grade Real Estate investment. Transactions under this investment type are handled by private equity firms, large pension funds, large insurance companies, Real Estate Investment Trusts (REITs), and syndicators, to name just a few. This means that the potential buyer should have huge financial resources to put up an investment.

The liquidity score would be slightly higher if the commercial property is highly sought after due to its location, brand, prestige, and other non-tangible positive attributes.

5/10

B. Scalability

Real estate investors usually start with residential properties by focusing on single family investments and gradually moving to duplexes, triplexes, and fourplexes. There comes a point when investors may feel the need to scale up and graduate from multifamily investment and move to other real estate investment vehicles to diversify their investment portfolios.

Investors would eventually set their eyes on the bigger prize and add a commercial property into the mix. There is a tendency to shift the investment focus when they feel that they have maximized their profits in the field of residential property.

The challenge lies in the financing of a commercial property. Although it is not impossible to own multiple properties under an investor's name, lenders might see this is as a red flag. The loan-to-value (LTV) ratio must be reasonably low for the investment portfolio to fund itself.

It would be highly unlikely for a single investor to finance a commercial property out of pocket, so the next option would be to find an investment partner with deeper pockets. Bringing in equity from other investors has its own set of issues that requires time and commitment to do due diligence.

Another thing to consider is that without a track record, the loan rate might be significantly higher, which eats up a portion of the profits.

Going the path of syndication is a form of crowdsourcing wherein a group of investors pool their resources to enable them to acquire properties that they could not afford as individuals. Without deeper pockets, the scalability for commercial real estate ranks low.

4/10

C. Potential Return On Investment

Commercial property investors look to the potential return on investment (ROI) as the key factor in making their investment decision. Achieving the desired ROI does not come easy. In fact, it comes with numerous risks. But if investors are able to identify the right opportunities, do their due diligence, and be comfortable with a certain degree of risk, then the ROI can be achieved.

If a high ROI compels investors to take the plunge into the competitive commercial real estate market, then it's important to look beyond the location, tenants, and lease terms, and think outside the common strategies. It is safe to say that the greater the risk, the greater the return.

The National Council of Real Estate Investment Fiduciaries (NCREIF) Property Index has reported that the average annual return in the commercial real estate sector over a 15-year period is 8.8%, which is higher by 200 basis points than the S&P 500 Index in the same time frame. In 2015, the annual return is 12.7%.

If an investor gets an ROI that is comparable to the sector average, or higher, then it's safe to say that the commercial property is performing well.

With a triple net lease in place, the lessee is solely responsible for the costs associated with the asset being leased on top of the rental fee. In this aspect, the investor is getting huge savings for the total upkeep cost of the property because the lion's share of the expenses is covered by the lessees.

There are complex factors that affect the ROI of a commercial property other than the operational expenses and some of them eat into the profit margin. Taxes associated with the commercial real estate rise when the assessed value of the property increases. So, the potential yield and the overall ROI will likely fall as well. The same effect can be expected with insurance premiums and interest rates.

Interest rate, in particular, has a significant effect on the cost of financing and cash flows. If interest rate is lowered, more funds flow into the investment, which, in turn, affects the demand and supply dynamics in the commercial real estate.

It is also worth noting that when the demand for commercial real estate skyrockets, the cost associated with acquiring a property also rises, which brings down the capital gain and total return. So, investors should be cautious about buying properties in a "hot market" because the market will eventually self-correct and prices will plummet. Rising interest rates usually trigger this correction.

In the commercial property sector, the ROI is tied largely to the rate of occupancy. If an investor can't get quality long-term tenants, the income is likely to suffer. Occupancy rates differ across cities and are affected by different factors including location, demand, and economic climate, among others. Under normal conditions, the commercial real estate is relatively stable and the ROI is favorable. This is why it remains a desirable investment.

9/10

D. Passivity

Most investors aim to generate passive income. It's essentially the "end goal" for commercial real estate investors. This is why many investors are moving away from single-family rentals and building a portfolio of passive commercial property investments. With a passive investment, there is more sustainable cash flow, considerably less risk, less reliance on direct oversight, and less expensive management cost.

The amount of capital required to become a direct owner or operator of a commercial real estate is too great for one investor. It is evidently a barrier to entry (albeit a good one as there is less competition!). To overcome such formidable deterrent, investors are opting to invest as a limited partner with commercial real estate operating companies. This way, they are co-investing with professionals who are experienced with dealing in sophisticated investment vehicles such as Real Estate Investment Trusts (REITs). Going this route diversifies the investment portfolio and opens the opportunity to choose different assets with less geographical and business limitations.

With REITs, investors looking to get a piece of the highly profitable commercial real estate pie can do so without actually having to purchase an expensive property and maintaining it like a landlord.

8/10

E. Simplicity

Getting started in commercial real estate investment is no walk in the park. Aside from the actual sale price of the property, there are other costs that will be incurred by the investor during the due diligence period. The cost will depend on the state or city the property is located as well as the size of the property.

Some of the costs to consider before purchasing include the environmental report, property appraisal fee, survey fee, and loan origination and fee, among others.

Financing the commercial property is a formidable barrier to entry that not many investors can overcome. Office buildings, apartment buildings, skyscrapers, and industrial properties require deeper pockets and necessitate pooling of resources. This is why large commercial properties are owned by private equity companies, banks, pension funds, real estate investment groups and investment institutions.

Even after securing the funds either through bank loans or crowdsourcing, the investor has to make improvements in the property to be outfitted for the new business. Sometimes the property is still in great condition that only minor renovations are necessary. However, there are times when a major renovation and retrofit are required. More often than not, investors underestimate the costs because they make wrong estimates. These additional costs add to the already complex nature of commercial investment.

5/10

Ten Tips for Successfully Investing in Commercial Real Estate

1. **Master the fundamentals** - Owning a commercial real estate is the first step to achieving financial freedom. However, investors must be able to first understand, appreciate, and apply the basic financial and investment concepts. The reality is that not all commercial real estate investments are lucrative. A bad decision can lead to a bad investment which could drag investors under.

Mastering the basic financial concepts allows investors to separate the good investment from the bad, to maximize profits and minimize costs, and to add value to the property. The core of an investor's decision-making process lies in the accurate evaluation of the commercial property's financials.

2. **Set investment goals** - It goes without saying that goal-setting is necessary for any investment or business venture. It helps investors keep track of their progress. It also allows them to determine if they are on the path to achieving their investment goals. Goals must be specific, measurable, attainable, relevant, and timely. Setting lofty goals isn't intrinsically bad, but it can lead to big disappointment if they are not achieved.

Setting a goal makes investors identify what they expect to have in a certain time period and allows them to gauge their risk tolerance for investment. It is a practice in self-discovery in the context of investment inclinations. Listing down the specific goals and the course of action to take to achieve them can help avoid emotional investing, which is largely influenced by trends, speculations, and overhyped markets.

3. **Use data to explore the market** - The commercial real estate industry is so diverse that selecting a high-performing property investment can be challenging. Data matters when it comes to making a sound decision. Investors must know how to read and interpret the key statistics and figures, so they can compare properties based on a number of indicators such as price per square meter, rate of occupancy, annual return, and population growth to name just a few.

4. **Don't be afraid to look beyond metropolitan areas** - Prime commercial properties are mostly located in metropolitan areas. They command a higher price tag because they are more lucrative and they carry a

certain level of prestige. Looking beyond one's own backyard can lead to more opportunities. There's nothing wrong with exploring and exploiting homefield advantage, but regional areas can be a haven for prime property investment.

Many investors fail to see that catchment population is big enough to sustain the business and the likelihood of closure is low. What's even more appealing is that it is likely isolated from competition. Well-situated businesses or properties can perform just as strongly as similar properties in the big cities, but they have the advantage of lower price tag, therefore, the yield is higher.

5. **Establish an exit strategy** - An exit strategy is crucial in investment, more so in commercial real estate. The absence of an exit strategy means gambling away the profits already earned and potentially wasting away future earnings. An escape plan must be developed before making the investment and it goes hand in hand with investment goals. This requires evaluating all options and weighing them against the goals.

Investors could opt to sell the property outright or hold on to it to passively create equity. The buy-and-hold strategy is appealing because properties increase in value and rental income can be sustained over time. Another option is seller financing, wherein interest income from loan is earned. The seller benefits from a monthly payment and a tax liability that is distributed over several years.

On the buyer side, it is an opportunity to legally acquire a commercial property if traditional financing channels refuse to lend. Another popular option is the 1031 tax-deferred exchange, wherein an investor can sell off his property without being required to pay capital gains taxes, provided that the equity is transferred to a property with a higher value.

6. **Find the right property** - The right property is the property that meets the investor's criteria. It can be an arduous process of finding as many prospective properties and narrowing down the list. Oftentimes, the key is building relationships with area brokers because they are the best source of information on properties, tenants, and business climate in the area. This makes analyzing the property easier because all the key indicators are locked in.

The choice of property must be carefully considered. What may seem to be a good choice can turn out to be a bust, and vice versa. Going against the grain can sometimes pay off big time. For example, many inventors ignore a property class (e.g. childcare centers or petrol stations) for simply being unpopular for a particular stretch of time, but they turn out to give above average returns. There is a certain degree of risk involved, but the investment can pay off.

7. **Look for alternative financing** - New investors may not be aware that they can seek for alternative financing if the traditional route is too constraining. Bank lending policies have become too cautious in the aftermath of the financial crisis in 2008. As a result, alternative sources of funding are on the rise. Alternatives include bridge loans, mezzanine loans, and hard money.

Bridge loans are considered as interim loans provided to individuals or companies until they secure a permanent financing arrangement or an existing obligation is removed. Some entities used bridge loans to fund short-term construction while waiting for a long-term financing to be secured.

8. **Add value** - Investors can directly impact their property's value by taking steps to boost income and cut expenses. This requires creativity and due diligence on the part of the investor. Some examples of adding value to a property include improving utility efficiencies, creating new sources of revenue, repurposing and upgrading the property, making improvements in the quality and image of the property, employing marketing strategies to boost occupancy levels, and improving property management.

9. **Re-evaluate investment goals** - Investors enter the real estate business with a set of investment goals, but priorities change and new milestones in life happen. It is important to review investment goals periodically to ensure that they are still on track and relevant.

Big life milestones such as getting married, having a child, kids moving to college, or moving to a new city can have a great impact on investment goals. The same is true when personal tragedies happen like a death in the family, getting sick, or going through a divorce. Having the opportunity to review and re-evaluate investment goals allow investors to make mid-course corrections.

It is recommended to review investment goals annually so that adjustments can be made when necessary. Investors should also take into account the changes in the real estate landscape to ensure that the goals are still realistic and attainable.

10. **Allow for adaptation in the future** - In real estate investing, it is necessary to be flexible and adapt to the changing business landscape. Investors must be ready to shift gears and move with the times. At present, investors may be focusing on a certain commercial property class, but this could change several years down the line.

Investors must always be on the lookout for more lucrative investment opportunities while maintaining and improving existing property investments. Exercising some flexibility will allow the investment to survive and thrive in the future.

Interesting Fact #8

In a competition to build the tallest building, the architect of the Chrysler Building secretly built it with a 125 ft spire inside. When his competitor's building was completed, the spire was pushed up through the building making it taller by 119 feet.

Chapter 29

Retail Real Estate

Retail real estate is one of the most diverse and biggest areas of the commercial real estate market. Retail real estate properties offer potential solid returns for investors.

Types of Retail Real Estate Properties

A retail property is used to sell consumer products and services. These properties range from pop-up shops and individual stores to shopping malls. Retail stores include cafes, supermarkets, fashion stores, pharmacies, etc. Investors can choose to put their money in these types of retail real estate properties:

1. Malls

These real estate properties are easy to identify. These are commercial properties that house several retailers and service businesses under one roof. These are normally enclosed areas although some malls have outdoor components.

In general, the size of a mall starts at 400,000 sq. ft. The size limit is still unknown. The largest shopping mall thus far is New South China Mall in Dongguan, China, with a gross leasable area of 7.1 million sq. ft..

2. Factory Outlets

These are also referred to as outlet malls. These are not usually a building or an enclosed area. They're more like clusters of outlet stores of different brands. What's common among these stores is that they sell at lower prices than the department stores. Sometimes, there are food options available, but they are usually limited.

The size of factory outlets is usually between 50,000 sq. ft. and 400,000 sq. ft. However, some of them can go bigger.

3. Lifestyle Centers

These became popular in the 1990s. They are basically malls that have more open spaces and smaller buildings. These are smaller commercial hubs that are intended to cater to the upscale market. Compared to malls, the atmosphere in lifestyle centers is more relaxed and intimate.

The average area of a lifestyle center covers about 150,000 sq. ft. to 500,000 sq. ft., but there those that are spread out over a bigger area.

4. Community Centers

Community centers are often categorized as what people call a strip mall. Their size ranges from 125,000 sq. ft. to 400,000 sq. ft.

Most of these properties have a grocery store. They can also have huge specialty shops and a discounter. Community centers can also have convenience retailers like a drugstore.

5. Neighborhood Centers

These are similar to community centers, but they are smaller. Neighborhood centers are commonly called grocery-anchored properties. They also have convenience retailers. Their size can be up to 125,000 sq. ft.

6. Power Centers

These are properties where you can usually find big-box stores such as home improvement retailers or furniture shops. They also have large specialty chains and discounters.

Some examples of power centers include Best Buy, Walmart, Dick's Sporting Goods, and The Home Depot. The pad sites in the parking lots of these properties often have fast food chains and other diners. The size of a power center starts at 200,000 sq. ft.

7. Convenience Centers

These retail properties are small, usually only less than 30,000 sq. ft. They have convenience-based stores, such as drugstores, salons, and dry cleaners. You can also find other kinds of stores where customers want to have a quick service or purchase.

8. Other Types of Retail Properties.

There are several other types of retail properties that do not fit into the categories above. Some of these are:

A. Urban Retail Properties – examples of these are the high-end shops along Manhattan's Fifth Avenue. They also include service shops and sales offices not necessarily located in a single building or complex. They are located right along the streets and are easily accessible to pedestrians. They usually do not have their own parking spaces.

B. Retail Stores in mixed-use properties – these are shops and restaurants located in commercial or office buildings and multistory residential condominiums or apartments.

C. Tourist/Traveler Retail Properties – these are retail properties that specifically cater to travelers and tourists. You normally see them in airports, entertainment hubs, and vacation spots.

The diverse selection of retail real estate properties gives you some flexibility in choosing where to put your money. The types of properties listed above vary in terms of investment requirement, income potential, and risks among others.

Pros and Cons

Generally, investing in the retail real estate market is a good long-term financial prospect. However, it is not something that you should get into carelessly. One wrong decision could jeopardize your income earning potential or even wipe out your money and leave you with nothing.

It is important to do a thorough research on the market. You also have to know the potential advantages and risks you might face. Furthermore, you need to have a complete understanding of the whole process of investing in retail real estate properties. This will guide you in making rational decisions while you work on closing deals.

Consider these in deciding if investing in retail real estate suits you:

The primary advantage of retail real estate investment is the high income potential. In the U.S., the average annual rental profit for residential real estate is 3% to 5%. This is considered to be beneficial. However, the annual gross rental profit for retail properties is much greater at anywhere from 9% to 12%.

Investors may also consider the potential of "turnover rents" that's unique to retail properties. This is an arrangement where the property owner takes a cut from the gross revenue of the tenant's business.

The longer lease terms also give investors an advantage. The average residential lease contract has a turnover of 6 to 12 months. A lease contract for a retail property is much longer. The average lease turnover is from 3 to 10 years.

This gives you a more stable 'basket' of tenant leases. Your property is also less likely to become unoccupied for long periods of time. Moreover, some tenants of retail properties invest money into the retail space. They usually customize their stores to fit their products and services.

Because of this, they tend to stay longer to ensure they get back what they invested. Giving your tenants some degree of freedom and flexibility in terms of customizing their retail space is an advantage. There is no additional expense on your part as the tenants would have to cover the cost of customizing the retail space from their own pocket.

Tenants are also likely to go for longer lease terms when you have a retail property that's in a high traffic location. This offers them a high level of visibility. Once their customers get used to doing business with them at your location, the business owners will not want to move their business elsewhere. Provided that there are no other issues and concerns with the property, they would renew their retail lease.

Investors in retail real estate enjoy limited hours of operations. The operating hours of shopping malls and retail stores are between 9 AM and 10 PM. Outside of this period, retail property owners are basically off the clock. On the other hand, residential property owners are expected to work any time of the day.

Bigger retail property investors usually hire property management companies. These companies take care of the day to day concerns of the retail tenants as well as any emergencies that could happen, particularly at nighttime.

Some retail properties also employ alarm companies. However, some tenants usually have their own people to handle such concerns.

Retail properties are usually less expensive than the average residential property. Because of this, you only have to pay a small capital amount in order to invest in a retail property.

For example, a small retail property can cost as little as $85,000. That is much cheaper than a small apartment that costs $200,000. The sooner you invest in a piece of retail real estate property, the sooner you will be able to reap financial gains from this segment of the real estate market.

Investors and tenants of retail properties have aligned interests. The tenants of a retail space are more likely to take care of the property than those who rent residential properties. The tenants/owners of retail stores know how important it is for them to keep their premises well-maintained. This affects their branding, customer satisfaction, and ultimately, business success. Both the investors and the tenants are working towards the same results.

As most retail leases are net leases, they require less in terms of maintenance work and costs. The tenant pays for most of the expenses that come with occupying your retail real estate property. These expenses include maintenance costs, property and personal accident insurance, and utility bills.

On the downside, economic conditions can drastically affect retail real estate. The real estate market and retail businesses prosper when the economy is strong. This means that commercial properties are highly in demand. In turn, the market value of retail properties will increase.

On the other hand, when the economy declines, the demand for these types of properties will drop. This is because the retail sector may be affected and business may fail. You may then experience a reverse in income.

As a retail property owner, be ready for possible long vacancy periods when the economy is down. To find tenants during difficult times, you can offer them incentives, such as reduced rents and internal fit-outs.

Before signing a lease, you must learn everything you can about your potential tenants. Find out how secure their business is. This will tell you how likely they are to succeed or fail and leave you when there is an economic downturn.

Changes in the area can affect the property. These include changes in the infrastructure of the surrounding area can increase the value of the property. It can also attract investments. However, there is also a possibility that these changes will swing the other way. Examples of these changes include traffic patterns, retail trends, and design.

This is why the location is crucial in retail real estate. The retail property has to be accessible, so it should have good public transport options and parking. Then, it should also have a lot of foot traffic. Lastly, the type of business has to fit the demographics in the area.

A retail shop can lose business if any of these changes occur. The value of the property can fall when the location becomes less desirable. You may also experience long vacancies.

It can be difficult to find tenants on certain conditions. It may seem like a simple task to find tenants, but this may not be the case for commercial properties. Retail spaces can acquire long-term lease contracts. However, it may be difficult to find a tenant who would commit to these contracts.

If this happens, you can have long vacancies on your property. During this period, you are liable for all the expenses related to it. This also includes the maintenance required to maintain the property.

There is often a need for quality professional assistance. Some retail property owners tend to be absentee investors. They are not hands-on in maintaining their real estate property. If you would like to do the same, you may need to get the services of a property management company. You have to be careful, however, in choosing a company to work with.

Do research on the property management group that you wish to hire. If you don't, you might miss out on important details that could cause bigger problems along the way. Make sure that you take time to evaluate everything before signing an agreement. You also have to check their progress every month.

Scoring Retail Properties

A. Liquidity

Selling a retail property is not easy. In fact, real estate in general is an illiquid asset because they are difficult to sell. They require higher capital to purchase.

It also takes long to sell retail properties. The process involves finding a buyer and completing the transaction process. Retail real estate is also limited to their location. They are affected by the changes on the local market.

There are still ways to sell your property fast. One way is through commercial property auctions. However, this has restrictions. Some of the disadvantages include uncertainty of a guaranteed sale and high auction fees. You can also give discounts to your buyer for a faster transaction.

3/10

B. Scalability

Scaling your retail real estate portfolio is important in achieving your investment goals. The first thing you have to do when scaling your portfolio is to assess your property. You can do this every quarter, but an in-depth assessment should be done every year.

There is a big chance that your retail property investment is doing well. This means it is giving you a steady stream of income. However, it will not be easy when it comes to scalability.

This is because scaling retail real estate involves buying more land. It also involves lots of other things, such as getting approval to build.

Just because you achieved success in your first investment does not mean you can simply invest in another retail property. Therefore, before scaling your retail real estate portfolio, you need to have a thorough research on the market once again.

You also have to do due diligence, so it is important to have a system. This system involves dealing with upcoming tenant vacancies, finding and evaluating property managers, etc.

3/10

C. Potential Return On Investment

Commercial real estate is the most lucrative sector of the real estate business. Among the types of commercial real estate, retail is one of the most profitable. Investing in retail properties is a great way to make profit, even for a novice investor.

Retail properties provide a stable income for investors. Tenants, such as government and businesses, lease spaces usually from three to 10 years or longer. As a retail property owner, you will have income security.

Retail real estate offers you higher ROI than residential real estate. If you want to invest in retail real estate, you need to learn how to determine the Net Operating Income (NOI).

NOI is the annual income generated by your property after you take into account all the earnings from operations. Then, you will deduct all expenses incurred from operations.

In retail real estate, NOI is usually positive because the operating income exceeds the operating expenses. The operating expenses include the costs of maintaining your retail property.

- Cleaning and Maintenance (CAM) – this fee is usually divided between the property owner and the tenant.
- Repairs – the property owner is often solely responsible for maintenance and repairs, unless it is specifically identified in the lease.
- Property taxes – some states tax businesses on their commercial property income. For federal taxes, you can deduct your expenses and pay tax based on your net profit.

In most situations, the property owner is responsible for the property taxes. However, in some cases, it can be stated in the lease agreement that the tenant will shoulder some of this expense.

Administrative costs – this is the payment for the property management company if you decide to hire one.

Property insurance – you pay for the insurance of the structure itself. Your tenant will pay for the commercial property insurance that covers the contents and other assets of their business.

8/10

D. Passivity

Passive income real estate is a great way to attain security in retirement. It will also help you have additional source of income and create a roadmap to attaining financial freedom.

If you do not want to take a more active role in your investment, then retail real estate is ideal for you. Retail real estate investing offers high passive income. Tenants can lease your retail properties with long-term contracts. This promises a more stable flow of income.

You do not have to invest much of your time managing your property. This is because you can hire a property manager to deal with everything, including maintenance, repairs, etc.

However, depending on the location of your property, retail tenants can be difficult to replace. They also tend to customize the retail space to their business needs.

9/10

E. Simplicity

While it offers greater cash flow than residential real estate, investing in retail real estate involves high initial costs. You also need to do a lot of research before proceeding and purchasing a retail property.

As an investor, you need to consider everything. This includes the location and the comparables in the area, which also include researching future development.

The comparables or "comps" are assets that refer to the prices paid for recently sold properties that are similar in style, location, and size. If you analyze comps, it will help you determine the market value of a property.

As a retail real estate investor, market research is important in the success of your business. The formulas on NOI, cap rate, and cash on cash can be confusing. However, if you master them, it will significantly boost your chances of success.

5/10

Ten Tips for Successfully Investing in Retail Real Estate

Like other industries that have a huge potential for success, you need to work hard in retail real estate investing in order to succeed. There are a lot of skills and information to learn.

The first requirement is for you to have a passion for retail real estate to excel in this business. You also have to learn all the methods you can use. Here are 10 proven tips on how to be successful in retail real estate.

1. **Get some training** - Learning as much as you can is the first thing you have to do. Professional organizations are available to teach you special skills you need to have for a commercial real estate business, including retail. They have courses that are required for you to be eligible for a real estate license.

Therefore, you have to look for a real estate course that you can take. You have options to do this at a physical location or enroll online. Then, you can work for acquiring a license to practice retail real estate. Your training will expose you to the following information:

General brokerage – this involves representing the sellers or buyers in real estate deals. The broker assists the client to sell or buy a retail property. They fill in for the client in meetings related to the real estate deals. Brokers are independent contractor. They are not employees of a real estate company. The compensation they receive is on commission terms. As real estate agents, they can deal in any type of commercial real estate. They also have an option to specialize in one type, such as retail commercial real estate.

Property management – in retail real estate business, you can also actively manage the day-to-day activities involved to maintain a retail property. Examples include contracting services, repairs, and maintenance.

The property manager receives a salary from the property owner for their managerial services.

Property development – this is the career path you can take when you want to invest in retail real estate. You will develop retail properties and lease them out to earn a profit.

As a retail real estate investor, you will arrange the financing and buy some land. You will then construct a commercial building for retail and rent it out to businesses. Property development is time-consuming and requires huge capital. However, it is financially rewarding.

2. **Organize your finances** - Buying a retail real estate property is not an easy task. Thus, you have to organize everything. More importantly, your finances should be in order before you even start your investment.

Your financial capability will determine the type of retail property you can purchase. If you go after a property that is not within your price range, the bank may decline you for financing.

To give you picture of what you can afford, you can consult with an accountant. He can also assist you in developing a budget. This includes any hidden costs that come with purchasing a retail property. He can also help you find tax benefits. This can be important to your financial state.

3. **Have a coach or a mentor** - In real estate, including the retail sector, you should avoid making mistakes as much as possible. Your business can grow much faster if your mistakes will not hold you back.

Having a mentor is the only way you can achieve that. This person is someone that you admire in the retail real estate business. You should be able to easily ask them for motivation and advice.

They should share their time with you while still making sure it also works for them. For example, you can accompany them during negotiations when they are closing deals.

This is a win-win situation for the both of you. Your mentor will be glad that they are able to impart their knowledge on you. They learn more by teaching. Then, you will also learn strategies about retail real estate investing. This will make you avoid mistakes that will waste your times.

4. **Create a solid plan of action** - It is always a good thing to have a plan when investing in retail real estate. Approaching real estate is the same as any business. You should have short-term and long-term goals.

If you have a solid plan of action, it will help you see the whole picture in retail real estate investing. You can also focus on your own goals. If you have a plan, it will make sure that you do not end up making hasty decisions. This is because your plan has all the actions you have to take to achieve your goals.

The retail real estate business demands your time and effort. Thus, having a plan will help you remain grounded. You can also get to focus on important matters.

5. **Work with a reliable company** - The name of the real estate company you work with is an instrumental factor in your success as a retail real estate investor. A reputable company provides their clients the security they need when investing in real estate.

Choose a company that has a good reputation in your city. This company may also have a good name in the state or national level. Therefore, you need to do some research about the real estate company you will work with. This will go a long way in boosting your chances of success.

6. **Choose your market wisely** - Like any type of commercial real estate, your market is important in retail real estate. Some areas are more profitable than others. For this reason, find one that has a huge potential for tenants and profit.

As a retail real estate investor, creating a successful career involves investing your money and time in the profitable areas. You should start by researching about your potential markets.

The market for retail real estate is usually better in the cities than in rural areas. This is because there is a higher demand for city properties. Furthermore, there are more business activities in the city and the properties command higher fees.

Try to enter city markets when investing in retail real estate. Also, make sure that you choose cities that have a strong market. Remember that some cities thrive more than the others.

Interestingly, real estate companies in thriving cities close deals and sign contracts on retail properties even before they are finished. The reason behind this is the high demand for retail spaces. Therefore, target an urban market or a city to succeed in retail real estate.

7. **Consider demographics and trends in the area** - When investing in retail real estate, you need to consider the demographics and the latest trends in the area. You can make smart investments by doing all of these. Moreover, you are also planning to have a secure future for yourself and for your interests.

If you have enough knowledge about the area, you can make informed decisions regarding your investment. So, to be successful in retail real estate, you should have a thorough understanding about the market you choose.

8. **Stay motivated** - Being motivated is one the characteristics you need to be successful in anything. You also need to be motivated in the retail real estate business. As you tackle the market, make sure that you find your motivation to work harder each day.

9. **Be patient** - In retail real estate, everything takes longer than investing in residential properties. It takes longer to find new tenants. Building or renovating a property is longer.

However, the leases are also longer. The key here is to be patient. It just takes longer, but the profit is higher than residential real estate.

10. **Select your tenants wisely** - The tenants on your retail property can either make or break your business. For this reason, you have to pick them wisely before closing the deal with them. First-come-first-served basis is not always the best option in choosing your tenants.

Interesting Fact #9

The designer of the Eiffel Tower, Gustav Eiffel, included a secret apartment at the top of the landmark that he could use whenever he needed to get away from the hustle and bustle of his daily life. This apartment is currently up for rent and a second one is being planned for the first floor of the tower.

Congratulations!

The sixth character of the password required to unlock the *Real Estate Business Scorecard* is letter z.

Chapter 30

Mixed Use

Another approach to earning a profitable income with real estate is to invest in mixed-use assets. While this is sometimes mistaken to exclusively refer to multi-story developments, a mixed-use asset actually goes beyond this description.

According to experts, these developments also focus on the integration and compatibility of property uses. These could also involve creating walkable communities that are supposed to ensure unhampered pedestrian connections.

You may choose to develop mixed-use assets in different ways. The primary requirement is that they should be an integral part of a place and be situated in locations with high densities.

You may develop them as neighborhood-based or site-specific projects. You may also incorporate them into redevelopment projects and smart growth initiatives both in rural and urban areas.

Overview of Business Model

The mixed-use business model makes use of real estate assets with meaningful components comprising of at least three revenue-producing uses in adjoining or similar structures. It combines commercial, residential, institutional, and entertainment uses.

You can develop mixed-use assets for a city block, a single building, or an entire community. These could be real estate projects by a government agency or a private developer.

An example of a mixed-use setting is a sky rise building with residential and retail spaces within. The area for residents is located at the upper portion while the retail spaces (that house fitness centers, medical clinics, hair salons, and other shared work spaces) occupy the lower half.

Historical Background

The preference for mixed-use developments is not a new idea. Ancient men have preferred mixed-use developments due to their practical nature. With multi-purpose structures, ancient men could conserve their resources. This is something that was difficult and maybe even impossible with single-purpose structures.

For example, they would build one structure that serves these three purposes:

1. An area where they can safely rest at night
2. An area for their day activities
3. An area where they can securely store their food

Building one structure instead of three saves building materials and occupies less space. Such a set up allowed them to be more efficient in the way they use space, move around, and perform their tasks.

Aside from practicality, mixed-use developments have the added appeal of being bigger and more interesting in terms of design. Through these developments, people were free to repurpose and redevelop their real estate assets.

People then had the freedom to decide if they want to operate multiple businesses in a single building with units that are mostly designated as residential areas. They could freely opt to add more commercial areas as they please or even incorporate entertainment centers inside residential buildings.

However, such arrangement was modified during the age of industrialism and introduction of the skyscraper in the late 1880s. From then on, laws and rules were written and applied for mixed-use development projects to regulate each structure's function.

Special Zoning Rights

The possibilities are exciting when it comes to developing mixed-use real estate assets. The owner and the investors are free to choose what types of establishments to have, the design of the structures, and the configuration or layout of the property units. However, their choices and plans will have to be in accordance with zoning rights for mixed-use assets.

In most countries, there are government and industry authorities who are tasked to draw up, implement, and enforce laws on property ownership and use. If you are not compliant with these laws, these authorities may revoke your permit to build and/or operate. You could be forced to terminate your project permanently.

The good thing is that most governments are in favor of having mixed use developments. Some regulators may even have incentives and relaxed rules for 'desirable' developers. This kind of environment is definitely an advantage for those who are interested in this type of real estate investment.

Specifically, here are the special zoning rights for mixed-use assets:

- Existing shopping malls are permitted to add adjacent offices and/or residential areas.
- Multi-story buildings with commercial areas on ground level and residential areas above are permitted to face main streets.
- Multi-story residential areas with civic and commercial uses can be developed in urban places.
- Multi-family residential areas can feature office buildings within.
- Neighborhood commercial zoning grants permission to convenience services in residential areas where these are normally prohibited.
- Office buildings that provide office-related convenience services can be developed.
- Parking structures can be erected.
- Shopping malls can feature detached (single-family) home districts.
- Suburban retail areas can be retrofitted to adapt a more aesthetically pleasing appearance and uses.
- The owners of residential areas can operate commercially. They can run small businesses in their building of residence.
- The owners of residential areas can use spaces in their building of residence for industrial agenda.

Built-In Diversification

Aside from their special zoning rights, mixed-use assets offer the advantage of diversification. This is great for those with significant investment in their real estate portfolio. It evens out their risks and offers great opportunities for more gains.

Mixed-use assets are already diversified in themselves. In one development, the investor enjoys several income streams coming from the different types of property occupants. You can have income from residential tenants as well as from commercial tenants in a mixed-use condominium building, for instance. When business is not doing good for your commercial spaces, you still have your residential units as your source of income.

A lifestyle complex, on the other hand, could give you even more sources of income. This, however, would require a lot more documentation and paper work. It would also be necessary for you to take a look at and comply with more regulations as the case may be. Specific use buildings would be governed by different laws and policies.

To demonstrate, here is an example of how mixed use assets can help control the impact of risk in your portfolio:

This example involves residential (1/3 of the asset) and commercial components (2/3 of the asset). If the residential component of a mixed-use property has sustained physical damages and fails to offer a decent return, an investor's income is still salvageable. The residential component may incur losses but the commercial components can gain high profits.

On the net, this investor ends up making a profit. The profits he was able to gain from the asset's components have compensated for the loss he suffered from the residential components.

Successful real estate investors diversify their portfolio with mixed-use assets and mitigate their risks. They are able to cover unexpected expenses and losses from one type of asset with gains from another asset type.

Pros and Cons

Mixed-use assets also have environmental advantages. They help reduce car and fuel usage, promote smart practices, and bring a positive impact to the environment. Some of the other advantages and disadvantages of mixed use real estate assets for both investors and tenants:

For investors:

They give more value to real estate investors. Because they can achieve better long-term returns, mixed-use assets are more favorable to real estate investors. These investors are willing to invest a larger amount of money due to the potential of a higher ROI.

With a lot of money allocated for their development, mixed-use buildings tend to be feature-rich and highly attractive. They are high-value properties that can help promote tourism and increase private investment.

Real estate investors incur lower infrastructure costs. Mixed-use assets are less expensive to develop compared to single-use assets. Since mixed-use assets allow the services for construction, design, and maintenance to be accomplished in one location, these services are delivered efficiently and cost-effectively.

If an investor wants to have residential units, fitness centers, and entertainment hubs, for instance, and he has to house all these in different properties, he would have separate infrastructure costs for each property. If they were housed in one mixed-use property, the costs would logically be lower for a single location development.

Mixed-use assets have better exposure. The more types of businesses in a single development, the more visibility it enjoys. Of course, these businesses have to be strategically positioned and marketed. Accessibility, security, and convenience are features that can easily make mixed-use properties more attractive both to investors and customers.

Mixed-use properties are easy to manage. Property management is more convenient with this type of real estate property. Everything is in one location and the property managers do not have to move from one place to another.

For tenants:

Tenants with active lifestyles are easily able to engage in the activities that they are interested in. Mixed-use properties often have several activity centers all in one location. Someone living in the development's residential units could easily walk to the gym, the pool, the library, or to the restaurant. They save energy, time, and money.

Likewise, these developments are accessible to public transportation so people living in or visiting the property can easily go to and from other locations.

Mixed-use real estate properties are healthier as these developments usually have enough open spaces for the tenants to enjoy. There are walkways, playgrounds, and hubs where tenants can have fun. The greenery also results in better air quality.

Tenants are likely to be more productive since everything is all in one place. Tenants do not waste a lot of time getting from one place to another. They do not have to commute far from their residence to their workspace and they can focus on their work and other important matters instead.

These living areas are great for extended families. Relatives do not have to live far from each other and get to see each other only during holidays and special occasions. They can live right next to each other in residential units in mixed-use properties. This set up allows them to preserve and strengthen family relations.

Business tenants will find mixed-use properties more practical. Businesses are closer to their customers when they are right where they live. Their employees can live right in the property as well, minimizing tardiness and absences in the workplace. The property is strategic for both the business and its customers.

However, despite the pros, mixed-use assets come with risks. They can offer challenging situations for real estate investors.

For investors, these properties can be difficult to market at first this is especially true when the area is still in the development stage. Not a lot of businesses and residents want to rent property in a place that is not thriving. The challenge for investors is to make their prospects realize the growth potential of the community.

The community might not always welcome the development as well. This happens when the development is seen to disrupt the life that the community has gotten used to.

Building a complex of tall structures in a mixed-use development, for instance, might not be a welcome change for a small quiet community. Some communities might also perceive the new development as a 'magnet' for heavy crime and traffic.

Among the issues that would make a mixed use property difficult to market are open and active resistance from the community, regulatory setbacks, and uncertainty in as far as the completion and delivery of the project.

Property managers who are used to managing single use properties might have a difficult time dealing with multiple types of establishments. While the need to hire several property managers specializing in each type of property might seem to be a good choice, it is not necessary to do so. It might take a little getting used to but it is not impossible.

There are tips and tricks that can be learned for managing multi use properties. The attitude of the property manager would be more important in acquiring the necessary skills to manage both residential and commercial spaces.

For tenants, a disadvantage lies in having too many people using the shared spaces. With the number of businesses and residents in one multi use property, it is expected that there will be a lot of users sharing the facilities and common areas.

Those who do not have rented parking space, for instance, could find it difficult to find a slot during times when there are a lot of people in the area. This could be managed by having dedicated parking spaces for residents and a separate area for visitors and customers.

Scoring Mixed Use Properties

A. Liquidity

If you want to get out of the business and cash out, you can't do it abruptly with these assets. Liquidating them might take you years and successfully transferring them to another's ownership usually requires a series of steps, proper documentation, and expenses.

A major factor that justifies the low rating is the fact that these assets come with multiple components. To put them out on the market, you would need to be on the lookout for mixed use property buyers as well as different types of buyers. This includes those who are on the hunt for commercial, residential, and industrial prospects. You cannot simply focus on just one type of buyer.

A redeeming factor that explains why this type of real estate asset did not receive a much lower rating is its value in real estate. If you find the right buyer, you can get great value for a mixed use property that's strategically located, built with excellent quality, and has great potential for growth.

3/10

B. Scalability

Just like how the rating based on liquidity is justified, a major factor that also justifies the low rating based on this criterion is the fact that there are multiple components that come with these assets.

Scaling mixed-use assets can be difficult because there are different types of property involved. Each type of property would have different business and regulatory requirements to alter or revise business wise or physically. You would have to worry about documentation, permits, zoning rights, and even community relations when you decide to scale your development up or down.

2/10

C. Potential Return On Investment

Mixed-use real estate assets have a high potential for growth and profitability. As an investor, you can look forward to higher ROI within a shorter period of time.

Despite the usually high overall operational costs of building, maintaining, and doing business with your mixed-use real estate property, you can still get a significant ROI. This is because the mixed income streams evens out your profitability. Whether or not a particular segment of your market is doing well, you are sure to reap benefits from other segments that are riding high.

It's another plus that this score on this criterion has already taken into consideration the investor's tax obligations for the ownership of these assets. Even with such expenses as property and income taxes, the ROI is still expected to be substantial.

9/10

D. Passivity

Once you succeed in building a mixed use setting and getting to full occupancy, you are assured of a steady income. The key is to have a sound marketing plan to attract both tenants and customers.

This potential to earn money passively is possible if you hire a skilled property manager. This professional will overlook the affairs in your building and supervise maintenance services.

An efficient maintenance services provider for mixed-use assets is important. Like any depreciable property, the income-earning potential of mixed-use property can dwindle over time if it is not managed properly. Conversely, you can increase its earning capacity when you improve the property prudently.

9/10

E. Simplicity

They can be a challenge to manage, although not impossible. They require expertise on multiple types of assets. The fact that they involve broad categories is a concern.

They are not ideal for novice developers because there is no "correct way" to work on them. Their purpose is to blend multiple land uses, which is up to your design to deliver. You shouldn't rush the development of these assets. A primary rule that you need to follow is to develop them so they can serve a vital part of their location.

Mixed-use assets are also not for developers with a tight budget. You need a large capital to acquire land and build the units, and enough funds during the ongoing development. Unfortunately, not a lot of financial companies and credit unions are open to the idea of funding the development of these assets. That is why most mixed-use developments are funded privately or through building authorities and redevelopment agencies.

The rating goes beyond average because mixed-use assets can be less challenging to get into for the experienced real estate developers. With expertise on the development of multiple types of property, it can be easy for them to dive into the field, work with flexibility, and succeed on the project.

They simply need to figure out a solid source of funding in the beginning. Once these developments are already built and occupied, getting conventional financing is easy.

6/10

Ten Tips for Successfully Investing in Mixed-Use Real Estate

Based on all the aforementioned information, you can conclude that developing mixed-use assets can be truly rewarding. It comes with a set of advantages and this outweighs the disadvantages.

Taking on the challenge of developing a mixed-use real estate property is not a walk in the park. However, its promising financial rewards make the hard work worthwhile. It would be a good idea to invest in mixed-use real estate development if you are willing to lay down the groundwork patiently and to have your investment tied up in the property until you achieve your ROI and establish a steady passive income stream.

Here are some tips that will help you succeed in mixed use real estate investing.

The Planning Stage

1. Establish a solid source of funding

The first tip for success in developing mixed-use assets is to secure your funding. This type of project is very costly. Unless you establish a solid (or unlimited, if possible) source of funding, you can find yourself stopping the development midway due to bankruptcy.

Even after calculating the initial costs for the development, you should be ready for all the possible expenses for its ongoing maintenance and operations. As you go through the construction process, some equipment may get damaged and you can run into manpower issues. These would result in unexpected expenses and setbacks. You need to factor these in when you draw up your financial plan.

2. Develop projects that respect their environment's heritage.

One of the top reasons why people succeed in the business of mixed use real estate investing is the fact that they are not completely oblivious to their project's neighborhood. It's a wise business move to commit to the preservation of the community's history and heritage.

The people in the community where you will develop your mixed-use real estate property should welcome you and perceive you as an ally rather than as an intruder. They should consider you as a corporate citizen who acknowledges their past and present and is committed to painting a better future for them.

An example of a successful development in this case is the prison that was turned into a mixed-use community in North Virginia. What once was merely a place of confinement has undergone progressive transformation. Old block cells are now loft-style apartments, a yoga studio, a fitness center, and a lounge room.

3. Develop mixed-use assets that are near public transportation.

Another tip is to leverage on public transportation. It's always good to be situated within easy access to the city's public transportation system. Even if you have a mixed-use property, your tenants would need to go to some other location. The customers of your business tenants would also most likely come from other places.

You need to make sure that customers are able to go to your property to do business with your tenants as they need to. Pay attention to the transportation network system and take note of the stations and terminals.

4. Establish good partnerships.

It has already been mentioned that investing in a mixed-use real estate development requires a lot of resources, not necessarily limited to financial. It would give you a lot of advantage to have other investors putting in more resources into the development.

Make sure that you partner with people who will share your vision and goals when it comes to the development. You need to want the same results and to agree on how you will achieve those results.

As the saying goes, "two heads are better than one." Having partners also means that you have people who will brainstorm with you and even argue with you as you find ways to gain maximum profitability from your investment.

Make sure that you partner with people you trust and respect. You need to be assured that you and your co-investors will be on the same page – even if you argue once in a while.

The Developing Stage

5. Focus on quality.

You need to ensure that the quality of your development will give you a competitive advantage. You cannot go half-baked on your investment. Otherwise, you are bound to spend even more or maybe even get into snags with the regulators and your customers themselves.

Invest in quality and make sure that your development more than meets the quality standards set by industry regulators and government agencies. The more that your property is perceived positively by your prospects, the more they will patronize you and the faster your asset's value will rise. The next tip is to focus on the quality of your mixed-use project. By ensuring quality, you have a competitive advantage.

If your project meets the standards in the real estate industry and comes with high quality, more and more people would want to check out what you have to offer. If they like what you have, they're likely to patronize you and your asset's value will rise.

6. Be willing to delegate responsibility.

There is no denying it. It takes a lot of work to build a mixed-use real estate business. When you attempt to do everything by yourself, you are bound to jeopardize quality and negatively affect your chances of success. You will end up with delayed outputs and you will get burnt out even before you are able to see any signs of returns flowing back into your pocket.

Just make sure to delegate the assignments to highly qualified people. Trust them to assist you and help you carry out your original plan. Among the professionals that you should consider hiring are property managers and financial advisers. You may also consult someone who specializes in mixed-use assets.

7. Stick to the plan.

Another tip is to be consistent and stick to your plan. You should always insist on seeing the bigger picture because it is how you'll receive high ROI. You might think that you need to rely on gut feel at times, but staying faithful to your business plan is always a good idea.

Stop second-guessing yourself every step of the way. For as long as you have exerted all your effort and exhausted your resources into drawing up a sound plan, you should trust that your plan is solid enough for you to rely on.

Assess risks and opportunities that you are likely to come face-to-face with as you develop your project and do business with your customers. Use the information to prepare your action plan so that you are ready with a response when these risks happen.

Finishing Up

8. Be more mindful of the quality of your tenants.

Even if you have the best buildings and the most promising business plans, you can lose out on your investment if you do not take care in choosing the kind of tenants who will occupy your units.

Just because a prospect has all the money to pay one year's rent in advance does not mean that he is a good tenant. He could be demanding and inconsiderate of other tenants and your own business.

Do business only with prospects with good intentions and have 'desirable' customer profiles. Remember that the quality of your tenants would also affect the way your business is patronized and perceived by your target customers.

9. Give importance to your tenants' concerns.

Establishing harmony among the tenants of your mixed-use property is important. This is why you need to have house rules for all areas of you property. Make sure everyone knows what's allowed and what's not.

Be open to comments, suggestions, and feedback. Check on your tenants every once in a while and find out how they're doing. Listen to their concerns and make sure that they are addressed accordingly as best you can.

10. Be up-to-date with trends.

Get updated really quick if you wish to be perceived as more attractive and appealing to your target market or prospects. The value and popularity of your business would definitely be much higher than if you do not ride the tide of trends.

Knowing what the trends are will allow you be more open to those who are looking to ride the tide of consumerism. A way to combat the market's unpredictable nature is to always know what's up in the real estate industry. You should be on the lookout for any new type of asset, as well as new approaches involving mixed-use developments and then address these concerns.

Interesting Fact #10

In California, buying real estate without water rights makes sewer and water hook-ups illegal.

Chapter 31

Residential Real Estate

Investing in residential real estate properties is a popular choice for the obvious reason that there will always be a demand for living spaces. There will always be a market for properties that provide the basic need for shelter. As such, you can also expect to be in competition with others who want to tap into this lucrative income source. You need a good business plan to successfully gain from residential real estate investing.

Processes Involved in Residential Real Estate Investing

There are basically three main processes involved in investing in residential real estate. The last process ultimately lets you decide on two possible outcomes for profit. Here's what you have to go through to earn from residential properties:

- **Purchase** – select and purchase a residential property. There are a lot of options for you and you have to be careful with where you put your money. You can go for traditional homes, practical apartments, or more modern condominium units.

  Spend some time doing research on the prices of properties as well as the possibilities and opportunities they present. Consider factors like location, population, and development in your evaluation of the properties you want to purchase.

- **Hold** – you would have to hold on to the property that you have purchased, at least for the meantime. This should allow you to set up your next steps. Your goal while you are holding on to your property is to boost your bottom line.

  This is the time for you to improve the property if necessary. You'll also be able to entertain potential buyers during this time as you already officially own the property. Depending on your goals and plans, you can hold on to a piece of property anywhere from a few weeks to several months.

- **Sell or Rent** – when you are ready, you can decide to either flip the residential property to get your investment back or rent it out for a steady stream of income. This decision would have to be based on what would give you the most profits. Consider current market conditions, consumer demand, and property trends.

Do these steps for each real estate property that you invest in. If you are planning on investing in more than just a handful of properties, you have to be systematic about your activities. You need to be sure that all your bases are covered and that you are able to factor in all the risks, rewards, and costs into your analysis. Be realistic in your estimates.

If you buy a property with the intent to sell, you should factor in manpower costs, taxes, and other expenses, plus your markup of course. You'll earn a significant profit with a piece of property that: you do not have to spend so much on to fix up, you can buy at way below market prices, and you can sell while the market is still hot.

You do not have to worry a lot if property values go down. You can draw up a plan to hold on to the property and wait for market prices to go back up again. In the meantime, think of ways to earn from the property while you wait. Renting it out on short term contracts would be a good option.

If you plan on renting out your property, you can look forward to regular monthly rental income. This can be allocated for expenses on the property like mortgage payments, maintenance costs, and taxes. To manage your risk, it would be best to choose your tenants carefully. You want to ensure that you will get paid and that your tenants will take care of your property.

Residential Real Estate Investment Strategies

You can choose from two strategies when you invest in residential real estate. You can either buy and hold or buy and flip. You can choose to concentrate on a single strategy or have a portfolio that combines both strategies.

1. Buy and Hold Strategy

When you choose this strategy, you take risks while you are holding on to the property. You've already put down your money on the property and you will have to wait until you recover your investment and gain earnings. Property values could go down and your property can deteriorate.

This strategy is best utilized when you are dealing with properties with long term prospects. You are banking on the expectation of being able to sell the property at higher prices at a later time. Or, you might also project a demand for rentals and plan to take advantage of the chance to charge higher rates.

With this strategy, you remain to be the owner of the property. Therefore, you will be responsible for payment financial obligations (mortgages, liens, utilities, taxes, etc.) on it. You will also have to take care of maintenance and repair needs.

If this is the only property you have, you have to ensure that your income on it is higher than your expenses. Earning rental income on a piece of property that you are holding on to is a good way to ensure that you have money to cover your regular expenses.

Whether you plan to rent out or re-sell the property in the future, you need to carefully choose the properties you invest in using this strategy. Locations where there is heavy competition are not ideal as you will not have much leeway in terms of rental rates or selling prices. There's a good chance that you will have to go lower in your pricing just to be competitive.

The buy and hold strategy is a good option for a portfolio of properties across different areas. This way, you even out your risk-reward potential.

2. Buy and Flip Strategy

This is a good strategy to make quick earnings on residential real estate. Flipping houses is fairly common these days especially with shows on mainstream television about it. These shows feature how properties can be bought, 'transformed,' and then sold at a much higher price.

In this strategy, you buy properties that are worn down or outdated but have a good potential for being renovated so they can be sold. These properties can be bought at really low prices. With the right improvements, you can quickly 'flip' these properties and sell them at thousands of dollars in profits.

Your calculations have to be spot-on when you use this strategy. You need to be able to estimate how much money you need to improve the property and jack up its price. You also need to accurately project how much you can sell the property for. Otherwise, you might end up selling the property for less than what you spent for repairs and renovations.

Note that flippers do not only look at the aesthetics of the properties they want to invest in. There are also 'hidden' flaws and damage that could make flipping expensive and jeopardize an investor's potential profits. Even if the properties are selling at rock bottom prices, a flipper still has to take steps to do a thorough inspection.

These strategies appeal to different types of investors. Your choice on which strategy to use depends on how much risk you want to take, what you are willing to do, and how soon you wish to reap gains among others.

Comparing Investment Strategies

It is recommended to compare the two real estate investment strategies first to evaluate which one is best for you. There are a lot of things to consider, but they are mostly about your own goals and resources as well as what you are comfortable with.

Here are some things for you to consider when you compare the two strategies:

1. The buy and hold strategy is a good way to set up a positive cash flow.

This is particularly true for rentals. While you are holding on to a piece of property until it appreciates in value, you can rent it out and collect regular income from your tenants. Once you are ready to sell, you can decide not to renew your rental agreement and put the property in the market.

2. The buy and flip strategy could be risky.

It's easy to get drawn to flipping because of its media exposure. When you plunge into this kind of undertaking without knowing exactly what you are supposed to do, you are exposing yourself to risks.

3. Upgrades do not always boost a property's value.

Flipping, therefore, is not always a good option. Not all rundown property has a good potential for being flipped. Before you put down your money on a property for flipping, thoroughly evaluate the work that needs to be done, the amount of money you need to spend, and the prospective selling price.

4. Both strategies entail costs as you retain ownership.

In the buy and hold strategy, you need to make sure that the property generates enough income to cover these costs. In a buy and flip strategy, you have to ensure that you impute these costs into your selling price.

5. The longer it takes for you to do your renovations, the more expensive it could be for you.

Costs can easily skyrocket when your renovations drag on. At the same time, the market could just as easily turn unfavorable for you. That's why you need a good plan when you decide to buy a piece of residential property for flipping.

6. Keep in mind that the market can easily change

So if you're left holding the property longer than you expected, you might be in it for a loss. In such a situation, you lose your advantage and may be turned into the type of seller that buyers can easily take advantage of.

7. Dealing with third-party suppliers and contractors

When you flip a property, you have to deal with third-party suppliers and contractors. Instead of acting as an investor, you can easily turn into a project manager. And if you're not up for the task, it can be quite a pain in the neck.

8. Pricing Correctly

Apart from mortgage payments and upgrades, you have to factor in man hours when you reprice the home for sale. Add to these taxes, fees, and other legal costs and you might not even break even. This is why you shouldn't just jump in when you see a home you'd think you'll make a buck on.

If you are looking for a solid real estate investment, you should always focus on realistic return figures that factor all elements in. Do not get blinded by the potential for huge returns. Consider what you need to do or spend to actually realize these gains.

The property that you buy should match the strategy that you want to use. If you are new to real estate investing, find a pro or mentor who can help you out especially with the calculations.

The Pros and Cons of Investing in Residential Real Estate

Weigh these pros and cons before you invest in real estate properties:

The Pros

A great thing about investing in residential real estate is that you have direct control over the properties you buy. Whether you decide to buy and hold, rent, upgrade, or flip, what happens to your property will be according to your own discretion. You have the freedom to decide on what you want to do.

Investing in residential real estate gives you several options to earn income. You can also determine how much income to make on a piece of property. The property becomes part of your assets and you can determine how you use it while it is within your ownership and control.

The Cons

Buying real estate property can eat away a large chunk of your money. You need to have cash to make such a hefty investment. Given that markets can be fickle and there are no guarantees of making profits whether from holding or from flipping, you'll be taking a huge risk here.

If you decide to secure funding for any property, expect it to be quite challenging if you don't have a regular line of credit with a bank or financial institution. Especially when it comes to pure investments like these, the lack of any guarantees may disqualify you from being granted an adequate amount of financing.

It takes more work than just putting down the money as an investor in order to profit from residential real estate. You'll have to be willing and able to put on other 'hats' too. You might have to act as a property manager, a contractor, or even an interior decorator in the process of making your investment more appealing to your potential clients.

If you decide to hold and rent, you may also experience problems with finding tenants. In some cases, you might even have to deal with vacancies. When your calculations allocate your rental income to paying for your monthly expenses and month obligations, vacancies can easily affect your monthly balance.

There are also legal concerns to be aware of when you invest in residential real estate properties. Laws differ depending on where the properties are located. In most cases, having professionals around to give you sound advice is necessary.

Scoring Residential Real Estate

A. Liquidity

With residential real estate, you are looking at anywhere from several months to years to dispose of properties at the right price. This also accounts for the time necessary to fix the properties up for flipping. This means that your money is tied up until you sell the property. Even if you decide to rent out the property, it is not likely for you to recover your principal investment in the near future.

Investing in residential real estate does not give you a lot of liquidity. If you need to recover your investment right away, you might want to think twice about putting it in this asset class. If you are not in a hurry, you can benefit from the high potential income residential real estate investing can give you.

3/10

B. Scalability

It is not easy to scale your residential real estate portfolio up or down. You cannot just decide to pare down your portfolio or expand it within a number of days or even weeks.

To add more properties to the mix, you'll need to have a lot of additional funding add to that spend hours searching and studying locations and available homes. In this case, considering that you're an average investor, it may not be the most scalable option there is.

3/10

C. Potential Return On Investment

Your potential ROI will depend on the market, demand, and your choice of location. But provided that you do things right and invest at a proper time, you can earn a lot from an investment in residential real estate whether you choose to go for a sale or decide to rent out your property.

Of course there will be certain fees that will affect your bottom line. There are taxes, permits, construction expenses, interest rates, mortgage payments, and additional expenses that you have to include in your final figures.

7/10

D. Passivity

Those who are looking for a passive income stream would have to choose the right strategy for their residential real estate portfolio. It is possible to set up a passive income stream from a portfolio of rental properties on long term contracts and lease agreements.

The buy and flip strategy might be intimidating for those who simply want to invest and then wait for steady returns on their money. This strategy also requires investors to be more hands-on and involved in the improvements that need to be done. Investors need to put in ample time and resources to profit from residential real estate investing.

6/10

E. Simplicity

It's easy enough to do business in residential real estate. You only need to have enough money to buy your first property. There really are no barriers to entry.

Even earning from your investment is simple enough since you can actually just buy and then sell the property outright as is. When you have had enough experience and learned the ropes, you can venture into more strategic residential real estate investing for long term yields.

The residential real estate market holds a lot of earning potential for every investor who is willing to put in the money, time, and effort. If these scores are aligned with your own investment objectives, knowledge, and risk appetite, then go ahead and look for worthwhile residential properties to earn income from.

8/10

Ten Tips for Successfully Investing in Residential Real Estate

Even if it is simple enough to get into residential real estate investing, you still have to put in your share of time and effort to be successful in it. As in any worthwhile investment, a combination of preparation, strategy, and good business sense are necessary. Here are 10 tips to help you succeed in this particular business endeavor:

1. Research about the properties you are interested in.

Due diligence can be a lifesaver when it comes to property investments. Do not take things at face value. Evaluate your options thoroughly to avoid wasting your money on duds and properties that could end up worth a lot less than what you bought them for.

Look into titles and liens. Check on past ownership and property history. Everything should be transparent and any risk that comes with the property should be clear to you. Weigh your options and make sure that any risk you will be taking on is worth the potential profit.

Do not hesitate to consult with professionals if you have doubts or if you need to clarify some issues before you move forward with your investment.

2. Invest in house inspections prior to purchasing any piece of property.

You might hesitate in incurring any costs before you even own the property, but it's an insignificant expense that could save you from more losses.

Through an inspection, you can spot issues that need to be addressed. You can demand to have these fixed first before you continue with your transaction or you can negotiate for a lower price because of these issues.

You may also decide that the issues discovered during the inspection are deal-breakers for you. In this case, you can go and look at other properties instead of wasting your time hovering over a piece of property that you are unsure of buying.

3. Make sure there isn't any serious structural damage in any property you are investing in.

Watch out for this if you are looking to flip properties. Rundown does not necessarily mean unsafe and inhabitable. Unless you are willing to rebuild the property from the ground up, it is best to stay away from properties that are not structurally sound anymore.

Wall gaps, uneven windows, and cracked floors are some of the signs that indicate possible structural damage. It is best to consult experts and engineers about these issues. You cannot just base your decisions on your own speculations.

4. Focus on minimal improvements first.

When looking for properties to flip, choose those that require minimal improvements or those that will not require a lot of money to fix up. Simple upgrades like a fresh coat of paint, updated hardware, and refurbished fixtures can already give you a lot of room to jack up your selling price.

5. Do not over-improve the property.

You might get carried away with your ideas for renovation. The temptation to turn whatever is in your imagination into reality might be too strong. Resist the urge to go all out in your improvements.

Focus your attention on making basic improvements and, as much as possible, leave your personal preferences out of it. Let the new homeowners worry about the major details and highlights. Buyers would appreciate having a 'blank slate' that they can paint on according to their own image of an ideal home.

6. Do the math and estimate your potential profits.

Take the time to make your calculations on what your costs are and how much you can expect to earn from your investment. It's not the same with all the properties that you buy. You have to consider variable costs for items like repairs and permits.

Add the costs to the selling price and compare it with the property's market value. Ideally, you should be able to sell the property at a price that covers your principal investment, the expenses you incurred to improve the property, and your markup. If the market values are below this price, it's not worth investing in the property unless you foresee a future time when it will be profitable.

7. Include miscellaneous costs in your budget.

Don't make the mistake of using up all your investment funds for buying a piece of property. Leave enough cash for repairs and other expenses necessary to boost the value of the property. Consider this as your 'operating' budget.

When you sell the property, you can include your operating costs in you selling price. You can do the same thing when you compute for your rental rates.

8. Work with a knowledgeable local realtor.

Make your property search easier by working with a local realtor. While you can look for properties to invest in on your own, a local realtor can point you in the right direction and show you the properties that fit your criteria. This way, you do not waste your time and energy scouring the market for great deals and profitable investment prospects.

9. Don't fall in love with any property.

It's all for profit. You are not investing in properties to have and to hold for your own personal use. Don't get too attached as it will be difficult for you to remain objective especially during negotiations. You might love the property strong enough to not want to sell it or let go of it anymore.

10. Be open to selling under market value.

Your goal for investing in residential real estate is to make profits, of course. There are times, however, when you need to take a loss. This happens in most investment instruments. You just have to be ready to cut your losses as soon as they become imminent.

It is possible for you to sell under market value and still profit from the transaction. This would put cash back into your investment budget so you can use it for more profitable undertakings.

Conclusion II

Before anything else, I would like to thank you for reading this book up to this point. That only shows that you are truly serious in achieving success with real estate investing. Being serious about it is a good start. It also prepares you in developing the right mindset.

Furthermore, I want to share with you something that I find terribly sad. Once people start reading a book, they typically only read 10 percent of it before they give up or forget about it. Only 10 percent. What's sad about this is that from this statistic, we can see that very few people actually follow through on what they commit to (at least when it comes to reading). The reason for this is harsh but understandable: most people are not willing to hold themselves accountable. People "want" and "want" all day, but very few actually have the fortitude to put in the work.

So what's my point? First, I am trying to tell you that if you're reading these words, you are a statistical anomaly (and I am grateful for you). But here's the kicker: in order to become successful as a result of this book, you are going to have to be in the .1 percent. You need to take action.

Finally..

There is great potential for investment earnings and growth in the real estate market. The range of available real estate investments gives something for all types of investors. All of these have their pros and cons that any investor can successfully manage with the right preparation and strategy. Given time, money, and effort, you can put together a portfolio of real estate investments that will give you substantial gains both in the short term and over the long term.

You have publicly-traded investments known as REITs (Real Estate Investment Trust), company-owned properties via REIGs (Real Estate Investment Groups), and RELPs (Real Estate Limited Partnership). You can also invest in tax lien certificates, direct purchase of land or industrial properties, direct purchase of commercial and residential lots, as well as retail and mixed-used facilities.

Investing in real estate regardless of the type can be quite daunting indeed. To wrap things up, here are some final tips:

- Start by choosing a property type to invest in and research viable funding options. Take a look at your current credit score, investor relations, and of course taxes and other potential costs.
- Also make sure that you take a closer look into trends. How is the market doing? Which areas are best to invest in? Where do people desire to live? What types of facilities are people looking for these days? These are just some of the questions that you should be answering early on in the process.
- Learn as much as you can about the trade and all processes involved. If you have to work with an expert then do so. If you need to take a class or seminar then don't be afraid to sign up. The thing about real estate investing is that's it's a long-term endeavor and commitment so make sure it's an industry that you really want to get into before making that big leap.
- If borrowing money becomes an option, study your options and see where it's best to facilitate such a transaction. It is possible for your personal assets to become collaterals if you're not working under corporate terms. Just make sure that you secure yourself before putting any payments down on a property.

Remember that no investment can give you substantial and sustainable gains overnight. You have to be willing to do some amount of work even to set up passive streams of income. Investing in the real estate market can only be worthwhile if you put in your share of work. Having read this book from beginning to end, I have no doubt you're the type that's willing to put in the work. With that, I wish you the very best of luck with your investments!

The End

Thank you very much for taking the time to read this book. I tried my best to cover as much information as I could without overwhelming you. If you found it useful please let me know by leaving a review on Amazon! Your support really does make a difference and I read all the reviews personally so can I understand what my readers particularly enjoyed and then feature more of that in future books.

I also pride myself on giving my readers the best information out there, being super responsive to them and providing the best customer service. If you feel I have fallen short of this standard in any way, please kindly email me at **michael@michaelezeanaka.com** so I can get a chance to make it right to you. I wish you all the best with your business!

Book(s) By Michael Ezeanaka

Affiliate Marketing: Learn How to Make $10,000+ Each Month On Autopilot

Are you looking for an online business that you can start today? Do you feel like no matter how hard you try - you never seem to make money online? If so, this book has you covered. If you correctly implement the strategies in this book, you can make commissions of up to $10,000 (or more) per month in extra income.

- WITHOUT creating your own products
- WITHOUT any business or management experience
- WITHOUT too much start up capital or investors
- WITHOUT dealing with customers, returns, or fulfillment
- WITHOUT building websites
- WITHOUT selling anything over the phone or in person
- WITHOUT any computer skills at all
- WITHOUT leaving the comfort of your own home

In addition, because I enrolled this book in the kindle matchbook program, **Amazon will make the kindle edition available to you for FREE** after you purchase the paperback edition from Amazon.com, saving you roughly $6.99!!

Available In Kindle, Paperback and **Audio**

Passive Income Ideas: 50 Ways To Make Money Online Analyzed

How many times have you started a business only to later realise it wasn't what you expected? Would you like to go into business knowing beforehand the potential of the business and what you need to do to scale it? If so, this book can help you

In Passive Income Ideas, you'll discover

- A concise, step-by-step analysis of **50 business models** you can leverage to earn passive income (Including one that allows you to earn money watching TV!)
- Strategies that'll help you greatly simplify some of the business models (and in the process **make them more passive!**)
- What you can do to scale your earnings (regardless of which business you choose)
- Strategies you can implement to **minimize the level of competition** you face in each marketplace
- Myths that tend to hold people back from succeeding in their business (**we debunk more than 100 such myths!)**
- Well over 150 Insightful tips that'll give you an edge and help you succeed in whichever business you chose to pursue
- More than 100 frequently asked questions (**with answers**)

- 50 positive vitamins for the mind (in the form of inspirational quotes that'll keep you going during the tough times)
- A business scorecard that neatly summarizes, in alphabetical order, each business models score across 4 criteria i.e. simplicity, passivity, scalability and competitiveness
- ...and much much more!

What's more? Because the book is enrolled in kindle matchbook program, **Amazon will make the kindle edition available to you for FREE** after you purchase the paperback edition from Amazon.com, saving you roughly $6.99!!

Available In Kindle, Paperback and **Audio**

Work From Home: 50 Ways To Make Money Online Analyzed

This is a **2-in-1 book bundle** consisting of the below books. Amazon will make the kindle edition available to you for FREE when you purchase the print version of this bundle from Amazon.com - **saving you roughly 35%** from the price of the individual books.

- Passive Income Ideas – 50 Ways to Make Money Online Analyzed (Part I)
- Affiliate Marketing – Learn How to Make $10,000+ Each Month on Autopilot (Part 2)

Get this bundle at a 35% discount from Amazon.com

Available In Kindle, Paperback and **Audio**

Dropshipping: Discover How to Make Money Online, Build Sustainable Streams of Passive Income and Gain Financial Freedom Using The Dropshipping E-Commerce Business Model

How many times have you started a business only to later realise you had to spend a fortune to get the products manufactured, hold inventory and eventually ship the products to customers all over the globe?

Would you like to start your very own e-commerce business that gets right to making money without having to deal with all of these issues? If so, this book can help you

In this book, you'll discover:

- A simple, step-by-step explanation of what the dropshipping business is all about (**Chapter 1**)
- 8 reasons why you should build a dropshipping business (**Chapter 2**)
- Disadvantages of the dropshipping business model and what you need to look out for before making a decision (**Chapter 3**)

- How to start your own dropshipping business including the potential business structure to consider, how to set up a company if you're living outside the US, how much you'll need to start and sources of funding (**Chapter 4**)
- How the supply chain and fulfilment process works – illustrated with an example transaction (**Chapter 5**)
- Analysis of 3 potential sales channel for your dropshipping business - including their respective pros and cons (**Chapter 6**)
- How to do niche research and select winning products – including the tools you need and where to get them (**Chapter 7**)
- How to find reliable suppliers and manufacturers. As well as 6 things you need to look out for in fake suppliers (**Chapter 8**)
- How to manage multiple suppliers and the inventory they hold for you (**Chapter 9**)
- How to deal with security and fraud issues (**Chapter 10**)
- What you need to do to minimize chargebacks i.e. refund rates (**Chapter 11**)
- How to price accordingly especially when your supplier offers international shipment (**Chapter 12**)
- 10 beginner mistakes and how to avoid them (**Chapter 13**)
- 7 powerful strategies you can leverage to scale up your dropshipping business (**Chapter 14**)
- 15 practical tips and lessons from successful dropshippers (**Chapter 15**)

And much, much more!

Finally, because this book is enrolled in Kindle Matchbook Program, the **kindle edition of this book will be available to you for free** when you purchase the paperback version from Amazon.com.

If you're ready to take charge of your financial future, grab your copy of this book today! Start taking control of your life by learning how to create a stream of passive income that'll take care of you and your loved ones.

Available In Kindle, Paperback and **Audio**

Dropshipping and Facebook Advertising: Discover How to Make Money Online and Create Passive Income Streams With Dropshipping and Social Media Marketing

This is a **2-in-1 book bundle** consisting of the below books and split into 2 parts. Amazon will make the kindle edition available to you for FREE when you purchase the print version of this bundle from Amazon.com - **saving you roughly 25%** from the price of the individual paperbacks.

- Dropshipping – Discover How to Make Money Online, Build Sustainable Streams of Passive Income and Gain Financial Freedom Using The Dropshipping E-Commerce Business Model (Part 1)
- Facebook Advertising – Learn How to Make $10,000+ Each Month with Facebook Marketing (Part 2)

Available In Kindle, Paperback and **Audio**

Get this bundle at a 35% discount from Amazon.com

Real Estate Investing For Beginners: Earn Passive Income With Reits, Tax Lien Certificates, Lease, Residential & Commercial Real Estate

In this book, Amazon bestselling author, Michael Ezeanaka, provides a step-by-step analysis of 10 Real Estate business models that have the potential to earn you passive income. A quick overview of each business is presented and their liquidity, scalability, potential return on investment, passivity and simplicity are explored.

In this book, you'll discover:

- How to make money with Real Estate Investment Trusts – including an analysis of the impact of the economy on the income from REITs (**Chapter 1**)
- A step-by-step description of how a Real Estate Investment Groups works and how to make money with this business model (**Chapter 2**)
- How to become a limited partner and why stakeholders can influence the running of a Real Estate Limited Partnership even though they have no direct ownership control in it (**Chapter 3**)
- How to protect yourself as a general partner (**Chapter 3**)
- Why tax lien certificates are one of the most secure investments you can make and how to diversify your portfolio of tax lien certificates (**Chapter 4**)
- Strategies you can employ to earn passive income from an empty land (**Chapter 5**)
- Two critical factors that are currently boosting the industrial real estate market and how you can take advantage of them (**Chapter 6**)
- Some of the most ideal locations to set up industrial real estate properties in the US, Asia and Europe (**Chapter 6**)
- Why going for long term leases (instead of short term ones) can significantly increase you return on investment from your industrial real estate properties (**Chapter 6**)
- Why commercial properties can serve as an excellent hedge against inflation – including two ways you can make money with commercial properties (**Chapter 7**)
- How long term leases and potential 'turnover rents' can earn you significant sums of money from Retail real estate properties and why they are very sensitive to the state of the economy (**Chapter 8**)
- More than 10 zoning rights you need to be aware of when considering investing in Mixed-Use properties (**Chapter 9**)
- 100 Tips for success that will help you minimize risks and maximize returns on your real estate investments

And much, much more!

PLUS, **BONUS MATERIALS**: you can download the author's Real Estate Business Scorecard which neatly summarizes, in alphabetical order, each business model's score across those 5 criteria i.e. liquidity, scalability, potential return on investment, passivity and simplicity!

Finally, because this book is enrolled in Kindle Matchbook Program, the **kindle edition of this book will be available to you for free** when you purchase the paperback version from Amazon.com.

If you're ready to take charge of your financial future, grab your copy of This Book today!

Available In Kindle, Paperback and **Audio**

Credit Card And Credit Repair Secrets: Discover How To Repair Your Credit, Get A 700+ Credit Score, Access Business Startup Funding, And Travel For Free Using Reward Cards

Are you sick and tired of paying huge interests on loans due to poor credit scores? Are you frustrated with not knowing where or how to get the necessary capital you need to start your business? Would you like to get all these as well as discover how you can travel the world for FREE?

If so, you'll love Credit Card and Credit Repair Secrets.

Imagine knowing simple do-it-yourself strategies you can employ to repair your credit profile, protect it from identity theft, access very cheap and affordable funding for your business and travel the world without any out of pocket expense!

This can be your reality. You can learn how to do all these and more. Moreover, you may be surprised by how simple doing so is.

In this book, you'll discover:

- **3 Types of consumer credit (And How You Can Access Them!)**
- How To Read, Review and Understand Your Credit Report (Including a Sample Letter You Can Send To Dispute Any Inaccuracy In It)
- **How To Achieve a 700+ Credit Score (And What To Do If You Have No FICO Score)**
- How To Monitor Your Credit Score (Including the difference between hard and soft inquiries)
- **What The VantageScore Model Is, It's Purpose, And How It Differs From The FICO Score Model**
- The Factors That Impact Your Credit Rating. Including The Ones That Certainly Don't - Despite What People Say!
- **Which Is More Important: Payment History Or Credit Utilization? (The Answer May Surprise You)**
- Why You Should Always Check Your Credit Report (At least Once A Month!)
- **How Credit Cards Work (From The Business And Consumer Perspective)**
- Factors You Need To Consider When Choosing A Credit Card (Including How To Avoid A Finance Charge on Your Credit Card)

- **How To Climb The Credit Card Ladder And Unlock Reward Points**
- Which Is More Appropriate: A Personal or Business Credit Card? (Find Out!)
- **How to Protect Your Credit Card From Identity Theft**
- Sources of Fund You Can Leverage To Grow Your Business

And much, much more!

An Identity Theft Resource Center (ITRC) report shows that 1,579 data breaches exposed about 179 million identity records in 2017. Being a victim of an identity scam can cause you a lot of problems. One of the worst cases would be the downfall of your credit score. You don't have to fall victim to it.

This book gives you a simple, but incredibly effective, step-by-step process you can use to build, protect and leverage your stellar credit profile to enjoy a financially stress-free life! It's practical. It's actionable. And if you follow it closely, it'll deliver extraordinary results!

PLUS BONUS - because this book is enrolled in Kindle Matchbook Program, the **kindle edition of this book will be available to you for free** when you purchase the paperback version from Amazon.com.

If you're ready to take charge of your financial future, grab your copy of This Book today!

Available In Kindle, Paperback and **Audio**

Real Estate Investing And Credit Repair: Discover How To Earn Passive Income With Real Estate, Repair Your Credit, Fund Your Business, And Travel For Free Using Reward Credit Cards

This is a **2-in-1 book bundle** consisting of the below books and split into 2 parts. Amazon will make the kindle edition available to you for FREE when you purchase the print version of this bundle from Amazon.com - **saving you roughly 25%** from the price of the individual paperbacks.

- Real Estate Investing For Beginners – Earn Passive Income With Reits, Tax Lien Certificates, Lease, Residential & Commercial Real Estate (Part 1)
- Credit Card And Credit Repair Secrets – Discover How To Repair Your Credit, Get A 700+ Credit Score, Access Business Startup Funding, And Travel For Free Using Reward Cards (Part 2)

Available In Kindle, Paperback and **Audio**

Get this bundle at a 35% discount from Amazon.com

Passive Income With Dividend Investing: Your Step-By-Step Guide To Make Money In The Stock Market Using Dividend Stocks

Have you always wanted to put your money to work in the stock market and earn passive income with dividend stocks?

What would you be able to achieve with a step-by-step guide designed to help you grow your money, navigate the dangers in the stock market and minimize the chance of losing your capital?

Imagine not having to rely solely on a salary or a pension to survive. Imagine having the time, money and freedom to pursue things you're passionate about, whether it's gardening, hiking, reading, restoring a classic car or simply spending time with your loved ones.

This book can help you can create this lifestyle for yourself and your loved ones!

Amazon bestselling author, Michael Ezeanaka, takes you through a proven system that'll help you to build and grow a sustainable stream of passive dividend income. He'll show you, step by step, how to identify stocks to purchase, do accurate due diligence, analyze the impact of the economy on your portfolio and when to consider selling.

In this book, you'll discover:

- Why investing in dividend stocks can position you to benefit tremendously from the "Baby Boomer Boost" (Chapter 1)
- **Which certain industry sectors tend to have a higher dividend payout ratio and why? (Chapter 2)**
- How to time your stock purchase around ex-dividend dates so as to take advantage of discounted share prices (Chapter 2)
- **Why a stock that is showing growth beyond its sustainable rate may indicate some red flags. (Chapter 2)**
- 5 critical questions you need to ask in order to assess if a company's debt volume will affect your dividend payment (Chapter 3)
- **How high dividend yield strategy can result in low capital gain taxes (Chapter 4)**
- Reasons why the average lifespan of a company included in the S&P 500 plummeted from 67 years in the 1920s to just 15 years in 2015. (Chapter 5)
- **A blueprint for selecting good dividend paying stocks (Chapter 6)**
- The vital information you need to look out for when reading company financial statements (Chapter 7)
- **A strategy you can use to remove the emotion from investing, as well as, build wealth cost efficiently (Chapter 8)**
- An affordable way to diversify your portfolio if you have limited funds (Chapter 9)
- **Why you may want to think carefully before selling cyclical stocks with high P/E ratio (Chapter 10)**

And much, much more!

PLUS BONUS - because this book is enrolled in Kindle Matchbook Program, the **kindle edition of this book will be available to you for free** when you purchase the paperback version from Amazon.com.

Whether you're a student, corporate executive, entrepreneur, or stay-at-home parent, the tactics described in this book can set the stage for a financial transformation.

If you're ready to build and grow a steady stream of passive dividend income, Grab your copy of this book today!

Available In Kindle, Paperback and **Audio**

Books In The Business and Money Series	
Series #	**Book Title**
1	Affiliate Marketing
2	Passive Income Ideas
3	Affiliate Marketing + Passive Income Ideas (2-in-1 Bundle)
4	Facebook Advertising
5	Dropshipping
6	Dropshipping + Facebook Advertising (2-in-1 Bundle)
7	Real Estate Investing For Beginners
8	Credit Cards and Credit Repair Secrets
9	Real Estate Investing And Credit Repair Strategies (2-in-1 Bundle)
10	Passive Income With Affiliate Marketing (2nd Edition)
11	Passive Income With Dividend Investing
12	Stock Market Investing For Beginners
13	The Simple Stock Market Investing Blueprint (2-in-1 Bundle)
The kindle edition will be available to you for FREE when you purchase the paperback version from Amazon.com (The US Store)	

Download The Audio Versions Along With The Complementary PDF Document For FREE from www.MichaelEzeanaka.com > My Audiobooks

www.ingramcontent.com/pod-product-compliance
Lightning Source LLC
Chambersburg PA
CBHW061323190326
41458CB00011B/3879

* 9 7 8 1 9 1 3 3 6 1 6 7 9 *